The New West Coast Cuisine

Also by Linda West Eckhardt:

The Only Texas Cookbook
An American Gumbo

The New West Coast Cuisine

Linda West Eckhardt

JEREMY P. TARCHER, INC.
Los Angeles
Distributed by St. Martin's Press
New York

Library of Congress Cataloging in Publication Data

Eckhardt, Linda West, 1939–
    The new West Coast cuisine.

    Includes index.
    1. Food supply—Pacific Coast (U.S.)   2. Food
supply—Pacific Coast (B.C.)   3. Cookery, American—
Western style.   4. Cookery, Canadian.   5. Food—
Catalogs.   6. Grocery trade—Pacific Coast (U.S.)—
Directories.   7. Grocery trade—Pacific Coast (B.C.)—
Directories.   I. Title.
TX733.E27   1985   641.3′0979   85-9785
ISBN 0-87477-358-X
ISBN 0-87477-359-8 (pbk.)

Jeremy P. Tarcher, Inc.
9110 Sunset Blvd.
Los Angeles, CA 90069

Design by Thom Dower
Illustration by Cathi Gunderson

Manufactured in the United States of America
10 9 8 7 6 5 4 3 2 1

First Edition

This book is fondly dedicated to the memory of
James Beard
Big Daddy-Mama of us all

CONTENTS

Acknowledgments

I THANK THE PEOPLE who handed me their cities on a silver plate: Portland, Anne Siegel and Ginger Johnson. Seattle, Virginia Parks. Vancouver, B.C., Betsy Kirkpatrick. San Francisco, Katherine DeFoyd and Danielle Lapp. Los Angeles, Mary Anne and Suzy Tinker. These people know how to eat and where to live and they showed me the best there is in their own backyards.

To all the food professionals and dedicated amateurs that I pestered to death for help and information, I say thank you for your patience and for coming through.

To my agent, Ron Bernstein, my editor, Janice Gallagher, and my publisher, Jeremy Tarcher, thanks for believing in the project and giving it the benefit of your not inconsiderable experience.

Thanks to the word processor for not breaking down. Thanks to my weak but persistent will power that kept nudging me not to eat from daylight to dark just because the food being tested around here was so irresistible. Thanks to the German Shorthair for inhaling all the failures, and thanks to my husband, Joe, and my son, Jay, who kept a modicum of reality intact by saying wow or yuck when I'd become too tired to tell the difference.

The New West Coast Cuisine

THE GREAT PORTS OF THE WEST COAST—Los Angeles, San Francisco, Oakland, Seattle, and Vancouver—welcome ethnic influences and raw ingredients from all over the world. From South San Diego County, California, to the rare green pastures north of Vancouver, British Columbia, immigrant farmers, grocers, and restaurant operators have found mini-climate zones within the geography of the region that make it possible for them to grow, produce, and process almost any foodstuff imaginable. And so, here on the West Coast, we are constantly seeing new things and through experimentation are beginning to evolve a new style of cuisine, a style in its infancy, a style that, at the moment, can only be described as new.

A marriage between the natural-foods movement and classic cooking techniques has produced a new generation of cooks. These new cooks—young, daring, innovative—have stormed the kitchen armed with everything from their mothers' beat-up copies of *Mastering the Art of French Cooking* to their own spotted paperbacks of *Laurel's Kitchen*. They know their way around a wok and have mail order addresses for morels. They are developing a cuisine based firmly on the premise of invention and goodness, a style we call *The New West Coast Cuisine*.

This splendid, fresh, easy, and elegant style of cooking makes good use of the Garden of Eden that is the West Coast. It draws on cooking principles from the venerated trinity—French, Italian, and Chinese. It is underpinned with the orthodoxy of the natural-foods movement, pays homage to Japanese and Mexican contributions, and goes beyond Judy Chicago by composing not only the place setting but also the plate.

One significant aspect of this posture regarding the kitchen comes in its attitude toward ingredients. The new chefs have fanned out into the community to acquire the best local food products available. In Berkeley, the chefs and farmers and cottage kitchen operators joined together and developed a newsletter so that chefs would know who was growing what and when it would peak. Once the chefs got to know the growers, they began to request that the growers plant specific items; soon the number and kinds of fruits and vegetables had increased dramatically. Then farmers—who might have planted more than a restaurant could use—began selling to home cooks through farmer's markets and ultimately through produce buyers for the big chains. The result is that once-exotic or nearly impossible-to-find food products are turning up on supermarket shelves.

And that leads to the reason that I wrote this book. I needed information I couldn't find in my own cookbook collection. And once I had ferreted out the answers to my own kitchen problems, I thought I might as well share them with you.

To state the problem most simply: grocery stores have outrun cookbooks. I find in my neighborhood store items I have barely heard of, have never before seen, and have only the faintest notion of what to do with. And, mind you, I do not live in some cosmopolitan urban center; I live in Ashland, Oregon, population 15,000. If arugula and radicchio and California chèvre have reached Ashland, just imagine what you'll find in L.A.!

Speaking of California, you may be wondering why this book isn't called *California Cuisine.* Besides the fact that some of the most succulent West Coast ingredients are grown in Oregon, Washington, and Vancouver, where quality wins out over quantity, there is also a basic difference in food philosophy. Most California Cuisine experts, it seems to me, were classically trained in French cuisine and then adopted Nouvelle techniques, adding the best of Asian cuisines and, lately, some Latin ones. In my opinion, that's just part of what is happening on the West Coast. What I have found, in my West Coast travels, are cooks who began as natural-foods students, who got to know a family of Vietnamese immigrants, say, perhaps in a neighborhood cafe, and who investigated with joy and vigor the endless possibilities using whole unprocessed foods and techniques from the world's peasant cuisines. This style of cooking is more robust and frequently more boldly seasoned than the more restrained California version. It is a style of cooking in which health and fitness are a given, where adventure is prized but not overemphasized. The New West Coast Cuisine tastes as good as it looks and is good for you besides.

I have divided the book into three sections. First, you'll find a products list. Think of this as your field guide to the grocery store. You can look up that exotic-looking green and see just what it is, how to buy it, store it, and prepare it—and then read about some suggestions for its use.

To find recipes using each ingredient, check the index under the name of the ingredient. There, you will also find cross references to where to buy it, in the mail order section.

The second section is made up of recipes. To gather these, I have traveled from my home on the Oregon-California border up and down the coast from San Diego to Vancouver. I have visited every major farmer's market on the West Coast. These markets offer the best and freshest foodstuffs available here. I have seen scallops swimming in briny bathtubs, eels and salmon, and carp and God only knows what all kinds of Pacific sea creatures. I have seen fresh local cheeses, butters and jams and fresh herbs, fruit vinegars and honeys and rabbit sausages, brown eggs and a dazzling array of fresh produce. I have talked with food editors, restaurant chefs, caterers, home cooks, produce people, fishermen, cooks in cafes. You will note names under some of the recipes; these are the good cooks I found in my travels.

In the recipe section, you also will find cross-references to the ingredients and mail order sections.

And that brings me to the final part of the book, the mail order section. This has been the most fun I've had in the food business in ten years. What I have discovered, traveling up and down the coast, are a host of small cottage kitchens working on the basic premise of goodness. Freshness. No chemicals. No pesticides. No preservatives. Wonder of wonders. It's real home cooking and you don't have to do it.

Also, what I have discovered is that local foods don't reach very far from their own neighborhoods. This mail order section makes the entire West Coast one big neighborhood. Now you will know where to order morels and chanterelles, razor clams, Oregon filberts, Bosc pears, even a salad with wild herbs and edible flowers. Whatever your heart desires. Pick up the phone. You can get it.

So what I offer here is three books in one, a guide to the New West Coast foodstuffs—what they are; how to cook them; and where to get them. Welcome to the Garden.

Special Ingredients

TWENTY YEARS AGO, people chose a grocery store on the basis of its meat department. Today, the produce section is the key. And right next to all that wonderful produce are ethnic sections offering staple ingredients for Latin, Asian, European, and an ever-growing number of lesser-known cuisines.

During the seventies we had an enormous influx of Latins and Asians into the country. Many of these people planted and grew the foodstuffs with which they were familiar. Some opened mom-and-pop restaurants, a tried and true method for putting the whole family to work and keeping them fed at the same time. We learned to love exotic cuisine.

Running parallel to these changes was the natural-foods movement, which made us more health conscious. These West Coast influences began to co- alesce into a food philosophy that has changed the way America sets its table.

One person who typifies what is happening here on the West Coast is Frieda Caplan, a specialty-produce shipper based in Los Angeles. Frieda started out selling mushrooms on the floor of her uncle's produce shed. Later, she began her own business and brought the Chinese gooseberry, a fruit she liked the taste of but whose name she didn't care for, to American markets. She christened the fuzzy little import the "kiwi" and the rest, as they say, is history. Frieda, and all of those who follow, are channeling this exploding produce bonanza into ordinary chain grocery stores in a wave that rolls from the West to the East, carrying foodstuffs and ethnic ideas into the heartland of the country.

Before I even begin, I must apologize for the fact that this section isn't complete. Before the ink is dry on the page there will be new items. The choices grow daily. But what I have attempted to do is describe the food products that are now grown, produced, or funneled through the West Coast. Not all of these products are exotic. At least not any more. I have tried to explain which foodstuffs are routinely available to West Coast cooks, as well as those that are precious and harder to find.

If you take the entire region—from South San Diego County, California, all the way up to the beautiful glacier-shadowed pastures north of Vancouver, British Columbia—you have encompassed nearly every climate zone there is that will support life. I am only beginning to become familiar with the range of products that are grown and are available here. I hope you'll enjoy learning about them with me.

Fruits

Apricots: In Steinbeck's time, the cot orchards were part of the revolving harvest that kept the Okies on the move. For two years I lived in one of those Steven Spielberg subdivisions that had grown up in a cot orchard. The grand- son of the original orchard rancher used to walk around our neighborhood, which still had little stunted trees all in rows, and tell us stories of the great harvests during the depression. Model Ts and broken-down trucks from the year one would line the orchard rows. Wooden boxes were spread every- where in the sunshine, and the privileged few who had mastered the skill would sit on stools, a great knife in their hands, and split the cots, tossing the pits over their shoulders, then spread the cots in the boxes to dry. Others would scramble through the orchard and climb the graceful fruit ladders to gather the fruit as fast as they could, because they were paid by the pound. Just like the sentimental old drunk says, as he squeezes the fruit in the front yards of houses, we grow the best apricots in the world in California. The best damn apricots in the world.

Apricots are delicate. If picked green, they just turn to mush and become what is generally referred to as potato fruit. If picked ripe, they last only three or four days. You can tell a ripe one by its aroma—it should have the full perfume of the apricot—and a golden look. There should be no hint of green, not even the slightest shadow of a green cast. That means it was picked too soon. And, of course, no bruising. To get the best apricot flavor, you still may be better off buying dried ones, unless you live in an area that gets prompt delivery from the California cot orchards, because the apricots for drying are allowed to mature fully on the trees. And are they delicious. (See mail order section for sources.)

Avocados: California produces two varieties of avocados, Fuerte and Hass. You can tell the difference immediately. The Fuerte is truly pear shaped and has a smooth green skin. The Hass is fatter, rounder, and has a blackish pebbly skin. The Hass is, without doubt, the preferred avocado. It is more creamy, more yellow, and more butterlike in texture, with none of the watery cucumberish qualities of the Fuerte. In choosing the best of the bunch, take the whole avocado in the palm of you hand and give a little squeeze. A perfectly ripe avocado will yield slightly—all over, not just at the stem end. If you must buy a green one, because that's all that's available, you can take it home and bury it in the flour bin. In twenty-four hours it will be ripe. Don't ask me why. I only know it because a produce man gave me this tip.

Don't forget avocados are for cooking as well as for eating raw in salads or guacamole. (See avocado in index.) Try the Chicken Avocado Velvet. Avocado in Cold Lime & Garlic soup. Avocado Advocate bread. However, if you go to the store and find they only have avocados from Florida, change the menu. They are not worth the paper bag it takes to get them home.

This Christmas season I also saw these little runty things about as big as your thumb called cocktail avocados. Do you want to know what these poor little things really are? They are Fuertes known to producers as "aborts," because they're so little and they have no seed. They don't taste any better than a big Fuerte and they're hell to peel. Save your money.

Blackberries: When we moved to Oregon, I was appalled at all the blackberries going to waste by the side of the highway. Later I learned that they were sprayed by the highway department and unfit to eat. If you are going to pick blackberries, take care that the spot you choose has neither been sprayed nor had too much car exhaust nearby. And do wear long sleeves and jeans. Blackberries are prickly. Sometimes we take a big piece of cardboard, like the cutout side of a refrigerator shipping carton, and lay it up against the vines. Then you can reach in and get the best ones. You know: the best ones, always just out of reach. If you do your blackberry picking in a market, choose ones that are uniformly black but have not stained the bottom of the basket (too ripe, going). Use within a day or two. You will find good blackberries from the Fourth of July to Labor Day.

Blueberries: Related to the huckleberry, these hardy berries grow well on the West Coast and are available fresh from the middle of July to the middle of September. You can freeze them more successfully than other berries because their tough skin keeps them from collapsing when they're thawed. Choose firm blueberries with a faint dusting of white on the skin, and store in the refrigerator without washing for up to a week. Made into a sauce, they produce a tart, bluish delicious glaze for pheasant, Cornish game hens, or plain old chickens. (See mail order, Canter-Berry Farms for fine blueberry vinegar, chutney and jam.)

The New Fruits

Here's a rundown on the new fruits available in West Coast markets. These fruits are in the same family with the kiwi, the guava, the papaya, and other tropical fruits. Use them interchangeably in recipes for different but exotic results. (See recipe for Fruited Cornish Game Hens.)

Carambola: Star Fruit. A five-sided yellow waxy fruit with a sweet-sour taste, it works admirably with meat dishes. May be too tart to be enjoyed out of hand.

Cherimoya: Looks like an immature swollen pine cone, it's the fruit that Mark Twain called "deliciousness itself." The plants have to be hand pollinated so it seems unlikely that this will ever proliferate like the kiwis have. If you let one ripen fully (feels soft around the stem end) and cut into it, you get a banana-pineapple-papaya taste. Cut into wedges and squeeze with the juice of a blood orange. Serve the cherimoya and a wedge of blood orange side by side. Gorgeous.

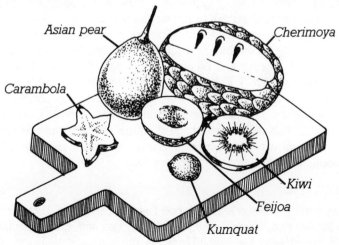

Asian pear

Cherimoya

Carambola

Kiwi

Feijoa

Kumquat

Feijoa: Sometimes known as the pineapple-guava, because that's what it tastes like, this New Zealand fruit has lower sugar than most fruits and is loaded with vitamin C. They're planting them in Southern California, so we hope that the prices will soon come down.

Cranberries: Did you know that those fresh packages of cranberries you buy from Thanksgiving to Christmas that say they come from the East Coast generally have been mixed with cranberries from Oregon, because Oregon cranberries are larger, brighter, and redder? Cranberries are wonderfully stable, keeping well for weeks in the refrigerator and months in the freezer. You will find many recipes for cranberries in this book because I love their tart, acidic fruit taste. (See index.) I especially would steer you to the recipe for Mama Stamberg's Cranberry-Horseradish Sauce, a splendid combination of cranberries, horseradish, onions, sugar, and yogurt. Don't knock it until you try it. And see mail order section for a cranberry candy from Oregon that is made right next to the bogs, using only the freshest Oregon cranberries.

Kiwi: Remember when kiwis were a buck and a half apiece? And only imported from New Zealand? Now, at Safeway, they are six for a dollar and come straight from Southern California. If you asked ten people walking the streets of Des Moines today where the kiwi hailed from, I bet you eight of them would say California. And aren't we glad. For this silly-looking fuzzy brown fruit with the bright green flesh that looks like a reject from a tennis ball factory offers a tart fresh-fruit addition to desserts and salads. It pairs well with chocolate and appears atop some fabulous desserts. The kiwi sliced thin and tossed with fresh strawberries, then topped with crème fraîche, is a dessert to die for.

Choose firm kiwis. Let them ripen in your warm kitchen until they yield slightly to a squeeze, then pare and eat them.

Kumquats: Just because of the mania for baby vegetables, don't rush out and buy a sack full of little kumquats to serve at your next dinner party. The kumquat, which looks like an orange but is about the size of an Emperor grape, makes a marvelous garnish or centerpiece, but as it is, raw, it's something like eating grapefruit rinds for fun. Somebody once told me that if you rub the skin vigorously, all the bitter oil comes off on your hand and you really can eat it. Yes. And Reagan will balance the budget this year. The neighborhood kids used to have kumquat wars, wherein they pelted each other and the mailman with these pretty little fruits. So what are they good for? They make divine preserves. They are good in fruit vinegars. Frieda Caplan sells a sugared kumquat that resembles candied ginger and is simply delicious.

By the way, if kumquats are your favorite fruit, don't write me a hate letter. This is my book and I am entitled to my opinion.

Lemons: Why can't you buy a lemon as good as you can grow? This has been my constant lament ever since moving from the house with the lemon tree in the backyard. The smell of the lemon blossoms, the beauty of the bright green shiny leaves, the utter here-we-are-in-paradise feeling of gamboling out into the backyard to snatch a lemon off the tree whenever you needed one for cooking. The backyard lemon, allowed to fully ripen on the branch, is tart but not so greeny sour, and just plucked, it is heavy for its size and simply drips with juice. When I was writing my last cookbook and using backyard lemons, I realized that I could not say "juice of a lemon," because my lemons were about the size of readers' oranges and had as much juice as three commercial lemons. So, I say to all of you, find a friend with a lemon tree. Cultivate that friend. Offer to pay the freight if they'll send you some. You know. I wish I had sold everything except the lemon rights when we got rid of that house. To me, it would have been more valuable than mineral rights.

Pears: Four pear varieties come from the Rogue Valley of Southern Oregon— Bartlett, Comice, Bosc, and d'Anjou. The Bartlett ripens first, is sold most, and appears in markets all across the country. It is usually known in other parts of the country as the great potato pear, being generally tasteless. The first year we lived here, we bought a peck of these from an orchard, and they were so delicious that I ate nothing but Bartletts for three days. Great God. What a difference. Now those were pears. But unless you live near a pear orchard, the Bartlett is not the one to choose.

The Comice is the best traveler. Sold by Harry and David for years as the Royal Riviera, the Comice is more round, seductively sweet, drips with juice, and is quite stable.

The Bosc, known as the "ugly" pear, is truly pear shaped but has a bronze-colored skin. It is a wonderful keeper and is beautiful to cook with. I use the Bosc in Ashland Avenue Pears and Ribs. (See index.)

Newest on the market is the Asian pear, which usually comes in a thing that looks like a hair net. Oh, those Japanese are persnickety. This pear is apple shaped and apple crisp. Its wonderful sweet pearish flavor coupled with crisp flesh and good keeping qualities make it a winner. Try it in salads. Pears are always picked green, so buy pears and let them ripen in your warm kitchen for a few days to complete the sweetening process.

Vegetables

Artichokes: Practically the entire American artichoke crop comes from the fog-kissed central coast of California. Visit Watsonville or Castroville and you'll find all kinds of artichokes for sale—from ones no larger than your thumb to the purple thistle bloom that's the end result of the artichoke's growth period.

Artichokes are at their best twice a year. In April, the harvest peaks, and they generally are reasonably priced then. In the fall you'll notice a bronzing on the leaves that is the result of frost. Artichoke connoisseurs swear that these are the best.

Choose artichokes that are tightly closed. If the leaves spread out, it probably means that they have been too long off the plant. Avoid ones that have gray-looking discoloration. When you get them home and begin trimming the spiny ends off the leaves—I find this easiest with a pair of scissors—drop them into water in which you have squeezed some lemon juice or plain vinegar. This will prevent discoloration.

Use promptly. Store in the hydrator of your refrigerator. See index for recipes.

Asparagus: I belong to the pencil school of asparagus choosers. I like a long pencil-slim stalk. But there are other equally opinionated asparagusseurs who prefer the fat whitish stalks. Whichever you prefer, choose firm, straight stalks. Snap them off where they break naturally. (You don't necessarily have to throw away the woody stalks. They make a terrific soup when peeled and cooked in broth that is then thickened with cream.)

You can begin to get good California asparagus in March. Later, in May, you will find the best, most succulent crop, which comes from Washington.

Brussels Sprouts: Grown in the central coastal areas of California and in Southern Oregon, the brussels sprout is sometimes sold whole on the stalk around Christmastime. See vegetable section for good ideas on using the brussels sprout as an edible centerpiece.

When choosing fresh brussels sprouts, whether on the stalk or cut off, choose the smallest ones you see; as these little cabbages mature, they get stronger. Store in the hydrator of your refrigerator for up to two weeks.

Celery Root (Celeriac): Big, rough globular roots, pale whitish gold and generally seen with some dirt and hairs hanging about, the celery root has long been popular in French cuisine. You can usually find them all over the West Coast in winter. The intense flavor of celery is splendid for use in game stuffings, as well as in the more familiar winter salads combined with apples and now, more frequently, jícama.

One great instant winter salad combines equal parts grated celery root, green apple, and jícama. Moisten with fresh lemon juice and season to taste with freshly milled black pepper.

Choose a small one; a big one is a lifetime supply. It will keep up to a month in the hydrator. Be sure to dip the tubers in lemon-juiced water to prevent discoloration. Eat it raw. As crunchy as jícama or a raw sweet potato, it's fun to serve all three with a good curried yogurt dip.

Eggplant, Japanese: This small elongated eggplant with shiny purple skin and tender golden flesh can be used as you would use any eggplant. Excellent in caponata or stir-fried dishes. No need to peel, salt, or parboil these little gems; they are never bitter as their overblown relatives sometimes are. The Japanese eggplant grows well all along the West Coast.

Select firm, shiny eggplants with no soft spots. Store in the hydrator of your refrigerator and use within two or three days.

Jerusalem Artichokes: Here is a case of the prophet in his own land. For the humble, rough brown root so named is neither an artichoke nor is it from Jerusalem. What we have here is purely North American and is, in fact, nothing more than the tuberous root of one variety of sunflower. Can't you imagine the first inventive cook to serve the bottom end of a towering sunflower just grabbing the name out of the air when presenting it to some suspicious gourmand? Frieda Caplan markets them under her own trademarked name, Sunchokes, which comes a little closer to truth. However they are named, the taste is the same. A sweet, nutty, smooth, satisfying taste that makes a wonderfully complex addition to soups, stuffings, or side dishes. The produce person where I shop says that diabetics buy them to satisfy their sweet tooth. Scrub well, peel if desired, and eat raw or cooked. They truly are about as sweet as sugarcane, and not harmful at all.

Choose tubers without soft spots or mold and store like potatoes, in a cool dark place for up to two weeks.

The only note of caution about Sunchokes is this: At a very toney meeting of gastronomes in Santa Barbara, Julia Child complained to Frieda Caplan in front of 400 epicures that Sunchokes produced inordinate amounts of flatulence. After some discussion, they agreed that in ancient Rome a feast was not a feast to remember unless the guests were gaseous end to end. Manners and customs do change, eh?

Jícama: Jícama is a tuber, looks like a big root vegetable, and comes from Mexico. It has the texture and flesh color of a raw russet potato but a taste that is both sweet and bland. Pared and cut into french fry slices, tossed with lime juice, and dusted with chili powder, it makes a wonderful crunchy beginning to a meal. You can also cut it into fake water chestnut shapes and use it in Chinese preparations. You can even bake it, like a potato.

Choose the smallest one you can find for the best texture, or ask your produce person to divide a larger one, and store in a cool dark place, for up to two weeks.

Mushrooms: When we first moved to Oregon and began picnicking in the woods, I was fascinated by the variety of mushrooms I saw growing wild. Once I gathered a big variety and brought them home. I went to the bookstore

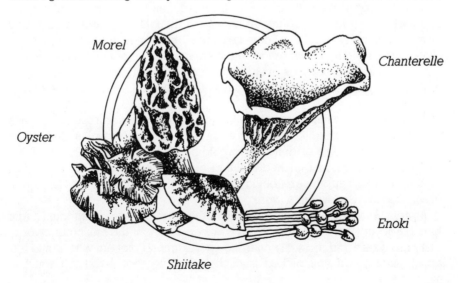

Morel

Chanterelle

Oyster

Enoki

Shiitake

and bought a field guide to mushrooms and tried to identify those I had picked. Just as I would find a picture that looked like the one I had before me, classified as "edible and common," I would turn a couple of pages and there would be another picture that also looked like it called "poisonous and rare." May I tell you that I simply dried all those first mushrooms and made a nice-looking table arrangement of them. I decided I had best go to a Mycological Society meeting so that we wouldn't get poisoned. I went. I learned two things about wild-mushroom pickers: they will never tell you where their favorite stash of morels is, and they will tell you story after story of experts, who, through a fluke, were poisoned. These kind of "drunk-a-log" stories like I used to hear in Texas from drunks who had walked away from flaming car crashes made me come to this conclusion: when I want wild mushrooms, I will buy them from a reputable produce person. Peter Hasson, for example, in the Pike Place Market, hires pickers to get chanterelles, boletas, morels, and the rare matsutake, which sells in Japan for $100 a pound and in Seattle for a mere $15. Here is a rundown on the newly available varieties you may see for sale. Full Moon Mushroom Co. grows and sells Shiitakes and oyster mushrooms (see mail order section).

To choose: all mushrooms should be plump, unshriveled, and with no odor other than that of the earth. Store in a paper sack rather than plastic, in the hydrator, and use promptly. Some cooks don't even wash them, just wipe them with a towel. Not me. I wash.

Boletus edulis: Sometimes known as cepes or porcini, you can buy these dried from Italy. They also are gathered and dried in Oregon. They're available fresh in the fall. Wonderful sautéed, you can use our own native mushrooms in any recipe calling for the porcini or cepe. Fresh ones are quite fragile and should be used promptly. To store, you may dry, pickle, or blanch and freeze.

Chanterelles: A golden reddish variety shaped like a trombone's bell, these wonderful fall mushrooms come to market by the boxful all along the Northwest Coast. They keep well in a brown bag in the refrigerator. I should know. I bought two big sacks of them in Seattle. More than I could cook. I smuggled one sackful into British Columbia, because I thought our room there would have a kitchen. No kitchen. Four days later I smuggled them back into the United States and home, where we ate them sautéed for our first dinner home. Still delicious. And perhaps even better for being smuggled. I used the last of those precious chanterelles ten days after I bought them, and they were still good.

Enoki: These are those funny little Japanese mushrooms you see in Nouvelle presentations that look like long thin white dandelion stalks with a little button on the end. These are so delicate, I would never cook them. Only nip off the woody end and serve bunched together on the plate. They look as good as they taste and, happily, are being cultivated all along the West Coast with great success. Use within a week.

Morels: Available from Oregon only in the spring, these mushrooms might best be described as intense. A Type A personality of the mushroom world. They are a rare and a closely guarded secret among pickers who would just about shoot you if you picked from their favorite spot. I did tell you that mushrooms of all varieties come up in the same spot year after year didn't I? The black morel, which is shaped kind of like a miniature pinecone, must be washed carefully before use. Rinse out the pockets and nip off the bulbous bottom end before cooking. If you are feeling entirely flush, one of the best ways to cook the morel is to simply cut it in half, dredge in seasoned flour, and sauté in butter until golden brown on both sides. Dried, these mushrooms are available year round at Irvine Ranch Market in Los Angeles for a mere $165 a pound.

Oyster Mushrooms: Named because of their distinct taste, and sometimes called "the shellfish of the forest," these firm white mushrooms should be used carefully and not combined with herbs that might mask their distinctive flavor. The oyster is another Asian mushroom that is now cultivated commercially in California, Oregon, and Washington. Just yesterday, I bought some locally cultivated oysters that cost less than buttons. I simply sautéed them along with a shallot and a couple of garlic buds in a little butter, then deglazed the pan with a teaspoon of raspberry vinegar. Was that wonderful. See Full Moon Mushroom in the mail order section, not only as a source for oyster mushrooms but for your very own oyster mushroom farm.

Shiitake: A Japanese staple, these are commonly found dried in Oriental markets and now are successfully cultivated commercially on the West Coast. They primarily are used in sautés and stir-fries. Full Moon also raises and ships Shittakes.

Onions, Walla Walla: The Pacific Northwest's claim to fame, these sweet white-fleshed onions can be eaten like an apple and are wonderful sliced thin in salads. They come to market from Eastern Washington in June and are not good keepers. Not long ago I saw an onion for sale in November that was marked Walla Walla. Now that was a good joke. That onion may have been grown in the same area, but it was not of the same variety. These are a summer-only onion, meant to be enjoyed for the brief moment that they are in season. Available from the Northwest produce shippers listed in the mail order section.

Potatoes:

Boniatos: A South American sweet potato, the boniato has a white, sweet-tasting flesh. Use interchangeably with yellow-fleshed North American yams. (See index for Boniatos con Limón.)

Yellow Finnish: A yellow-fleshed potato with a wonderful mealy texture similar to the russet. (See index for good recipe for roasted Finnish Potatoes.) Don't confuse these with Yellow Rose potatoes, which have a more gluey consistency and don't bake or fry as well. Don't be surprised if you know more about them than your produce person. At my market, they sometimes just put them out as "yellow" potatoes, and I have to ask them to check the box they came in to clarify.

German Purple: These potatoes are grown in the state of Washington and are fun for potato salads because they turn blue when cooked. Kids like them a lot. But then, kids like green gravy, too.

Radishes:

Black: These Japanese radishes are turning up more and more frequently in the produce market. They taste about the same as common red radishes and can be used interchangeably.

Daikon: This large, white Oriental radish looks like an enormous anemic carrot but has a mildly pungent taste. It is good raw, and great marinated in a rice wine vinegar. A natural with sashimi. If you shop in Hawaii, you may discover that the daikon sold there bears more resemblance to horseradish than to an icicle radish. Stateside, you will see daikons anywhere from 6 to 18 inches long and sometimes as big around as your wrist. As with other vegetables, go for the small ones. The taste is more subtle and pleasing than the big ones, which can become woody. Summer daikons are hotter than those offered in fall or winter.

Horseradish: Tulelake, California, grows the very best horseradish there is. If you are buying fresh whole root of horseradish, ask the produce person where it came from. If it's not from Tulelake you're better off buying the prepared stuff (see mail order section). Grate and mix the root with grated beets for your own delicious preparations. See recipe for Mama Stamberg's Cranberry-Horseradish Sauce.

Regardless of the variety, choose firm, blemish-free radishes and store for a week or so in the hydrator. If you can, buy radishes with tops. They'll keep better. Serve raw or stir-fried.

Salad Greens and Reds and Yellows

Arugula: When I first heard Alice Waters talking about rocket, I thought she was referring to some special Fourth of July salad she had invented. But rocket, or arugula, is a Mediterranean green as piquant as our own mustard green.

Buy the youngest, smallest one you see; otherwise, you might as well eat green persimmons marinated in cayenne. Mix with butter or red tip lettuce. Actually, I think the best posture to take toward arugula is to consider it as a

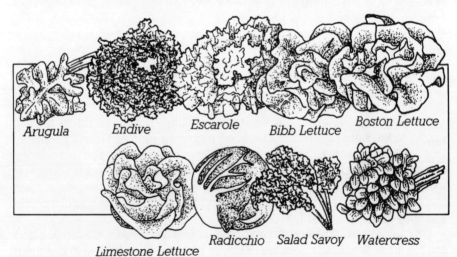

Arugula   Endive   Escarole   Bibb Lettuce   Boston Lettuce

Limestone Lettuce   Radicchio   Salad Savoy   Watercress

kind of herb. A little goes a long way. Highly perishable, use it the same day you buy it and only buy it if it is sold with the roots on. If you can't find it, substitute mustard greens or any bitter weed from your garden that isn't poisonous—say chickweed—for a similar effect.

Endive, Belgian: A real import, this small, tightly held chicory (C. intybus) looks rather like a pale bullet and does come from Belgium. Grown in a light-deprived state, the most anemic one you can find is the best example of the product. It is usually no more than 5 inches long, and it is excellent in salads. Mild in flavor, it combines well with radicchio for both a color and a taste contrast. Store in damp paper towel inside plastic wrap for up to a week.

Endive, Domestic: A member of the chicory family, like Belgian endive, this is a green loose-leafed lettuce that looks something like red-tipped lettuce except that it is as deep a green as parsley and has narrow leaves with white centers. Slightly bitter, it gives punch to mixed green salads.

Escarole: Yet another member of the chicory family, this loose-leafed lettuce is a broader-leafed version of endive. You will know it by its curly leaves and slightly bitter taste. Use as you would endive; they are interchangeable in any recipe.

It is interesting to note that New Orleans–style coffee is sometimes laced with the root of chicory not, as some believe, for economy's sake, but because of taste preference.

Lettuce, Bibb: Another name for butterhead lettuce, this variety is named for the man who developed the strain. Mr. Bibb's lettuce is dark green and soft, and a loose, mild, gentle head.

Lettuce, Boston: Still another name for butterhead lettuce, this variety of lettuce is usually a little larger than the Bibb and sometimes has red-tinged leaves. All of the butter lettuces, Boston, Bibb, Limestone, and butter, are interchangeable in a recipe. The differences in their tastes are subtle. The price differences are sometimes extreme.

Lettuce, Limestone: Another name for butterhead lettuce, this newly popular lettuce is pale green, soft, and buttery. I did discover that much of the California limestone lettuce crop hails from Southern Oregon and is shipped down under cover of night to Northern California markets and sold as a "California" product. I can't quite figure out the cloak-and-dagger posture toward this Oregon-grown and California-sold lettuce, since the word "limestone" only applies to butterhead lettuce that is grown in limestone soil, which is found mostly in Kentucky. The butterhead lettuce grown hydroponically in Southern California is usually priced as high as the occasional head of real Kentucky limestone lettuce that makes its way West, but you don't get that limestone-trace-mineral taste unless the lettuce is grown in limestone soil. So if you go to the grocer's and see "limestone" lettuce at $2 a head next to "butter" lettuce at $.59, just think about it before you cough up the two bucks. Remember the emperor's new clothes.

Lamb's Lettuce: Known by many names, it is sometimes called corn lettuce because it grows wild between rows of corn, or *mâche*. This splendid mild-flavored lettuce has slight overtones of filbert, and it is delicious by itself with just a subtle vinaigrette made with rice wine vinegar and daikon coins on the side.

Radicchio: My favorite story about radicchio comes from my cousin MaryAnne. She and her sister, Margaret, went to Europe and every salad they ordered came embellished with this reddish purple chicory. Margaret couldn't get over it. She kept telling MaryAnne, "You know they've banned the use of DDT in America. I can't imagine. Such a blatant disregard for human life. These salads are positively poisonous." After sending back two salads to stone-faced waiters, she finally was informed by one that the red ingredient, the one she thought had been dipped in DDT, was radicchio, the king of salads. I asked a produce shipper in Los Angeles about this, and she said that every food writer she knows secretly despises the stuff but hates to admit it. I'll say it. This is a prime example of the emperor's new clothes. Radicchio does taste like it's been dipped in DDT. If you like it, go for it, but don't serve it when I come to lunch. When you're buying it, choose the smallest one they have, for the larger they get the more poisonous they taste. And they don't keep well; they should be used within a day or so.

Salad Savoy (Kale): This is that gorgeous purple flowering cabbage like the stuff plant people are putting out into gardens just for looks. Pike Place Market in Seattle even made their annual poster using a fabulous watercolor of purple kale. It also comes in a creamy yellow white. It now is sold in produce sections along with the other salad greens and can be used in salads, or steamed, or in centerpieces. It is gorgeous *and* good to eat.

Watercress: Don't forget about this aristocratic green, a member of the nasturtium family, for when you are putting together fabulous salads. Besides being a good addition to a new mixed green salad, watercress goes well with green and red peppers and a fruit vinaigrette, say blueberry or raspberry. And while you are at it, plant some nasturtiums in the backyard and toss a few nasturtium flowers into your next salad. Their peppery fresh taste is as welcome an addition as their lovely good looks.

Squashes: In the supermarket today, there are at least fifteen varieties of squash. Besides the ubiquitous zucchini, there are bananas, buttercups, butternuts, delicatas, golden nuggets, hubbard, kabocha, and the beautiful turban, which looks more like a centerpiece than something to eat. And the list goes on. One of our favorites is the *chayote,* a green-and-white pear-shaped squash that has a taste like a mild cross between an apple and a cucumber. (See index for recipes.)

Choose firm squashes without soft spots. Use the summer varieties (zucchini, yellow crookneck) promptly. I am happy to report that the many new varieties are more stable, like their cousins the gourds, and stored in the hydrator may keep for months.

Tomatillo: These green tomatoes, sometimes known as *fresadillas,* look like little hard-green tomatoes in a brown paperlike husk. Although a cousin to the more familiar tomato, these little wonders have a tart, lemony tang that sets them apart. Substituting regular green tomatoes can be done, but you'll miss the lemony taste. If you do substitute green tomatoes in a recipe calling for tomatillos, add a squeeze of fresh lemon juice to approximate the taste. I call your attention to the recipe for Sopa de Tomatillo as the best example of the pure, fresh tomatillo taste.

Herbs and Flavorings

Basil: It wasn't long ago that the only place I saw basil growing was in the backs of small Italian restaurants in California mountain towns, where invariably it nestled in a half-buried whitewashed truck tire just outside the kitchen door. The cook would dash out the back door, nip off just what he needed for the day, and slam the screen door behind him on his way back to the stove. But with this popularity explosion, the cook probably will have to start fencing off his basil patch or the neighborhood housewives will steal it all. Everybody wants basil. Last week my neighborhood Safeway offered it as Basel. That's Switzerland, sweetheart, I wanted to say. But anyway, I was glad to see it, by any name.

If you grow basil, or if you buy more than you can use before it wilts, which seems to happen almost instantly, freeze it chopped in ice cube trays filled with olive oil. Then when you need to make a sauce, pop a cube in the skillet. Press a garlic clove or two in, cook and stir, and you are on your way to a great tomato sauce. Basil, fragile as a magnolia, does not dry well. Your best bet is to pick or buy only as much as you need that day, like the Italian chef in the Sierras.

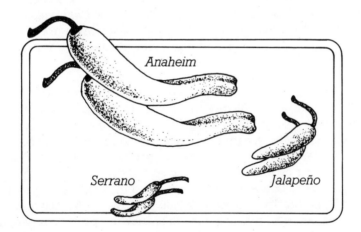

Anaheim

Serrano

Jalapeño

Chiles:

Sometimes I think the produce people are trying to drive me crazy when I go to buy fresh chili peppers. I swear, they will label them anything. I have seen jalapeños called chiles, I have seen jalapeños called serranos, and I have seen everything under the sun called jalapeños. If you find peppers mislabeled in your store, speak to the produce people. The catastrophe occurs if you use a hot jalapeño when the recipe called for a mild Anaheim, and you did it because they weren't properly labeled.

As a rule of thumb, think of it this way. Generally, the smaller the pepper, the hotter it is. The little ones you see that are usually green with some having ripened to red are probably

Serranos. Usually 1 to 1½ inches long, they are small cylinders with pointed tips and a light-green going into yellow. Beside those bigger, darker-green, and rounder cylinders are the

Jalapeños, which are roughly 2½ inches long and 1 inch in diameter. These are hot, but not so hot that pepper bellies can't eat them like apples. They are good both raw in salsas (see recipe for San Francisco Salsa) and cooked in any Mexican Nouvelle dish (see index). If you substitute serranos for these, use only half as much.

Up from the serranos and jalapeños are the nice, mild

Anaheims, or *California chiles,* which may be as long as 6 to 8 inches and 1½ inches in diameter. These are the good stuffers, good in salads, and great in dishes that call for "green chiles," which translates into a mild, green chile.

Cilantro (Fresh Coriander): You'll see this for sale next to the parsley. It looks similar, but has a flatter leaf and is a lighter green. It has become the in seasoning and is used in Mexican and Oriental preparations. In recipes, it is sometimes called "coriander," or "Chinese parsley." It is the leaf of coriander and is used by the Chinese instead of parsley. The taste of cilantro is cool and licoricelike. It should be used judiciously by beginners, for it can overwhelm other flavors. A lot of guacamole has been ruined by born-again cilantro zealots. . . . Pliny named this herb Coriandrum, a name derived from the Greek word "Koris," which means bedbug. Now, we no longer know what bedbugs smell like, but we can guess.

You can keep this fresh, interesting herb the same way you keep parsley—stuck like a posy in a jar of water on the refrigerator shelf with a plastic bonnet. But don't try to dry it. Like parsley, it loses all flavor when dried. Chop and mix with a high-grade olive oil and freeze in ice cube trays to preserve the intense cilantro flavor.

Fennel: Aniselike in flavor, this is a member of the carrot family. Long used as an herb, it is gaining popularity on the West Coast as a vegetable. You will find tightly held pale-green heads that look something like a stunted, flat celery plant with feathery, carrotlike leaves coming from the top. Take a whiff; the licoricelike aroma will let you know that you've found the right thing. Store fennel in hydrator or refrigerator for up to a week. What you don't use by then, you can hang upside down and dry, and then toss on the coals while grilling fish. The licorice, smoky taste will improve the fish flavor. Or steam the stalks and serve with lemon juice and a few drops of extra virgin olive oil for a great, warm salad. Raw fennel is delicious in salads cut up the way you would use celery. Combine fennel slivers with garlic and punch into the flesh of a pork loin before roasting.

Garlic: I went to the garlic festival in Ruch, Oregon, this fall, where everything from garlic braids to garlic wine was for sale (don't ask about the garlic wine). I met an eighty-year-old man who credited his health and vigor to eating an entire head of garlic every morning for breakfast. He claimed that his doctor said his blood pressure had dropped fifty points since he had begun to eat garlic by the head. Now, I don't want to take anything away from the garlic, but I am sure his stress level was reduced by this health practice, since, all during the day, I saw the crowd part for him as he wandered around the festival. The aromatic old boy had a happy buffer zone of about five feet in every direction. But after hearing a talk given by an herbalist, I must say, we came away convinced that garlic must be the rotorooter of the vessels, and we bought some garlic pills that very day. But after two days of belching, we decided we'd rather be dead. Now we just stick to garlic buds in recipes.

At the garlic festival I also learned that in addition to the usual Italian purple-husked garlic that is sold in the supermarket, there is a superior silver-husked variety that is pure white and highly desirable. I also learned that "elephant garlic" is not a true garlic, but actually milder and can be sliced and cooked along with vegetables with great success. You can eat a little parsley after garlic to get rid of garlic breath.

Store garlic in a cool, dry, dark place (not the refrigerator), and it will retain its aromatic personality for several months.

Gingerroot: These knobby brown tubers bear little resemblance to the powdered kind your mother used to make into gingerbread men. The fresh root has a pungent, sharp taste that fades to nothing more than a hot memory when dried and ground. Purchase plump, unshriveled roots, breaking off a moderate supply for yourself.

You can store ginger the way the Chinese do, buried in sand in a cool, dark place, or go the more convenient route, wrapped in plastic wrap in the refrigerator or freezer. In the refrigerator, it will keep for weeks, in the freezer, forever. You can slice it, julienne it, mince it, grate it, or press it through a garlic press. James Beard said that if he grated a small amount for a dish, he didn't even bother to peel it. A good plan, provided you scrub dirt from the root. Each process provides a slightly different result in a recipe. Try different procedures and see which one produces the result that best suits your own particular tastes.

Note: You can grow gingerroot easily from the very roots they sell at the grocery store. Cut the root into eyes, just as you would a seed potato, and let the eyes dry out for a day or so. Then plant in warm fertile soil. The plant requires plenty of moisture and good drainage and can't endure a freeze. It is an excellent choice for a winter crop in the greenhouse. To harvest, dig down about 4 inches below the earth's surface with a sharp paring knife and lop off what you need for cooking that day. This sort of root pruning seems to make the plant thrive.

Parsley: Besides the curly-leafed variety that is a staple in grocery stores, there is a flat-leafed Italian parsley that is more aromatic, less overbearing, and even prettier to look at. And it is as easy to grow and as good to eat as it is good for you. See recipe for Cold Parsley Soup.

Sun-dried tomatoes: Italian countryfolk have long dried the pear-shaped roma tomato for use in the winter (drying being the cheapest, most efficient way to preserve any comestible). Suddenly, here on the West Coast, we have discovered sun-dried tomatoes, as if they'd been invented the day before yesterday. They are delicious, intense, with a supertomato flavor. Next year, I'm going to try drying some myself. But until we all learn how to do it at home, we can buy them from Timbercrest or Frieda's Finest (see mail order section). See index for recipes.

The Moveable Feast

WHETHER MOVING DINERS from the dining room table to the living room, or from the house to the patio, or onto the Stanford parking lot for a tailgate party, you will want foods that can be eaten out of hand. Savory spreads to go with outstanding breads and crackers, and good handmade cheeses and fruits. You may discover, as I have, that a crockery pot filled with an aromatic spread makes for a better picnic entrée than a sandwich.

We do a great deal of alfresco dining on the West Coast because our alfresco, from San Diego to Seattle, is so gorgeous. In British Columbia they call picnics "cottage afternoons." The foods included here are suitable for your own cottage afternoons.

What you won't find in this chapter are canapés and hors d'oeuvres that require individual attention. Although pretty to look at, they seem to me a losing proposition. Whenever I have people at some set-up watering hole, where drinking and talking are central, the food doesn't get the attention it does when people are seated before a beautifully composed plate. I am not about to slave in the kitchen for eight hours just to watch people pop exquisitely executed canapés into their mouths like popcorn. I'll give them popcorn instead. Leave the canapé making to Las Vegas hotel chefs. I want to enjoy the moveable feast myself.

Oyster Mushroom Almond Pâté

If you can't get hold of oyster mushrooms (say, from Full Moon), then by all means make this pâté with grocery store button mushrooms. It's simply too good to miss. Make it a day ahead, store it in a French canning jar, serve with Janet Saghtelian's Armenian cracker bread, from Valley Bakery, and just sit back and watch your guests' faces after that first bite.

Makes 1 pint

3 cups fresh oyster mushrooms (in a pinch, plain mushrooms)
1 cup vermouth
⅔ cup chopped almonds
4 tablespoons sweet butter
⅔ cup freshly grated Parmesan cheese

2 tablespoons dry sherry
2 green onions and tops, minced
2 tablespoons minced parsley
2 teaspoons whipping cream
salt and white pepper to taste

Boil mushrooms in vermouth, covered, for five minutes or until tender. Meanwhile in skillet, brown almonds in butter, taking care not to burn them. In food processor, combine mushrooms, almonds, and remaining ingredients and process to a smooth purée, adjusting seasonings to taste. If texture appears dry, add vermouth, a tablespoon at a time, to create a smooth, spreadable purée.

Japanese Eggplant Caviar with Tamari Sunflower Seeds

The wonderful smooth texture and taste of the Japanese eggplant lends itself well to this old favorite. Using sunflower seeds marinated in Tamari soy sauce brings a new dimension to this lovely spread. (You'll find Tamari sunflower seeds in bulk bins.) This spread is good with cold meats, or on tomato slices, or as a dip. It keeps well, up to a week in the refrigerator, and can be made at your convenience.

Makes 4 cups in 20 minutes

2   pounds Japanese eggplant, peeled and cubed
2   cups Tamari sunflower seeds
6   tablespoons extra virgin olive oil
     freshly ground pepper to taste (be generous)

4   cloves garlic, pressed
4   to 8 shots of Tabasco
¼   teaspoon allspice
¼   teaspoon powdered ginger

Bring 5 quarts of water to a boil in large saucepan. Cook eggplant cubes, uncovered, for about 5 minutes, or until tender. Reduce seed to a coarse butter in blender or food processor, adding 2 tablespoons of olive oil to moisten. Add remaining ingredients (except 4 tablespoons of olive oil) to seeds, and blend.

Once eggplant is cooked, drain and place in mixing bowl. At high speed, beat eggplant until light and airy. Add seed mixture and, with mixer running at highest speed, dribble in remaining olive oil. Adjust seasonings to taste, adding a little more Tabasco or salt to bring flavor to a good potent pow of a taste. When you have a nice mayonnaiselike emulsion that hits you, transfer the mixture to a serving dish. Served best at room temperature.

Beefsteak Mushrooms Stuffed with Sun-dried Tomatoes
[Timber Crest Farms]

Good old California sunshine will dry tomatoes as well as the sun of Italy, and it is now possible to buy domestic dried tomatoes for less than the national deficit. If you have not yet tried tomatoes dried by the sun, I urge you to do so. The intensification that turns an insipid apricot into an outstanding dried fruit works the same on a tomato, giving it the most profoundly sweet flavor. Wonderful.

Serves 4 in 30 minutes

15 large mushrooms, about 2
    inches in diameter, wiped
    clean
2 tablespoons olive oil
5 sun-dried tomatoes
3 shallots
1 clove garlic
¼ cup grated Asiago

12 basil leaves, or 1 teaspoon
    dried
    generous pinch fresh
    oregano, or 1½ teaspoons
    dried
2 tablespoons red wine
    Italian bread crumbs

Preheat oven to 350°. Remove caps from mushrooms and set aside. Coat caps with 1 tablespoon olive oil, inside and out, and arrange in a lightly oiled baking dish.

Finely chop mushroom stems, tomatoes, shallots, and garlic. Sauté in a 10-inch skillet over medium heat until onion is clear; remove from heat. Combine with cheese and herbs, and place a spoonful of filling in each mushroom cap. Add red wine to pan and cook over medium heat, stirring until wine combines with pan drippings and reduces by half. Pour over mushroom caps and top with seasoned bread crumbs. Bake for 15 minutes. Serve hot.

Sonoma Sun-dried Tomato Spread

This one's too easy to prepare to call a recipe, but here's a quick, delicious canapé. Purée one 6-ounce jar of marinated tomatoes and oil in food processor or blender. Season to taste with freshly grated Parmesan and spread on freshly toasted sourdough slices. A rich, smoky ultraconcentrated essence of tomato, this is better than caponata. Try it.

Ginger-Grilled Shrimp on a Skewer
[Judyth's Mountain]

You can get 50 appetizers from this one recipe—or feed four people who happened to get a whiff of it cooking. It is best prepared over a charcoal or mesquite grill, because the spices that drip onto the flame and smoke up give it a pungency that cannot be matched if broiler-cooked. Remember, shrimp are about 90 percent water and cook in no more than two minutes over a properly preheated grill. If you are having a party, you can marinate and skewer up the whole batch, then hand them, uncooked, to your guests and let them grill their own. Be sure to save the marinade to dredge the grilled shrimp in after they are cooked. Hot flour tortillas are wonderful to catch the juices. Just lay a skewer full of shrimp on a tortilla, draw the skewer out, and slather with sauce.

Serve with guacamole, jícama with lime and chiles, and carambola, papayas, mangos, and/or other tropical fruits. A great white-wine cooler or rum knock-out punch also works nicely with this one.

*Makes 50 appetizers, or as a main
course serves 4*

2   pounds medium shrimp,
    cleaned and shelled
1   tablespoon white wine
    vinegar
1   tablespoon ginger jelly
    (Judyth's Mountain)
1   teaspoon chili powder
    (Gebhardt's)
1   clove garlic, pressed
12 fresh basil leaves, minced,
    or 1½ teaspoons dried

¼   teaspoon freshly milled
    black pepper
10 fresh mint leaves, minced, or
    1 teaspoon dried
¾   cup salad oil
    wooden skewers
12 flour tortillas (cut in quarters
    for appetizers; whole for
    main-dish service)

Place shrimp in glass baking dish. Combine all sauce ingredients, except oil, in small saucepan and heat to a boil over medium heat. Remove from heat. Add oil and stir to mix. Pour over shrimp and refrigerate, covered, marinating at least 4 hours but as long as overnight.

Thread shrimp onto wooden skewers and grill on preheated charcoal or wood grill. Baste with marinade and serve folded inside hot flour tortillas. The tortillas are best heated covered in a 200° oven for 5 to 10 minutes. If serving as an appetizer, cut the entire stack into quarters and offer 2 to 3 shrimps per quarter. If serving as a main course, divide the cooked shrimps into 4 portions and allot 3 tortillas per diner.

Smoked Salmon Pâté
with Jalapeño Hollandaise

Fine French restaurants include salmon pâtés on the menu as a matter of course. The success of such a pâté depends partly on the quality of the salmon the cook uses. On the West Coast, custom canners pack salmon that has been alder smoked, Indian style, which produces a superior product that ultimately will make for a smoky, complex pâté—no pale, tepid sissy stuff like they serve in four-star restaurants. When combined with Lime Jalapeño Hollandaise (see next recipe), this is a first course that will make them sit up and pay attention. (See mail order section for sources for custom-smoked salmon.)

Serves 12 in an hour

1   fresh jalapeño (1 ounce),
    stemmed and seeded but left
    whole
4   sprigs Italian parsley
½   teaspoon freshly milled
    black pepper
1   small (3-ounce) onion
1   7-ounce can custom-smoked
    salmon

½   pound fresh salmon fillets
½   teaspoon dried dillweed
2   teaspoons fresh lemon juice
    salt and pepper to taste
1¼ cup whipping cream
2   large eggs
1   cup Lime Jalapeño
    Hollandaise

Preheat oven to 250°. Generously butter a standard 9-by-5-inch bread pan. Cut parchment paper to fit bottom and butter one side of paper, laying it in the pan, buttered side up.

Combine jalapeño with parsley and drop into boiling water for 30 seconds. Remove and lay on paper towel to dry. Cut jalapeño into thin slices and rounds. Using all of the pepper and half of the parsley, make a design on the buttered paper at the bottom of the pan; fan it out like leaves, perhaps cutting some thin rounds, like flowers. Just make it look good. Once you are satisfied with the design, place the pan in the refrigerator to chill.

Combine onion, salmon (make sure there are no bones), dillweed, lemon juice, and pepper and salt to taste in a food processor or blender; whirl until a smooth purée. With the machine running, slowly pour in whipping cream, then eggs. Process 30 seconds.

Remove ¾ of the mixture. Add the reserved blanched parsley to the remaining quarter. Process 10 seconds to blend. Preheat oven to 250°.

Divide the larger portion in half; now you have three parts. Place the part without parsley in the bottom of the terrine, taking care not to disturb the design. Press down with the back of a spoon.

Layer over with the parsleyed portion, leaving a ½-inch boundary on all edges. Layer the final third of the mixture over this, smoothing the surface with the back of a spoon.

Cut another piece of parchment paper to fit over the top, butter generously, and lay it on top of the pâté.

Place bread pan in a larger pan filled ¾ full with warm water, taking care not to splash any into the pâté. Bake for 15 minutes. Turn heat down to 225° and bake for another 25 minutes.

Shake pan; the pâté should not tremble. Insert a straw or fork into center; it should come out clean. When the pâté is firm, like a well-cooked custard, remove from oven. Let stand until it reaches room temperature, then chill (at least two hours). Remove top piece of parchment paper and turn out onto serving plate. Carefully peel away parchment paper, not disturbing your design.

To serve: Cut pâté into thin slices. Puddle a tablespoon or so of Lime Jalapeño Hollandaise onto a small plate and place pâté on top. A little sprig of parsley and a jalapeño cutting beside it finishes the picture. And this, my friends, is more than just a pretty face. Even the most jaded of palates will perk up in anticipation of the main course after one small serving of this West Coast pâté.

Lime-Jalapeño Hollandaise

Here is a sauce so delicious, it could even transform fish sticks into something sublime. Basically, it is nothing more than plain old-fashioned hollandaise made zippy by using lime juice, instead of lemon, and by the pungent addition of diced jalapeños.

Try Lime-Jalapeño Hollandaise over grilled swordfish for a Mexican Nouvelle presentation. Or you can bring new life to an old standby by simply substituting this punched-up sauce into a classic eggs Benedict. One way I like to use it is over a couple of poached eggs resting on a hot corn tortilla. Pour it over leftover ratatouille, and yesterday's eggplant will spring back to life.

Whether you try this sauce with eggs, vegetables, fish, or grilled chicken, do serve it with a side of kiwi, pineapple, and mango slices. Looks good. Tastes good.

If you have a favorite procedure for making hollandaise, just skip my directions and stir in a minced jalapeño or two, but this new technique achieves a perfect hollandaise using a food processor and microwave, tools that many of today's kitchens are blessed with.

Makes 1 cup in 15 minutes

1 **to 2 fresh jalapeños,**
   stemmed and seeded
3 **egg yolks**
2 **tablespoons fresh lime juice**
½ **cup melted butter**
   few grains of salt to taste

Mince one jalapeño in bowl of food processor, using chopping blade. Add egg yolks and whirl 15 seconds. Add lime juice and whirl another 15 seconds.

Meanwhile, melt butter. Easy in a 2-cup Pyrex measure in microwave, or in a pan on the stove set on high. When butter begins to boil, pour into egg mixture with processor running, and whirl for 30 seconds.

Now it's a judgment call. Is the sauce thick enough that you can lay a teaspoon on top and it won't sink? If not, you still have a raw sauce on your hands (despite what all those cheerleading processor cooks have told you in the past). Here's the secret: return thin sauce to 2-cup Pyrex measuring cup. Set microwave on low and cook for 30 seconds. Stir thoroughly with fork. If still a little thin, repeat. Adjust seasonings to taste. If you wish, you may now add the other jalapeño, minced, to make it hotter. If needed, add a few grains of salt. And there's your smooth-as-satin, hot-as-the-devil hollandaise that will *make* your reputation.

Smoked Salmon–Pistachio Cheese Ball

The boys up at Norm Thompson in Portland, who sell an outstanding smoked salmon, recommend the following recipe to their customers. If you use those dyed pistachios along with the green parsley you'll wind up with a super-looking Christmas ball. Just try not to think about red dye number 2.

Makes one 6-inch ball

1   6-ounce can custom-smoked
    salmon
1   8-ounce package cream
    cheese
½   medium onion (2 ounces),
    minced

2   tablespoons fresh lemon
    juice
1   cup finely chopped pistachio
    nuts
¼   cup parsley, finely chopped

Combine salmon, cream cheese, onion, and lemon juice. Form into ball and coat first with pistachios, then with parsley. Refrigerate to set. Delicious with stone-ground crackers or Armenian cracker bread from Valley Bakery.

Hot Artichoke Soufflé Spread
[Rose Miller]

You wouldn't think that this would amount to much, just reading the recipe. But as a one judge of nine in a food show, we found it to be the best in its division, proving once again, that to be good, things needn't be complicated. Served from a pristine white soufflé dish, bubbling hot and steaming, with the pungent aroma of Parmesan cheese, this simple spread tasted better and looked more appetizing than twenty more-complicated entrants in the show.

Makes 2 cups in 30 minutes

1   8-ounce package cream
    cheese
½   cup Parmesan cheese,
    grated
½   cup mayonnaise
3   to 4 shots Tabasco sauce
1   small jar (6 ounces)
    marinated artichokes,
    drained and coarsely
    chopped

Preheat oven to 350°. Thoroughly blend cheeses, mayonnaise, and Tabasco. Fold in artichokes. Pour into 4-inch soufflé dish. Dust top with additional Parmesan. Place in preheated oven and bake 20 minutes until top is brown. Serve hot and bubbly with wheat crackers.

Bay Shrimp Butter

For a savory spread to have on hand for impromptu entertaining, the sweet, succulent Pacific bay shrimp comes to the fore. You can keep this in a crock in the refrigerator for up to a week. And the color is such a lovely shrimpy pink, that when combined with sourdough and perhaps just a touch of golden caviar from California, it becomes a bite fit for a feast.

Makes 1 cup

½ pound butter
¼ pound bay shrimp
shot of Tabasco

1 teaspoon fresh lemon juice
salt and freshly milled black
pepper to taste

Combine all ingredients in processor bowl and whirl to fine smooth pink purée. Pack into crock and chill, covered, for at least 2 hours. Serve with melba rounds or, even better, fresh-made toast from sourdough baguettes.

San Francisco Salsa
[Nancy Denny Phelps]

Here is a simple salsa that has become as much a staple at our house as brown rice. It keeps well in the refrigerator and can even fill in as a vegetable. It's great with fresh, hot homemade tortilla chips and avocado halves brimming with fresh lime juice.

Makes 2 quarts in 15 minutes

3 16-ounce cans stewed
   tomatoes
3 cloves garlic, pressed
½ medium onion (2 ounces),
   finely chopped
1 fresh tomatillo
5 small (2 ounces) fresh
   jalapeño peppers

1 tablespoon cumin seeds
1 teaspoon salt
scant ½ teaspoon black
pepper
juice and pulp of half a lime
(no white membrane)

Ideally, you can make this in a food processor by whirling together the ingredients into a rough purée. You can also make it in a blender, mixing half the ingredients at a time, or by pressing tomatoes through a food mill and fine-chopping the remaining ingredients. The sauce is better if allowed to mellow for 24 hours. Keeps a month in the refrigerator in sealed sterile mason jars.

Homemade Tortilla Chips

Here's a quick way to make tortilla chips at home, and without any oil. Made this way, you get a high-fiber, no-fat snack that, if combined with bean dip, provides a whole protein. It's almost too easy to call a recipe.

Preheat oven to 300°. Take a big stack of fresh corn tortillas and cut them in quarters. Lay them out, one layer deep, on cookie sheets. Sprinkle lightly with salt. Place in oven and bake about 20 minutes until they are well dried out and beginning to brown on the edges. Great hot . . . and think of the cost . . . fast food . . . no preservatives. No fat, and cheap, cheap, cheap.

The Soup Kitchen

THERE'S A NEW JOKE JOURNAL making the rounds of the scientific community that is called "The Journal of Irreproducible Results." Science being, after all, just what you learned in the fifth grade, a process that can be reproduced by the scientific method.

I'd almost like to call this chapter "The Art of Irreproducible Results," because that's what soup making really is—art, not science.

How can I help you make a good soup? It seems like such a simple question. But it is not. Some of the best soups I have ever made can never be duplicated. Why? Because I made them from leftovers. Today for lunch we had a soup so aromatic and delicately scented we all begged for more. There was no more. This soup was made from the contents of the refrigerator. But it well represents a posture toward soup that will go a long way to producing memorable soups for you. I only tell you this so you can see the method, not so that you can replicate this particular soup—I don't even aspire to this myself, I only relish its memory, which will be with me always.

Here's how it went. First, I pulled a quart of frozen stock from the freezer. Now this was no carefully conceived and prepared soup stock. This was the water I had used last week when I had boiled a pound of shrimp scented with bay leaves, lemon juice, peppercorns, salt, and cayenne pepper. After I'd boiled the shrimp, that scented water just looked too good to throw away, so I strained it and threw it into the freezer.

I set this on the stove to boil. Next, I tossed in one of those Manischewitz dry soup mixes—minus the MSG-laced seasonings—which added barley and dried limas to the simmering broth. I let this perk along for a while. I gave it a taste and decided it could use some onion. So I sautéed four coarsely chopped onions along with a whole head of pressed garlic in a little olive oil in a skillet, and then dumped it in with the rest.

The bubbling water was beginning to smell and taste like soup. It had some character and was beginning to have some depth. Finally, I took one more look in the refrigerator and spied a leftover square of Filbert phyllo that we had had for dinner last night. I figured: it's got spinach, the phyllo will probably dissolve and thicken the soup, and the butter couldn't hurt anything. So I cut this three-inch square of stuffed phyllo into little half-inch squares and tossed it in. Guess what? Those lovely little squares did not dissolve. They stayed intact, and that became the greatest surprise of all. Here were these delicious little cheese and nut and spinach filled squares in a soup that was beginning to be too good to be true.

Just before serving, I cut up some fresh parsley and tossed it in. What a soup. What a lunch.

You can create memorable soups yourself, if you'll just begin by saving the scented water used for cooking fish, chicken, or vegetables. (I swear to God, I am not going to repeat the directions for making broth in one more cookbook. If you don't know how, look in one of your big general cookbooks.) You can also create memorable soups using the recipes in this chapter as inspiration and varying the ingredients to taste.

The soups in this chapter represent well the West Coast foodstuffs and ethnic influences. Mendocino Miso, our own California version of a Japanese classic using California seaweed and chicken broth, is as good as any you'll find in a Japanese restaurant. Good garlic soup with guacamole will cure what ails you. I would swear the Cold Lime and Garlic Soup with Cilantro Guacamole is Jewish penicillin that passed through Spain and then Mexico en route to our own West Coast. Medicinal and curative, as well as delicious. Don't miss Heather Bryse-Harvey's Sunchoke Soup. They rave about it in Portland. Make it once and you'll see why.

Please forgive my indulgence in Latin-type soups. I have a weakness for Mexican food, and if asked to choose between Squash Blossom, Tomatillo, Green Chile and Corn, or Chayote Sopa, I simply could not do it. I'd take one of each. I hope you will, too.

Making soup is a joy. I hope you'll begin to create your own irreproducible results in the soup pot.

Cold Cream of Parsley Soup
[Betty Cier]

Betty Cier has been growing and selling herbs and herb vinegars from her home on the Oregon coast for a good many years. She says she knows nothing about herbs, but she studies all the time and knows a lot. Here is a tip she passed on to me about parsley that I found quite useful.

Parsley has one big advantage for winter. It lends its freshness to dried herbs, so that you can mince some and combine it with other dried herbs, at the rate of about one teaspoon dried herbs and one and a half teaspoons finely minced fresh parsley for the equivalent of two tablespoons of fresh herbs. No matter what combination of herbs you are using, basil, marjoram, or rosemary for example, just this little fresh boost of parsley will approximate what you can get during the fresh-herb growing season.

This cold soup of Betty's is really so West Coast. Refreshing, beautiful to look at, and loaded with vitamins to boot. I like to serve it with Italian Tomato bread and a hunk of raw milk Gouda. Raspberry sorbet for dessert with a black butter shortbread. The colors and textures are beautiful and varied. Makes a lunch that belies the simplicity of its ingredients.

Serves 4 in 30 minutes, chills in 1
hour

1   bunch parsley leaves (about   2   large egg yolks
    2 cups loosely packed)   salt and cayenne pepper to
3   cups rich chicken broth   taste
2   cups half and half

Mince parsley leaves. Add to broth in medium-size saucepan and bring to a boil. Simmer for 20 minutes. Strain and stir in cream and egg yolks. Stir over low heat just until mixture coats spoon. Do not boil. Adjust salt and cayenne to taste. Remember that because it will be served cold, the seasonings will tame, so season boldly. Cover and cool soup; then refrigerate to chill. Serve in clear cups with salted whipped cream topping (recipe follows) and a sprig of fresh parsley stuck in like a flag.

Whipped Cream Topping for Parsley and Other Soups

If you are out of sour cream or yogurt and would like a dollop of something to top soup, here is a choice that just may be better than either of the two original choices. I discovered this when—you guessed it—I looked in the refrigerator and saw that it was bare.

Serves 4 in 5 minutes

¾ cup whipping cream
2 tablespoons lemon juice

1 garlic clove, pressed
   salt to taste

Combine whipping cream and lemon juice and let stand a minute or two. Press garlic into it. Now whip until you have stiff peaks, adding just enough salt to taste. Drop this on the soup by the spoonful. Or spread it on bread. Or serve it with cold roast beef. Or stuff it into celery. Or use it for a dip. All-purpose. Pure white. Delicious.

Mendocino Miso Soup

Our very own seaweed, gathered from the beaches of Mendocino and dried, comes to the store looking less pressed and pretty than the seaweed that we get from Japan, but it also is less salty and perfectly splendid in this classic Japanese soup. The latter-day natural-food folks now refer to such seaweeds as sea *vegetables,* but they're still sea*weeds* to me. The Japanese make this soup using a broth made from bonito, a fish that's kin to the tuna. If you happen to have a fish stock around, you could, of course, make this soup using fish stock. A red miso works particularly well in this soup. Serve with rice crackers, the ones that are punched up with cayenne pepper.

Serves 4 in 30 minutes

¾ cup dried Mendocino
   seaweed sheets, broken into
   a cup
4 tablespoons red miso
1 quart rich chicken broth, or
   fish stock

   salt (only if you must)
4 green onions and tops, finely
   chopped

Soak seaweed in warm water for 15 minutes. Drain, rinse, and cut into fine slices. Place in soup pot. Combine miso with about ½ cup of broth to get thin, smooth mixture; then, add remaining broth. Bring to boil and simmer seaweed in broth for 15 minutes. Taste and add salt if seems to need it. Add green onions and tops and continue cooking for 3 minutes. Serve immediately.

Cold Lime and Garlic Soup
with Cilantro Guacamole

Hot garlic soup, with crusty French bread and Parmesan broiled on top, is as good as a classic French onion. This recipe came about because of some leftover soup I had, once again verifying the old maxim about leftovers: sometimes they're better than the original dish. This old leftover became new again, served cold, Mexican Nouvelle style. Olé. If you wish, just double the recipe and eat half hot, and half cold. Then you can compare and see which way you like it best. Actually, both are good and good for you. You know what they say: garlic is as good as ten mothers.

Serves 4 in 30 minutes

2 tablespoons olive oil
1 whole head garlic cloves, peeled and sliced paper thin
5 cups rich chicken broth
¼ cup fresh minced parsley
1 teaspoon Hungarian paprika

salt and freshly milled black pepper to taste
¼ cup fresh lime juice
1 cup Cilantro Guacamole

In the bottom of medium soup pot, sauté garlic in oil until it begins to brown. Add broth and raise to boil. Remove from heat, stir in parsley, and season to taste.

To serve cold: Chill soup and, just before serving, add freshly squeezed lime juice to taste (generally, about ¼ cup juice to 5 cups of broth seems right to me). Serve with a dollop of guacamole that has cilantro stirred in. Mexican Nouvelle. Olé.

To serve hot: Place soup in individual oven-proof soup bowls. Place a thick slice of crusty, generously buttered French bread on top of soup. Sprinkle heavily with freshly grated Parmesan cheese. Run under the broiler to brown, and serve.

Cilantro Guacamole:

2 very ripe Hass avocados
1 green chile, minced
4 tablespoons lemon or lime juice
1 medium tomato, finely chopped

1 small white onion, minced
salt to taste
⅛ cup fresh cilantro leaves, minced

Mash avocados with a fork, not too smooth. Add remaining ingredients. Mash with a potato masher. Serve immediately.

Jerusalem Artichoke Soup
[Heather Bryse-Harvey]

Cooking for company in a business known as "Yours Truly Catering," Heather has found that this soup's reputation precedes it. Her clients request Jerusalem Artichoke Soup for their most elegant affairs. This is a preparation whose sum exceeds its parts. It is so delicious that many diners may feel they'd just as soon skip the following courses and have another bowl of soup. It works admirably with fish or poultry entrées and is especially nice before duck.

Serves 12 in 1½ hours

2 pounds Jerusalem artichokes
¼ pound butter
3 large potatoes, about 2 pounds, peeled and coarsely chopped
½ large onion (¼ pound), coarsely chopped
1 pint (2 cups) rich chicken stock
1 well-packed cup parsley, washed and left whole

2 bay leaves
½ teaspoon dried thyme leaves
1 teaspoon celery salt
½ teaspoon white pepper
   salt to taste
¾ gallon (12 cups) milk
1 cup fresh croutons
   parsley for garnish

Scrub Jerusalem artichokes until most of the brown skin is rubbed off, then slice into ⅛-inch-thick pieces.

Melt butter in a large soup pot over medium heat. Sauté sunchokes until al dente, stirring frequently to prevent burning. Add potatoes and chopped onion and sauté until onion is clear but not brown. Add stock, whole parsley stalks, and seasonings. Simmer, stirring frequently, for a hour, or until potatoes are falling apart. Add milk and simmer an additional 30 minutes. Remove from heat; discard parsley and bay leaves.

Cool slightly, then purée in food processor. Finish by passing soup through fine-mesh sieve to remove lumps. Reheat before serving. Garnish with freshly made croutons and minced parsley.

Chayote Sopa

This wonderful Mexican squash tastes like a cross between an apple and a cucumber and, when combined with flavorful rich chicken broth seasoned with soy, sugar, and a whiff of *mirin* (a Japanese sweet rice wine used exclusively for cooking to give a distinctive sweet, sharp taste to soups) makes an outstanding soup. If you can't find *mirin,* you can substitute rice wine vinegar. Serve this soup as a first course in a many splendored meal.

Serves 4 in 20 minutes

4 medium chayotes (about 1½ pounds)
3 cups rich chicken broth

2 tablespoons sugar
1 tablespoon *mirin*
1½ tablespoons soy sauce

Peel and cut pear-shaped chayotes in half; then disgorge the big seed and discard it. Cut the squash crosswise into paper-thin slices.

In medium saucepan, bring broth to a boil. Season with sugar, *mirin,* and soy sauce. Add squash slices and simmer until squash is tender (no more than 6 or 7 minutes). Do not overcook, or the squash will disintegrate. Adjust seasonings to taste. Serve immediately.

Green Chile and Corn Soup with Crème Fraîche

The combination of green chiles and corn in a rich chicken broth topped with a pungent crème fraîche makes a delicious beginning to a Mexican Nouvelle dinner.

Serves 4 in 30 minutes

½ small onion (4 ounces), minced
2 cloves garlic
1 tablespoon oil
4 green chilies (5 ounces), stemmed and deseeded, or 1 4-ounce can green chilies, minced

2 ears of corn, kernels cut from cob
1 quart rich chicken broth
   salt and pepper to taste
½ teaspoon brown sugar
½ cup crème fraîche for top (See Sadie Kendall, M.O.)

Sauté onions in garlic and oil in soup pot over medium heat until onion begins to brown, about 3 minutes. Add green chiles and kernels of corn. Cook, stirring, until corn begins to brown, about 3 minutes. Add broth and bring to a boil. Season to taste. Simmer until corn is cooked through, about 10 minutes. Serve with a dollop of crème fraîche atop each bowlful.

Squash Blossom Soup

For a delicate, pale-gold cream soup with a flavor as evanescent as spring, you need to obtain squash or pumpkin blossoms. Any farmer's market that sells courgettes, those baby squashes with the blossoms intact, probably will sell you the blossoms alone. If you have your own pumpkin patch, check Squash Blossom Chicken (see index for recipe) for instructions on how to pick your own.

This Mexican Nouvelle soup, available only in the summer when the squash crop is on, tastes splendid out in the backyard, while you are grilling fish or poultry. I have served it before the Oysters Hot-Cha-Cha, along with a loaf of sourdough bread and a bottle of Oregon Perry.

Serves 4 in 15 minutes

4 tablespoons butter
1 medium onion (4 ounces), coarsely chopped
1 quart squash or pumpkin blossoms (about a dozen)
2 cups rich chicken broth

2 cups half and half
salt and white pepper to taste
1 perfect squash blossom for garnish

Sauté onion and blossoms in butter in medium soup pot, over medium heat, until onion is clear, blossoms collapse, and stems appear tender, about five minutes.

Purée, either in processor, blender, or food mill. Return purée to soup pot and stir in broth and cream. Raise to a simmer, but do not boil. Salt and pepper to taste, but gently, gently. . . . Don't let the pepper overwhelm the blossom's delicate aroma. Serve immediately. Float a luscious whole squash blossom on top of the soup.

Thyme Mushroom Soup
[Danielle Lapp]

Thyme waits for no man, and if this soup is allowed to stand, thyme takes over. So make it, serve it, and be out of the kitchen in less than half an hour. It makes for a lovely lunch with assorted field greens, a good brown bread, and fruit of the season for dessert.

Serves 4 in 15 minutes

2 tablespoons butter
½ pound mushrooms, coarsely chopped
1 medium (¼-pound) onion, coarsely chopped
2 tablespoons flour

2 cups milk
1 cup yogurt
1 cup rich chicken broth
1 teaspoon fresh thyme leaves, or ¼ teaspoon dried thyme leaves

In a 10- to 12-inch skillet, heat butter over medium heat. Add chopped mushrooms and onion and sauté until onion is clear and browning on edges and juice evaporates. Sprinkle flour over vegetables, stir, and cook for a couple of minutes. Add milk, yogurt, broth, and thyme. Cook, stirring constantly until thickened. Do not boil. Purée soup in processor. Adjust seasonings to taste. Reheat only if necessary. Serve immediately.

Sopa de Tomatillo

Here is a clear, bright astringent soup that is a luscious yellow green and so pungent you'll swear it has lemon juice in it. Not so. Just good old tomatillos, those green Mexican tomatoes in the paperlike husks. (See Special Ingredients section for further description.) Serve this soup by itself for a diet lunch, or to begin a Mexican Nouvelle dinner. Follow with Pollo Margarita, Sesame Tortillas, and sliced cherimoyas with lime for dessert.

Serves 4 in 15 minutes

2   tablespoons olive oil
½   cup chopped onion
4   cloves garlic, pressed
1   pound fresh tomatillos, husked and coarsely chopped

1   quart rich chicken broth
    salt and fresh ground black pepper to taste
½   cup plain yogurt for top

Heat olive oil in medium saucepan until sizzling. Add onion and garlic and sauté until onion turns clear. Add chopped tomatillos and cook, stirring, until tomatillos begin to lose their shape, about 10 minutes. Add chicken broth and raise to a boil. Season to taste. Serve immediately with a dollop of yogurt on top. Delicious with Sesame Tortillas.

Chicken and Shellfish Provençal in Broth
[Chef Ross Pullen for Belinda's in Portland]

Here is a classic Mediterranean dish that makes use of local products in the best tradition of peasant cuisine. (Lucky are the peasants who live in such a neighborhood, no?) Serve with garlic French bread and a good rosé. Gelato for dessert. Cup of espresso. Do I hear you moaning with pleasure?

Serves 2 in 20 minutes

¼   cup olive oil
½   cup sliced fresh mushrooms
4   sliced artichoke bottoms
2   tablespoons finely minced bell peppers
2   tablespoons finely minced garlic
2   tablespoons finely minced shallots
4   ounces chicken breast, boned, skinned, and cut julienne
6   ounces fresh Oregon scallops
3   tablespoons Herbes de Provence (Pocket Creek Farm)

4   tablespoons chopped parsley
¼   cup peeled, seeded, and chopped fresh tomato
¼   cup dry white wine
4   tablespoons hot chicken broth
4   small shrimp, peeled and deveined
    salt and freshly milled black pepper to taste
8   cooked Dungeness crab legs in the shell
8   Oregon mussels, steamed

Heat olive oil in a 12-inch skillet over high heat. Add mushrooms, artichoke bottoms, and bell peppers and sauté lightly over high heat, shaking the pan to prevent sticking. Add garlic, shallots, chicken, and scallops. Continue to sauté until chicken, garlic, and shallots begin to brown. Add Herbes de Provence, parsley, tomatoes, white wine, chicken stock, shrimp, and salt and pepper to taste. Simmer for 5 minutes, uncovered. Add crab legs and mussels; adjust seasonings to taste. Divide into heated stoneware bowls.

This is the end of a day's work for me. I am off to the fishmonger's, and if he is out of even one of these ingredients I will reach across the counter and throttle him.

California Onion Soup Zinfandel

The basic French onion soup, spiked with the zip of a California Zinfandel and made with the patience of a French farm wife, will bring results as good as any four-star restaurant's. The main thing with the procedure of this recipe is to be patient. When you are cooking the onions in the butter, keep the temperature low and cook them until they are absolutely shapeless. You will smell a great caramel aroma wafting up as the onions release their sugars. Shortcut this procedure and you won't get the same result, because this soup relies on the chemistry of what happens in the equation: onions + heat + wine + broth. Buy the best quality Swiss cheese you can find, use only top-of-the-line French bread, and select a good Zinfandel. Look, you can drink the rest of it with the soup. The results are worth every minute of your careful attention.

Serves 8 in an hour

4 large yellow onions (2 pounds), thinly sliced
¼ pound butter
4 tablespoons unbleached white flour
2 quarts rich beef broth
1 cup Zinfandel

salt and cayenne pepper to taste
8 thick slices French bread, toasted and slathered with butter
1 cup grated Swiss cheese

In a medium-size soup pot, sauté onions in butter over very low heat, stirring from time to time, until onions completely lose their shape, turn a lovely golden caramel hue, and give off a divine browned-sugar aroma (takes about 20 minutes). Sprinkle flour over, and cook, stirring, for 3 minutes. Pour in stock and wine and simmer, uncovered, for 30 minutes. Season to taste. Pour servings into heat-proof soup bowls in which you have placed a piece of toasted, buttered French bread. Top with generous sprinkle of cheese. Run under the broiler to brown. Serve immediately.

Pacific Salmon Chowder

Pacific coast fishmongers who routinely sell salmon steaks generally have for sale the heads, tails, scraps, and chunks of fish that are too small to sell otherwise. These pieces make a perfectly delicious chowder. The only cautionary note I can offer is to take a good deep sniff to make sure that the fish pieces you buy are as fresh as the steaks on ice at six bucks a pound. If you are buying fish heads and chunks to make chowder, purchase *1½ times* as much weight as the recipe calls for in order to get the required amount of fish meat. This recipe produces the most gorgeous salmon-pink cream you ever saw. Serve with Gloria's Whole Meal Bread (see index for recipe) and a bottle of beer.

Serves 8 in an hour

2 pounds salmon meat
2 quarts water, lightly salted
1 bay leaf
1 medium onion, quartered
1 celery stalk, cut into three pieces
2 medium potatoes (1 pound), cut into ½-inch cubes
1 cup finely chopped onion
1 cup finely chopped celery
1 1-pound can tomatoes, finely chopped with juice

½ teaspoon celery seed
3 tablespoons butter
3 tablespoons unbleached white flour
1 pint half and half
   salt and freshly milled black pepper to taste
   butter and fresh chopped chives for garnish

Combine salmon, water, bay leaf, onion, and celery in large soup pot. Salt water to taste. Heat just to simmer and cook until salmon flakes off the bone (no more than 15 to 20 minutes). Remove from heat. Lift salmon from broth and separate meat from skin and bones. Reserve meat; discard skin and bones. Pour broth through strainer and reserve.

Wipe out soup pot. Measure out 2 cups of reserved broth and replace in soup pot. (Cover and freeze the rest of this precious scented water for another fabulous soup.) Add potatoes, onion, and celery. Cover and simmer until vegetables are tender, about 15 minutes. Add tomatoes, juice, and celery seed, and continue to simmer.

In a medium saucepan, make a golden roux using flour and butter; then pour in half and half and heat to a boil, stirring. Adjust seasonings to taste. Cook and stir until sauce is smooth and thick. Add white sauce to vegetables and broth and stir. Heat, but do not boil (remember, tomato and milk curdle when boiled together). Add salmon. Adjust seasonings to taste. Serve immediately. Swirl a little butter on top and dust with chives.

Halibut–Bay Shrimp Chowder

The combination of pearly white firm-fleshed halibut chunks and delicate bay shrimp in a classic chowder, underscored by bacon, onions, and potatoes, makes a hearty winter-menu item. This chowder should be so thick that your spoon will rest comfortably on top without sinking. Serve it with condiments including freshly made croutons, riced hard-cooked egg, minced green onions and tops, and minced bell pepper pumped up by the addition of some finely minced jalapeño. Serve with crusty French bread, thick slices of Brie, winter pears, and the Spinach Salad with Peanuts (see index for recipe).

Serves 8 in an hour

4 thick slices of bacon, diced	1 pint half and half
½ cup diced onion	3 tablespoons butter
3 medium potatoes (¾ pound), diced	3 tablespoons flour
water to cover	¼ pound cooked bay shrimp
1½ pounds halibut, cut into 1-inch chunks	2 tablespoons fresh lemon juice
salt and white pepper to taste	1 tablespoon lemon zest, minced
1 quart milk	2 tablespoons dry sherry

Cook bacon in a soup pot over medium-low heat until fat is rendered and bacon is browned. Add onion and cook until clear. Add potatoes and water to cover. Add salt to taste. Heat to a boil and cook, uncovered, until potatoes are tender, about 15 minutes. Add halibut chunks, milk, and half and half. Simmer, uncovered, for 5 minutes.

Make a golden roux of flour and butter in a 6-inch skillet. Scoop a cup of hot milk into roux and make thick sauce; pour sauce into soup. Adjust seasonings to taste.

Finally, add shrimp, lemon juice and zest, and sherry. Serve immediately.

Hearty Lamb-Barley Stew

A robust, rich, winter main-dish stew, this requires little attention and will warm you up after a day out in the snow, or the rain, or with the IRS. I'd call this the ultimate comfort stew, and it takes advantage of the outstanding "spring" lamb that comes to our West Coast markets right in the teeth of winter. Serve with Gloria's Whole Meal Bread (see index for recipe), a salad of pomegranate and grapefruit, and a glass of robust red wine. A memorable West Coast winter meal.

Serves 8 in 1½ hours

1 pound lamb stew meat, visible fat removed, and cut into chunks
2 medium onions (½ pound), finely chopped
2 tablespoons oil
2 medium carrots (½ pound), grated
2 cups rich broth; beef, mushroom, or vegetable
1 cup dry red wine
1 28-ounce can tomatoes and juice
1 8-ounce can tomato sauce
2 tablespoons brown sugar
½ cup dry uncooked barley
12 sprigs fresh rosemary, or 1 teaspoon dried
   salt and freshly ground pepper to taste
½ cup fresh minced parsley

Sauté lamb chunks and onions in oil in a large soup pot until both begin to brown. Stir in grated carrot and cook for 3 minutes. Add stock, wine, tomatoes and juice, tomato sauce, brown sugar, barley, rosemary, salt and pepper. Bring to boil, cover, and simmer, stirring occasionally, until meat is thoroughly tender, about 45 minutes. Add chopped parsley and serve.

Old Hollywood Star Potion
Potassium Power Purée

Back in the thirties, the movie stars were the ones who figured out that it was in their best interest to live forever and to remain, if possible, forever twenty-eight years old, seamless, wrinkle-free, and steamy. To that end, the health food business began in America. Here's an old Hollywood recipe that I find quite good for lunch, and new again in that it is pure complex carbohydrate and high in potassium and vitamin C.

*Serves 2 potential stars or 1
superstar*

1 large russet potato (½ pound), sliced but unpeeled
1 medium yellow onion (¼ pound), peeled and roughly chopped
2 large stalks celery with leaves, cut in 5 or 6 pieces
6 medium carrots (¾ pound), unpeeled and cut into 5 or 6 pieces each
   cold water to cover
¼ cup shoyu tamari soy sauce
¼ cup minced parsley leaves
   juice of half a lemon
   salt and pepper to taste

Cook vegetables in open pan with water to cover until tender, about 30 minutes. Purée in blender or food processor; return to pan and season with soy sauce, parsley, and lemon juice. Bring to a simmer. Adjust seasonings to taste. Now drink a toast to Gloria Swanson, Mae West, and all the good old girls.

All-Vegetable Chili

This is it. Now I'll have to stay on the West Coast forever. The real chili heads in the country's heartland would shoot me on sight at the very mention of chili without meat. But I'm telling you. This is rich. It's satisfying and I promise you that not one person you serve it to will ask, where's the beef?

Textured vegetable protein (TVP) is a 100 percent soy product that looks like rolled oats and is sold in natural-foods stores. Although you may have to hunt for it, you'll find it to be more successful than tofu, which is the usual addition to vegetarian chili. If, however, you are stumped completely, do substitute a pound of tofu, broken into small bits, for the TVP. The chili, like all chilis, is better the next day.

Adapted from The Ashland Bakery
Serves 10 to 12 in an hour

2   cups (1 pound) dry kidney or pinto beans
7   cups water, slightly salted
¼   cup cooking oil
4   garlic cloves, pressed
1   small (4-ounce) finely chopped onion
2   stalks (2 ounces) finely chopped celery
1   bell pepper (4 ounces), finely chopped
1   jalapeño (1 ounce), finely chopped
2   cans stewed tomatoes (1 28-ounce can plus 1 16-ounce can)
1   7-ounce can chopped black olives

2   tablespoons Worcestershire sauce
½   cup TVP (textured vegetable protein) or 1 pound tofu, crumbled
2   tablespoons chili powder (Gebhardt's is best)
½   teaspoon red pepper flakes
1   tablespoon cumin seeds salt and black pepper to taste
1   12-ounce bottle of beer (Labatts Canadian is perfect)
¼   cup corn meal masa dissolved in
1   cup cold water

Cook the beans in water until tender (quick in a pressure cooker). In soup pot, heat oil until water sizzles when dropped into it; then sauté garlic, onion, celery, and peppers. Add tomatoes and juice, breaking them up with a spoon.

Add olives, Worcestershire sauce, TVP, beans, and all remaining ingredients except beer, corn meal masa, and 1 cup water.

Bring to a gentle boil. Cook, uncovered and stir occasionally, for 30 minutes, adding beer as you go along to maintain thin soupy consistency. Just chugalug any that's left over.

Mix masa and water and stir in to bind the chili. Cook for 5 minutes. Adjust seasoning. You may eat immediately or, if you can stand it, let it sit. It will be better in 1 hour and too good to be true in 1 day.

Black Bean Gumbo

When I told my South Louisiana friend that out here on the West Coast I had begun making gumbo from black beans, there was a shocked silence on the other end of the phone. At last she spoke. If you want beans, she began, have red beans and rice. If you want gumbo, use meat—even coon or alligator—but *something* to flavor the gumbo. Now, wait a minute, I told her. Think about this. What flavors the gumbo? Well, she said, Really, I guess it's the roux. Precisely, I said. You know the roux is so delicious that you could make a meal out of an old tennis shoe if you had to. Yes, she laughed. Some of those old Cajuns have pulled up worse than that from the bayous and made a decent gumbo from it. Amen, I said.

Like lots of soups and bean dishes, this one also is better the second day. And it freezes well. So, even though it makes a lot and is some trouble, you'll get several meals from it. So here it is. A bean dish that is savory, well seasoned, and pungent, not like any other bean dish you've ever had. Great for vegetarians but equally satisfactory to carnivores. Good with a Roman Romaine Salad, Gloria's Whole Meal Bread, and Chocolate Silk Pie for dessert (see index for recipes).

Serves 8 to 10 in 1 hour

2 cups (1 pound) dry black turtle beans

7 cups lightly salted water

Cook beans in boiling water until tender (quick in a pressure cooker)

4 onions (1½ pounds), chopped

4 celery stalks (6 ounces), chopped

1 bell pepper (4 ounces), chopped

7 garlic cloves, pressed

1 cup cooking oil

1 cup flour

2 quarts vegetable (or chicken) broth

¼ cup Worcestershire sauce salt to taste

generous amount black and red pepper

¼ teaspoon thyme

3 cups cooked rice (white or brown)

1 tablespoon filé

1 cup fresh parsley, cut fine with scissors

½ cup finely sliced green onions and tops

½ cup finely chopped fresh tomato

Chop onions, celery, bell pepper, and garlic and set aside. In a 5-quart cast-iron Dutch oven, over low heat, make a dark brown roux using oil and flour. When it is just this side of burning, add chopped vegetables and stir vigorously. Keeping heat low, cook and stir until vegetables seem to blend completely with roux. (This entire process will take about a half-hour.) Add broth and Worcestershire sauce. Season with salt, peppers, and thyme. Lift beans from cooking liquid and add to soup. Cover and simmer for 30 minutes, adding bean juice as needed to maintain a thin, soupy consistency. Stir frequently during cooking period so that beans don't stick to the bottom. Meanwhile, remember to cook the rice.

When 30 minutes is up, stir in the filé and let it cook for 3 to 4 minutes to bind gumbo. Just before serving, stir in parsley and green onion. Adjust seasonings. Serve over rice with dollop of chopped tomato on top. Begs for corn bread and a bottle of beer. Umm. Ummmm.

Cold Strawberry Rhubarb Soup

You will need to have on hand Strawberry Rhubarb Sauce to begin, but once you have the sauce made, the soup goes together in five minutes flat. And what a soup. Serve with Pistachio Puffs, cold sliced breast of turkey, and Riesling to drink. Now that's a summertime lunch.

Serves 4 in 5 minutes flat

1 cup chilled Strawberry
   Rhubarb Sauce
1 cup plain yogurt

1 cup half and half
1 cup cold rich chicken broth
1 cup dry white wine

Whisk together and serve.

Strawberry Rhubarb Sauce

A good portion of the nation's rhubarb crop is grown and processed on the West Coast. Frieda Caplan says that it's one of her best-sellers. For a sauce like this one, you will only need a stalk or two of fresh rhubarb. Choose one that is not too big, one that, if you pierce it with your thumbnail, yields readily. The amazing thing about this sauce, made from just-ripe berries and rhubarb, is that it's good on almost *everything*. Grilled poultry. Vanilla ice cream. Custard. Even pan-grilled fillet of sole. It is amazing. The sauce keeps well in the refrigerator and in the summer is more useful than mayonnaise. Try it as a side dish with curried chicken-fruit salad. Kiwi. Flame grapes, almonds, and bananas. And don't forget to try the soup that is based on this sauce.

Makes 1 pint in 20 minutes

1 cup chunked fresh rhubarb
1 cup sliced strawberries
¼ cup water

⅔ cup sugar
   few grains salt

Combine all ingredients in saucepan. Cover and bring to a simmer. Cook slowly until rhubarb is tender, about 10 minutes. Cover and refrigerate. Good cold or room temperature.

Quick Two-Melon Soup

This takes only as long as it takes you to peel, seed, and toss two melons into a food processor. Nothing to it, and it's a perfect beginning to an outdoor summer meal. Choose this soothing, bland soup to accompany a pungent chile-spiked entrée, like the San Diego Chicken or a grilled fish with Lime Jalapeño Hollandaise and a Spiked Polenta (see index for recipes).

Serves 4 in 10 minutes

1 perfectly ripe cantaloupe (about 1 pound)
1 perfectly ripe honeydew melon (about 1 pound)

½ cup fresh lemon juice
  zest of ½ lemon, minced
4 sprigs fresh mint

Peel, seed, and coarsely chop the two melons. Purée in processor, blender, or food mill. Stir in lemon juice and zest. Refrigerate. Serve cold with a sprig of fresh mint on top.

The
Farmer's
Market

TO PREPARE FOR THIS BOOK, I visited every major farmer's market on the West Coast: The Farmer's Market, Irvine Ranch, and Grand Central in Los Angeles; The Farmer's Market and Produce Terminal in San Francisco; The Yamhill in Portland; The Pike Place in Seattle; and the Granville Island in Vancouver. If you want to understand the minute, idiosyncratic nuances of the West Coast food scene, just visit these markets.

The abundance and variety call Fellini to mind. Trays full of lambs' tongues. Eye-high pyramids of cherimoyas. Acres of green groceries. Living geoduck clams that draw back when you touch them. Eggs. Fresh flowers. Jams. Honeys. Boxes stacked to the ceiling. Cold cement floors washed clean with a hose. To walk through a market in a West Coast city is to get the real picture of the abundance of our life out here in the Garden of Eatin'. When visiting a farmer's market, you get a firsthand look at the ethnic influences that eventually find their way to the suburbs.

While visiting Pike Place, for example, Oriental farmers offered not only the familiar bok choy and pak choy but also bundles of sweet pea leaves and vines, lemon grass, and other greens that I couldn't identify, and they couldn't say, in English. Hang around a farmer's market, ask questions, and you'll get answers—maybe only in halting English—but you can learn about new foodstuffs and cooking techniques if you'll just ask. Like the Thai fellow I asked about the wonderful marinade he was using on some skewered chicken he had grilling in Pike Place Market. He looked up at me and grinned from ear to ear. Is made from soy sauce and 7-Up, he said. So much for ethnic purity.

In this chapter, I have included not only vegetables but fruits. The sorbets can be used, as we all know, for both desserts and between-courses items. I do think that when you shop farmer's markets in summer, sorbets become a real possibility if you're a bargain hunter. Fruits or berries at their last gasp of ripeness make the best sorbets, and you can usually get them for low prices. I don't keep sorbets on hand during the summer for anything grand, like a seven-course dinner. I keep them because they are cool, refreshing, and handy to have around, just for the family.

The one thing I must say about the fabulous fruits and vegetables we have here on the West Coast is that they require the fewest recipes. For most of them can be eaten as is, or with just a little steaming or stir-frying. If you were so inclined to become a vegetarian, there'd be no better place on earth to live than the West Coast of North America. It's all here. It's all fresh. It's all at the farmer's markets.

Avocado Advocate Salad

One day I was in the supermarket, poring over the avocados, giving them the standard ripeness test—you know, press in at the stem end. When who should step up but this big burly fellow with a perfectly groomed handlebar mustache, looking for all the world like that silver-haired daddy of mine. Turns out he had just sold his avocado ranch near San Diego and moved north. Now he was into trees, he said. But anyway, he said that I was testing all wrong. He picked up an avocado in a hand that looked like a ham, and holding it in the palm of that paw, just gave the whole thing a little squeeze. Now that's the way to test for a ripe avocado, he said, leering. The man did love his fruits. And judging from the jangle of gold chains around his neck, the avocado had been good to him. He was unhappy about kiwi fruits, though. Why ever' damn school teacher's buyin' up pieces of land for kiwis. They'll drive the price clear through the floor, he went on. He was out of kiwis too, he said. Then he gave me advice about buying land in Oregon for farming trees and offered me a ride home. Poor old devil. I guess he'd discovered that trees don't talk.

But he did know a good way to serve avocados. This is the way we do it down in San Diego, he said. Thanks, I said, trotting into place at the checkout counter. I wonder what happened to him? I never even got his name to credit him for this recipe.

Serves 4 in 15 minutes

2 **large perfectly ripe Hass avocados, peeled, deseeded, and sliced**

1 **papaya, peeled, deseeded, and sliced**

1 **head limestone (or butter) lettuce**

Fan alternating slices of avocado and papaya onto a bed of butter lettuce set on individual salad plates.

The Dressing:

4 **ounces plain yogurt**

1 **tablespoon shelled roasted peanuts, coarsely chopped**

1 **tablespoon sunflower seeds**

1 **tablespoon fresh minced mint leaves**

3 **tablespoons orange juice**

Mix ingredients in jar. Cover and shake. Pour over salad.

Four-Pepper Salad

Monterey Bay once was teeming with sardines. As Steinbeck informed us, the waterfront was choked with canneries. But one day, mysteriously, the sardines vanished from Monterey Bay. Visit the boardwalk today and you'll see shops, restaurants, and tourists instead of the fishery business that once occupied those huge, plain structures. Californians did, however, develop a taste for sardines, and in their customary, innovative fashion, incorporated them into the standard vinaigrette, much as the Italians have done with their beloved anchovies.

This dressing works well in any vegetable salad where the vegetables would be improved upon by marinating. Blanched green beans. Mushrooms. Just look around. The produce section will probably suggest more possibilities than I could. I get a little delirious over the produce section in my plain old West Coast Safeway store. Just last week they had four kinds of bell peppers, not to mention the hot ones. So I picked up one of each color and had the makings for a salad that looked as good as it tasted.

I fanned the peppers onto individual serving plates, alternating the different color peppers. Then I drizzled the vinaigrette over each serving. Gorgeous and a taste that really woke 'em up.

Serves 4 in 10 minutes
(plus 2 hours for marinade)

1 **each: red, yellow, purple, and green bell pepper, seeded and thinly sliced**

Sardine Vinaigrette:

¼ **cup red wine vinegar**
1 **teaspoon brown German-style mustard**
1 **medium shallot, minced**

4 **sardines**
½ **cup olive oil**
   salt and pepper to taste

Place peppers in glass dish, taking care to keep each color separate.

Whisk together vinegar, mustard, and shallot. Mash sardine into mixture, using fork. Now add oil, drop at a time, whisking, to make a fine emulsion.

Spoon over peppers. Cover and refrigerate for at least two hours.

To serve: Fan peppers onto individual serving plates, making wide bands of each color for dazzling red, purple, yellow, and green crescents. Wow. Good with a simple, basically bland bean entrée (see index for Baked Lentils with Cheddar recipe).

Alfalfa Sprout and Artichoke Salad

When I sent this in to my editor, she commented that it seemed a bit too easy. To which I reply, honey, there's no such thing as "too easy." A jar of marinated artichoke hearts put up in California and for sale in every grocery store west of the Mississippi has saved the day for many a harried cook. I'll tell you the truth: if I'm really desperate, I just eat them for lunch right out of the jar.

Serves 4 in 10 minutes

½ **head cauliflower (½ pound), broken into flowerets**
2 **green onions and tops, cut into 1-inch segments**

2 **cups (4 ounces) alfalfa sprouts**
1 **6-ounce jar marinated artichoke hearts and juice**

Combine all ingredients in a salad bowl. Toss to mix. Just pour juice from the artichoke jar over for dressing. Easy, no? White and green, crunchy and soft. And ready in no time at all.

Belgian Endive with California Wild Rice Topping

Remember that wild rice expands up to four times its dry volume. In order to get two cups of cooked wild rice, you just begin with half a cup dry rice and simmer it, covered, in two cups barely salted water until it is tender (about forty minutes). You can make this ahead, even a day ahead, and only top the greens at serving time. Delicious with roast poultry.

You will find American pine nuts in markets, or you can get them through mail order from Meadow Farms Country Smokehouse. You may see Portuguese and Chinese ones; avoid the Chinese. They taste as if they've been marinating in turpentine across the Pacific.

Serves 4 in 15 minutes

2 cups cooked wild rice	⅓ cup mayonnaise
⅓ cup toasted chopped pine nuts	⅓ cup plain yogurt
	¼ teaspoon curry powder
½ cup golden raisins	1 head Belgian endive

Combine rice, pine nuts, and raisins in medium bowl. Mix together mayonnaise, yogurt, and curry powder and pour over rice mixture. Stir to mix. At this point, you may refrigerate and hold until serving time, even the next day. Just before serving, divide endive among 4 salad plates, making a nice design, and place a serving of chilled rice mixture on each.

Warm Carrot Salad with a Blueberry Vinaigrette
[Canter-Berry Farms]

Carrots and blueberries are a marriage made in heaven. This warm salad, of luscious carrot orange, blue berry, and bright green Italian flat leaf parsley, is a natural complement to grilled fish entrées. Thick slices of good brown bread, sweet butter, a bottle of dry white California zinfandel . . . now, that is a dinner.

Serves 4 in 20 minutes

1 pound carrots, scraped and sliced into thin coins	½ cup finely chopped flat Italian parsley leaves
⅓ cup extra virgin California olive oil	2 teaspoons blueberry jam salt and freshly milled black pepper to taste
¼ cup less a tablespoon blueberry vinegar (Canterberry)	

Place carrots in medium saucepan with barely salted water just covering. Cover and boil until barely tender, about 15 minutes. Meanwhile, in serving bowl, combine oil and vinegar. Whisk into an emulsion and add parsley leaves and jam. Adjust seasonings to taste. Stir to mix and let stand until carrots are cooked. Once carrots are al dente, remove from heat, drain, and pour dressing over. Stir to mix. Serve warm.

California Christmas Fruit Salad

For an astringent, light complement to a winter's roast poultry meal, try this one.

Serves 4 in 10 minutes

2 navel oranges
1 perfectly ripe Hass avocado
1 pomegranate

1 banana
½ cup coarsely chopped walnuts

Section oranges, slice avocado, seed pomegranate, and slice banana; and combine all with walnuts. Toss to mix.

The Dressing:

1 tablespoon honey
1 tablespoon Madras curry powder

1 tablespoon poppy seeds
4 tablespoons rice wine vinegar

Whisk ingredients together and pour over fruits. Toss to mix.

Mustard-dressed Brown Rice Salad

This whole-meal salad is best served at room temperature. Make the dressing while the rice is cooking, and let the dressing blend. I usually add the remaining ingredients to the dressing before the rice is done, and let that marinate a while as well. One nice alternative is to use about ¼ cup of California wild rice along with the brown rice. You would think, here on the West Coast, that we had just invented brown rice. It is prominent on the menus of Los Angeles Thai restaurants and some Chinese and Japanese ones, as well as the conventional natural-foods restaurants. When I see an item like this on a menu, I believe that the natural-foods folks really have won the war.

This salad is good for two or three days, and we like it with pan-fried brook trout laid on a bed of watercress. Makes a very pretty plate.

Serves 4 in an hour

1   cup brown rice
2½ cups barely salted water
½   cup olive oil
1   egg
2   tablespoons white wine
    vinegar
1   tablespoon Dijon mustard
    salt and fresh cracked
    pepper to taste

½   cup (2 ounces) raw milk
    cheddar cheese, cut in bite-
    size cubes
½   cup finely chopped fresh
    Italian parsley
6   green onions and tops, cut in
    1-inch lengths and sliced
    vertically into shards
1   red bell pepper, cut in fine
    julienne

Cook rice, covered, in simmering water until just al dente, about 50 minutes. Place in sieve, then refresh under warm running water. Drain thoroughly.

While rice is cooking, whisk together dressing ingredients to a mayonnaiselike emulsion. Add other ingredients and stir to mix. Cover and set aside until rice is done.

Toss cooked, drained rice with cheese, parsley, onion, and red pepper. Pour dressing over salad and toss.

Sonoma Sun-dried Tomato and Wilted Lettuce Salad

Marinated sun-dried tomatoes have the most divine, smoky quality, and when combined with lettuce, they make an outstanding salad. For a main-dish salad, simply add *pancetta* (Italian dry-cured unsmoked bacon) or cooked, crumbled bacon. A loaf of sourdough and sweet butter. Pinot Noir to drink. Gelato. Can you stand it?

Serves 4 in 15 minutes

½   cup marinated sun-dried
    tomatoes, cut into slivers
1   head torn butter lettuce
    leaves
¼   cup seasoned tomato oil,
    from tomato jar

½   cup thinly sliced fresh
    mushrooms
2   tablespoons red wine
    vinegar
    salt and pepper to taste

Combine tomato slivers with lettuce leaves. Heat oil with mushrooms until smoking hot in a 6-inch skillet. Add vinegar, season to taste. Stir to mix and pour at once over tomatoes and lettuce. Serve immediately.

Sonoma Sun-dried Tomato
and Rosemary Chèvre Salad
[Timber Crest Farms]

Sadie Kendall sells the most outstanding California goat *(chèvre)* cheese with dried rosemary impressed into its sides. Sadie's cheese is as white as first-fallen snow, and as mild and creamy as any chèvre you'll find. As Sadie once told me, goat cheese is not supposed to taste "funny." Believe me, Sadie's cheese does not taste "funny." It is sublime. If you ask her to ship you some, it will come carefully wrapped, tucked in with a cold pack, shrouded by plastic foam. You know the Kendalls are careful, even before you open the cheese. And then you eat it. Wow. No wonder Kenneth Frank, chef of the famous Los Angeles restaurant, La Toque, orders it every week. I have to tell you, it's Christmas every day here. Because of mail order food supplies, that is. And today, I not only have Sadie's cheese but Rancher Waltenspiel's marinated sun-dried tomatoes to cook with. I hope you can read this. I am writing lying down, because I am too weak with joy to sit up.

Serves 4 in 15 minutes

1   **cup crumbled goat cheese with rosemary (add ½ teaspoon dried rosemary when using plain, uncoated goat cheese)**
½   **cup marinated sun-dried tomatoes, drained and cut into ½-inch pieces**

1   **tablespoon red wine vinegar**
1   **teaspoon Dijon mustard**
1   **tablespoon olive oil salt and freshly milled black pepper to taste**
1   **head butter lettuce, separated into leaves**

Combine crumbled cheese, rosemary, and tomato pieces.
Whisk together vinegar, mustard, and oil. Season to taste.
Arrange washed and dried lettuce leaves on chilled salad plates, spoon equal portions of cheese-tomato mixture into center of lettuce beds, and top with dressing.

California Chèvre Orange Salad

The explosion of greens and reds in the lettuce section of the produce department has changed forever our ideas about what lettuce means. Pale, buttery Boston lettuce, combined with red peppery Radicchio and bleached Belgian endive, combine to provide a salad plate with visual pleasure as well as taste excitement. Making a luxurious bed for *chèvre* (goat) cheese and succulent oranges, well, that's "California Nouvelle" at its finest. (See mail order section for goat cheese and exotic lettuce sources.)

Serves 4 in 15 minutes

12 leaves Boston lettuce
12 leaves Radicchio or red
    cabbage
2   whole Belgian endives
½   cup olive oil
½   cup whole blanched
    almonds
½   cup walnut halves

8   ounces California chèvre
    cheese, cut in thin slices and
    then divided into 4 equal
    parts
8   thick slices navel oranges,
    peeled and thinly sliced
¼   cup rice wine vinegar
    salt and pepper to taste

Arrange washed and dried lettuce, Radicchio, and endive leaves on chilled salad plates in an alternating-spoke pattern.

In an 8-inch skillet, heat oil, then sauté almonds and walnuts until lightly browned, stirring constantly. Drain on paper towel. Now, in same skillet, heat cheese slices until warmed through and beginning to soften. Remove and arrange over salad greens and reds. Top with orange slices and sprinkle with nuts. Add vinegar and salt and pepper to skillet. Bring to a boil, pour over salads, and serve.

Pistachio Pasta Salad

Here's a whole-meal, yellow, green, red, and white, crunchy, soft salad. Quick and satisfying.

Serves 4 in 20 minutes

1   medium yellow squash (¼
    pound), cut julienne
2   medium carrots (½ pound),
    scraped and cut julienne
½   cup (2 ounces) mushrooms,
    sliced vertically
6   cherry tomatoes (3 ounces),
    halved
4   green onions and tops, cut in
    1-inch lengths, then sliced
    finely

8   ounces small seashell pasta,
    cooked al dente and drained
⅔   cup pistachios, shelled, chop
    half and reserve other half
    whole for garnish
¼   cup Italian parsley leaves,
    packed loosely
½   cup vinaigrette

Wash, cut, and prepare all vegetables.

Bring 4 quarts of water to a rolling boil in a large sauce pot. Place julienned squash and carrots in a large colander and drop into boiling water. When water reaches a boil again, count to 30, then remove colander and vegetables from water. Refresh under cold, running water. Drain and reserve.

Combine blanched vegetables with mushrooms, tomatoes, onions, and cooked pasta. Toss to mix. (At this time, you may cover and refrigerate until serving.) Just before serving, toss in chopped pistachios and parsley. Pour a standard vinaigrette over, and toss to mix. Top with whole pistachios.

Japanese Green Salad
[Katherine DeFoyd]

Combining California's finest lettuces and the French method of fine chopping fresh ingredients (for maximum flavor) with a dressing of Japanese origins makes for an outstanding salad to serve with grilled fish. Do note that the dressing should be allowed to stand for fifteen minutes before it's poured over the greens. Then, the salad itself, which is best at room temperature, should stand for ten minutes before serving.

Serves 4 in 30 minutes

½ head red tip lettuce, washed and torn into bite-size pieces

1 head butter lettuce, washed and torn into bite-size pieces

12 spinach leaves, washed and torn into fine pieces

3 green onions and tops, cut white part paper-thin and green part into ½-inch lengths

2 celery ribs, strung and finely chopped

1 3-inch piece of daikon, cut into fine slivers

Dressing:

¼ cup oil

¼ cup rice wine vinegar

1 teaspoon saké

1 teaspoon water

2 tablespoons chicken broth

¾ teaspoon German-style brown mustard

2 teaspoons sugar

2 teaspoons toasted sesame seeds

2 drops sesame oil

Combine all dressing ingredients in jar, cover, and shake to mix thoroughly. Let stand for 15 minutes.

Combine salad ingredients, cover, and set aside.

Pour dressing over greens, and toss to mix. For maximum marriage of flavors, let dressed salad stand for 10 minutes before serving.

Roman Romaine Salad

Here is a salad particularly well suited to pasta entrées, and ideal with Sonoma sun-dried tomato main dishes. You will find it best to allow the greens to marinate in the dressing for at least 10 minutes before serving.

Serves 4 in 20 minutes

15 large Romaine lettuce leaves, washed and torn into bite-size pieces

1 medium carrot, scraped and grated

1 6-inch piece of English cucumber, finely sliced

½ cup pine nuts

Dressing:

½ cup extra virgin olive oil

¼ cup red wine vinegar

1 teaspoon water

¾ teaspoon German-style brown mustard

½ teaspoon brown sugar

3 garlic cloves, finely chopped

1 teaspoon Worcestershire sauce

salt and freshly milled black pepper to taste

Combine torn greens with carrot, cucumber, and pine nuts in a wooden salad bowl.

Combine dressing ingredients in jar, cover, shake to mix, and pour over salad. Allow to stand for 10 minutes before serving. Toss well.

Spinach Salad with Peanuts in a Citrus Vinaigrette

The first time I ate this salad, I couldn't figure out what the little brown things were. Undercooked garbanzos? Big lentils? It finally hit me. Plain old peanuts. What a lovely combination.

Serves 4 in 20 minutes

4 cups packed fresh spinach leaves (1 pound)

½ red onion (3 ounces), thinly sliced

1 cup roasted peanuts

½ cup sesame seeds

1 grapefruit

2 teaspoons fresh lemon juice

2 teaspoons Dijon mustard

2 tablespoons vegetable oil

salt and pepper to taste

Wash spinach carefully (remember, they grow the stuff in pure sand). Break into bite-size pieces, discard stems, and place in large salad bowl. Toss red onion rings with spinach. Sprinkle in nuts and seeds and toss.

Working over a bowl to catch the juice, cut peel from grapefruit, removing all of white peel and membrane. Cut grapefruit into wedges, discarding all membrane. Add grapefruit to spinach.

In small jar with tight-fitting lid, combine 2 tablespoons grapefruit juice, lemon juice, mustard, and oil. Cover and shake vigorously. Season to taste. Chill dressing and salad separately until ready to serve.

To serve, pour vinaigrette over salad, toss gently, and serve immediately.

Alaskan King Crab and Vegetable Salad

Alaskan King crab remains a popular item on West Coast menus. If you get a fresh one, there is nothing better. But nine times out of ten, this particular crab seems to taste remarkably like rubber bands. Why? The Alaskan King, along with *all* of its shell-covered cousins, begins to lose flavor within 24 hours of being plucked from the water. If you purchase crab meat that has been removed from the shell and—god forbid—frozen, you'll be eating a product that bears little resemblance to the succulent fresh version. Oxidation causes a chemical change to take place in shellfish, and the premature loss of shell is fatal to flavor.

The problem with Alaskan King crab is that it just doesn't get to market quick enough in the lower forty-eight. If you have a reliable fishmonger who will tell you the truth about delivery times and whether or not the crab was ever frozen, then by all means try this delicious salad with Alaskan King crab. Otherwise, just substitute a shellfish that you *can* get impeccably fresh—Dungeness crab, scallops, shrimp, or prawns.

Serves 4 in 30 minutes

1 cup (6 ounces) small young Blue Lake green beans, snapped and cut into 1-inch lengths

1 cup (6 ounces) small yellow wax beans, snapped and cut into 1-inch lengths

8 baby or 4 regular carrots (½ pound) scraped and cut into ¼-by-2-inch julienne

2 celery ribs (3 ounces), cut into 2-inch lengths, then into ¼-inch julienne

1 medium (¼-pound) zucchini, cut into medium ¼-inch coins

1 medium (¼-pound) yellow squash, cut into ¼-by-2-inch julienne

¾ cup (6 ounces) whole snow pea pods, with blossom end snapped off and strung

1 medium red bell pepper (3 ounces), cut into paper-thin julienne

½ medium English cucumber (¼ pound), cut into thin ⅛-inch coins

1½ to 2 pounds Alaskan King crab, or other shellfish, boiled just until done and removed from the shell

Arrange the cut and prepared beans, carrots, and celery on an expanded vegetable steamer. Place steamer in a 10-inch skillet with an inch of water lining the bottom and bring water, over high heat, to a boil. Cover, reduce heat, and steam for 4 minutes.

Pour ½ cup cold water into skillet to stop boiling and add green and yellow squashes, layering snow pea pods over the top. Isn't that a picture? Recover and continue steaming for three minutes.

Remove vegetables and place in colander; refresh under cold water. Drain and set aside while you make the dressing.

Dressing:

1 tablespoon rice wine vinegar	¼ cup vegetable oil
1 teaspoon fresh lemon juice	generous grating of fresh
1 tablespoon brown German-	black pepper
type mustard	

Whisk together vinegar, lemon juice, and mustard. Add oil, a little at a time, whisking to make a nice vinaigrette emulsion. Season to taste with pepper.

To assemble: Combine cooked vegetables with raw bell pepper and cucumber in a good-looking serving dish. Toss in cooked, shelled crab meat, reserving a little to place on top for garnish. Add dressing to salad and toss. Garnish with reserved crab and serve.

Cole Slaw with Bay Shrimp

Remember cole slaw? That ever-present addition to fried-fish plates? Sometimes good, sometimes slimy, sometimes totally forgettable? Well here's a West Coast version, using precooked bay shrimp, that is pungent, lower in calories, higher in taste value, and quick to prepare. Did you ever wonder how they shell those little suckers? Boy, I'd hate to be a shrimp shucker on the West Coast.

Serves 4 in 10 minutes

4 cups shredded cabbage	1 green apple, diced (pippin
(Savoy's the best)	or Granny Smith preferred)
1 green onion and top, finely	1 cup cooked bay shrimp
sliced	

Dressing:

¼ cup mayonnaise	2 drops Worcestershire sauce
½ cup plain yogurt	1 tablespoon honey
1 tablespoon Japanese rice	
vinegar	

Mix vegetables, apple, and shrimp. Combine dressing ingredients and whisk to mix. Pour over salad, toss to mix, and chill.

Sashimi Salad

The key to any Japanese raw fish dish is freshness. Buy the albacore from a reliable fishmonger. Sniff it carefully; it should have a clean, almost vinegary smell to it. The least hint of ammonia and it's too old to eat. If you have access to fresh fish, you can add some of the following varieties and make the plate even more beautiful: halibut for a compact, firm chewy texture; squid for nice pinwheel shapes, or salmon for lovely color. Our own Tulelake horseradish, about as pungent as Japanese wasabi (see mail order section), makes a good dipper. In California, East can meet West with this salad, as it might well precede an entrée of grilled red meat and a French mousseline of the season. Try it. It really works.

Serves 4 in 15 minutes

4 tablespoons rice wine vinegar
3 tablespoons brown, German-type mustard
   salt and pepper to taste
½ cup salad oil
12 stalks pencil-slim fresh asparagus, woody stem snapped off
1 6-inch piece Daikon radish, peeled and cut in 3-inch match-stick julienne
1 6-inch piece English cucumber, peeled and cut in match-stick julienne

2 medium carrots, peeled and cut in match-stick julienne
1 medium tomato, finely diced and reserved separately
   vegetable oil for deep frying
8 won ton skins
1 pound fresh raw albacore tuna, cut in paper-thin slices
12 sprigs fresh chervil, or ½ teaspoon dry

Make salad dressing of vinegar, mustard, salt and pepper, and oil. Whisk to blend and set aside.

Blanch asparagus in boiling salted water for 3 minutes; douse in cold-water bath. Cover and set aside.

Combine radish, cucumber, and carrot in bowl. Cover and refrigerate.

Dice tomato and refrigerate separately in a covered bowl.

About 10 minutes before serving, pour oil into heavy, medium saucepan to a depth of 3 inches and heat to 365°, using a candy thermometer. Using kitchen tongs, deep fry won ton skins until golden. Drain on paper towels.

At serving time, divide mixed vegetables onto 4 plates. Place a won ton skin atop vegetables; then place thin slices of albacore on each skin. Cover tuna with another won ton skin and top with a second layer of tuna. Use remaining tuna around edges. Top with blanched asparagus, 3 to the plate, a portion of diced tomato, and some fresh chervil sprigs. Drizzle dressing over and serve. They'll love it.

Braised Artichoke Halves, Family Style

In Castroville, California, the artichoke capital of the world, artichokes are as common at the family table as bread and butter. But the natives figured out long ago that a big, beautiful whole one, weighing close to a pound, serves two people.

So, if you prepare a big multicourse dinner and have, at hand, a supply of large green globe artichokes, you may discover that you needn't serve an entire artichoke to each person—it actually may be too much of a good thing—and that you can present the artichokes in an arresting fashion by cutting them in half before cooking and serving them.

I love to serve these artichokes with a course of fresh pasta in a butter-and-garlic sauce. For a party of eight, after the artichokes are cooked, arrange them in a handsome design on a round platter and pass the platter along with a heaping bowl of pungent pasta. The picture presented by eight artichoke halves, looking for all the world like some minimalist painting on a plate, followed by a staggering bowl of butter-garlic-sauced pasta (see Judyth's Mtn. in mail order section), freshly grated Parmesan cheese, and freshly minced Italian parsley, is enough to make you skip the rest of the dinner. The following proportions are for four people, but you can double it, triple it, or whatever you need, depending on the size of your dinner.

Serves 4

2 large green globe artichokes	¼ cup fresh lemon juice (about
2 tablespoons olive oil	½ lemon)
4 cloves garlic, pressed	½ cup water
¼ cup minced parsley	

Prepare artichokes for cooking. First, use scissors to cut off spiny ends of leaves; then cut off woody-stemmed end. Using a long thin-bladed fillet knife, cut artichoke in half, lengthwise. As you look into the cut flower, you will see leaves, pale small leaves with prickly tips, and the solid, white heart. Using a paring knife, cut away small prickly leaves and fuzzy "choke." Do not cut into the heart.

Over medium heat, in a 12-inch skillet, sauté garlic in oil until it begins to brown. Now add artichokes, the cut side down, and sauté until beginning to brown. Sprinkle with parsley and lemon juice. Reduce heat to lowest setting, add water, cover, and steam until just tender (from 10 to 20 minutes, depending on size and maturity of artichokes). To determine doneness, give one leaf a tug; it should come off quite easily.

To serve, arrange on a serving plate in an interesting spoke pattern, pass along with lemon, garlic, parsley butter, or Lime Jalapeño Hollandaise (see index for recipe).

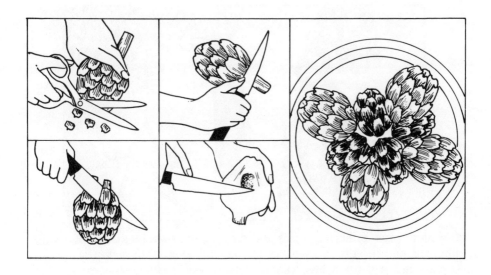

Boniatos con Limón

The South American sweet potato, *boniato*, is a white-fleshed, pale-red-skinned tuber. Combined with the tart addition of lemon, it makes a sweet, satisfying starch dish that goes well with stir-fried entrées. (You can substitute a regular sweet potato or yam with good results.)

Serves 4 in 45 minutes

2   medium *boniatos* or sweet
   potatoes (about 1 pound)
1   lemon

4   tablespoons sugar
   water to cover
   pinch of salt

Peel sweet potatoes and cut into 1-inch cubes. Drop immediately into pan of water to cover that has been scented with juice of half the lemon, sugar, and salt. Place over high heat and bring to a boil. Cook, uncovered, for about 20 minutes.

Meanwhile, slice remaining lemon half into very thin slices. After 20 minutes of cooking, add lemon slices to boiling syrup. Continue to cook until potatoes are tender and lemon syrup has reduced to a clear, thick consistency (about 20 minutes longer). Serve hot or at room temperature with glazed lemon slices. Drizzle a spoonful of hot syrup over each serving.

The Brussels Sprouts Christmas Tree with Two Dipping Sauces

In the fog-kissed coastal mountains around Half Moon Bay, in California, you can tell it's winter when the hills turn green again. And the carefully cultivated fields that bloom in the bottom crevices of the hills begin to yield

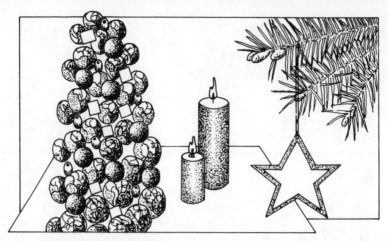

up winter crops, brilliant in color and dazzling in array. Fields full of orange pumpkins and flowers of every color that will soon stock flower shops nationwide, acres of artichokes, as bountiful and regal as their silver green color promises. And standing in rows, bright green, 3-foot-high, cone-shaped plants that, on closer inspection, turn out to be brussels sprouts on the stalk.

As Christmas approaches, you will find brussels sprouts still on the stalk for sale in West Coast grocery stores. Brilliant green, a fine whorled design of little cabbages entwining stalks as sturdy as walking sticks. You can take the entire 2-foot stalk home, steam it, stand it up, and have your own edible festival tree. Sometimes, when we're having a holiday party, I poke holes in the stalk with an ice pick and "trim" the tree with cherry tomatoes, radish roses, carrot curls, Westphalian ham rolls, and anything else that strikes my fancy.

Presented cold, and with a couple of good dipping sauces, this makes a nice edible centerpiece that gives partygoers the familiar feeling of something to dip without that same tired crudités platter.

I've also given you a couple of good dipping sauces that are good both on vegetables and meats; and both also work well as salad dressings. In fact, I first tasted them in a fine Eastern European restaurant, where they were ribboned over plain old romaine lettuce with alfalfa sprouts on top. (Now there is Californizing for you. Hay sprouts, indeed.)

One stalk serves 8 to 10
in 20 minutes

  1 **whole stalk brussels sprouts**
     barely salted water to cover
     bottom of pan

Place a steamer rack inside the biggest roasting pan you've got. Trim the stalk end from the brussels sprout to make level, so that it will stand up. You may discover that you need a saw to do it. Gads, the thing is as tough as a tree. Pull out the remaining leaves tucked between the sprouts. Using an ice pick, make holes where the leaves were, for later, when you can plug in toothpicks for alternate vegetables. Place stalk in roaster on a rack, add 1 inch of water, cover, and steam over medium heat until sprouts are just tender, about 15 minutes. Once cooked, remove and cool. Trim the "tree" with whatever edible baubles you can think of—cherry tomatoes, black radishes, hard cheese squares, cucumber chunks, carrot curls, stuffed green olives. Accompany with dipping sauces.

Makes 1½ cups in 5 minutes

Parsley Dressing:

1 cup loosely packed Italian parsley leaves	⅔ cup best-quality mayonnaise
	⅓ cup plain yogurt
1 tablespoon lemon juice	

In a blender—not a processor—blend completely parsley leaves and lemon juice. Whirl in mayonnaise and yogurt. This dazzling lime green sauce is good for dipping cold vegetables or for dressing a green salad.

Makes 1½ cups in 5 minutes

Mustard Sauce:

1 green onion and top	½ cup plain yogurt
1 tablespoon rice vinegar	½ cup mayonnaise
2 tablespoons brown German-style mustard	

In blender, whirl onion with vinegar until puréed. Add remaining ingredients and whirl into a smooth sauce. This nice, tan speckled sauce looks good beside the parsley sauce, yet has a distinctive taste all its own. The two can be used together and won't run together or fight one another.

Calabasitas
[Betty Hunt]

Here is a nice, light Saturday lunch. Serve it with Sangrita, homemade tortilla chips, and Black Bean Gumbo.

Serves 4 in 20 minutes

1 red bell pepper (3 ounces), cut into fine julienne	8 corn tortillas, cooked until crisp
1 green bell pepper (3 ounces), cut into fine julienne	4 finely chopped green onions and tops
4 small zucchini (½ pound), cut into fine julienne	2 cups (¼ pound) grated Swiss cheese
1 cup fresh mushrooms (¼ pound), sliced vertically	1 tablespoon chili powder (Gebhardt's is best)
1 tablespoon cooking oil salt to taste	1 perfectly ripe Hass avocado, peeled, pitted, and cut into fine slices

In a 10-inch skillet, sauté peppers, zucchini, and mushrooms in oil over medium-high heat until just crisp and beginning to brown—careful not to overdo it. Salt to taste.

Crisp-cook the tortillas in a 6-inch skillet, barely wiped with oil, over high heat (about 30 seconds on each side). Place on warmed plates and reserve.

In a mixing bowl, combine green onions with half the cheese. Add chili powder and stir to mix thoroughly. Add sautéed vegetables. Toss and place on crisp tortilla. Top with remaining cheese. Garnish with avocado slices. You might like a shot of picante sauce or the San Francisco Salsa on this as well.

Vegetable Chalupa

Chalupa means little boat in Spanish. And this little boat is brimming with sautéed vegetables, crisp and delicious. Here is a vegetarian entrée that grows like the fabled loaves and fishes. Simply multiply the vegetables at a rate of one piece for every diner, and you can create a banquet for anyone who shows up for supper.

Serves 4 in 15 minutes

2 tablespoons olive oil	1 cup grated cheddar cheese
1 medium zucchini (½ pound), sliced in thin coins	½ cup plain yogurt
1 onion (4 ounces), coarsely chopped	1 fresh ripe tomato (4 ounces), chopped
2 cups mushrooms (¼ pound), sliced vertically	1 very ripe Hass avocado (¼ pound), peeled and thinly sliced
2 celery ribs (2 ounces), thinly sliced on the slant	Picante sauce or San Francisco Salsa
4 corn tortillas	

Heat oil to sizzling in a 10- to 12-inch skillet. Sauté zucchini, onion, mushrooms, and celery until onion is clear, about 5 minutes. While doing this, warm 4 dinner plates in the oven.

Warm tortillas in a dry 6-inch skillet over high heat, about 15 seconds on each side. Place 1 on each warmed dinner plate and pile on the sautéed vegetables. Top with cheese and run under the broiler until bubbly and brown, about 3 minutes.

Top with a dollop of yogurt, tomatoes, and avocado. Spoon on a little salsa and serve. This is one of those great all-in-one dishes. Hot and cold and crisp and soft and a picante taste that makes you sit up and take notice.

Chayotes Rellenos
(Stuffed Individual Squash)

The chayote is a small hard squash, popular in Central America and now being cultivated in Southern California. Its smooth green flesh lends itself to stuffing for a good vegetarian lunch. Serve with fresh fruit of the season, crusty French bread, and ginger-lemon tea.

Serves 4 in an hour

2 chayote squash (1½ pounds)
1 small onion (3 ounces), finely chopped
3 tablespoons butter
1 hard-cooked egg, chopped
½ cup grated raw milk cheddar

¼ cup plain yogurt
1 raw egg, beaten until frothy salt and freshly milled black pepper to taste
⅓ cup bread crumbs

Preheat oven to 350°.

Choose firm, light yellow green squashes. Split them down the middle and scoop out flesh, leaving about a ⅓-inch shell. Mince squash meat and reserve. Sauté onion in half the butter. Add squash meat and cook, stirring, until squash begins to brown on edges, about 5 minutes. Add hard-cooked egg and cheese, stirring to melt cheese. Remove from heat and mix with yogurt and raw egg to bind it. Season to taste, and stuff into squash shells. Sprinkle with bread crumbs and dot with remaining butter.

Place in a greased baking dish, cover, and bake for 25 minutes, or until tender. Remove cover and continue to bake until brown, about 5 more minutes.

Eggplant in a Szechwan Sauce
[Hilary Miller]

I am fond of this eggplant side dish not only with Chinese dinners but also with leg of lamb. The recipe, as it stands, is fiery hot. If you're timid, first try it with only one jalapeño and a half-teaspoon of white pepper. But do try it, at least once, in all its glory. Janice Gallagher, my editor, and I agree that once in a while, you should eat something that makes your nose run. This capsicum hot eggplant preparation will do just that. Another reason it's one of my favorites is because it can be made ahead, even a day ahead. I just had leftovers of it for breakfast; I swear it was better than it was last night. What a great way to start the day. Serve at room temperature.

Serves 4 in 45 minutes

1   eggplant (about 1½ pounds)
2   fresh jalapeños (about 3
inches long), stemmed,
deseeded, and chopped
4   medium-size garlic cloves,
chopped medium fine

1   large green onion and top,
chopped into ½-inch pieces
½   cup oil

Sauce:

¼   cup soy sauce
½   cup water
½   to 1 teaspoon white pepper

1   teaspoon sugar
1   tablespoon cornstarch

Cut eggplant into 1-by-3-inch julienne pieces. Soak in ice water to close pores, about 15 minutes. While eggplant is soaking, cut peppers and garlic and make sauce.

Mix sauce ingredients together in cup and set aside, leaving a spoon in mixture to stir once more before adding to vegetables.

After 15 minutes, drain eggplant and dry by paper toweling; pieces should be firm and have shiny skins. Heat wok until just smoking around bottom; add ½ cup oil and heat. Add eggplant and toss a couple of times in oil to thoroughly coat, then cover and cook for 2 minutes. Uncover and continue cooking for another minute.

Add chopped peppers, garlic, and onion, and cook until eggplant is tender. Pieces must be completely limp before sauce is added. Stir sauce again, then add to eggplant mixture. Stir until thick. Remove to serving dish. Let dish stand until reaches room temperature for optimum taste.

Garlic Braised Fennel

Here is a wonderful, bright vegetable to serve with pastas. Although it takes an hour, slow cooking makes the combination of cool licorice-like fennel, sometimes known as sweet anise, and the hot sweet taste of slow-cooked garlic buds so delicious that you may find yourself mopping the pot liquor up with a piece of french bread, because this marriage was made in the slow-cooking skillet and deserves to be savored.

Cut the feathery tops off the fennel bulbs, tie a string around them and hang them upside down to dry in your warm kitchen. Then, the next time you are grilling fish, break off a few sprigs and toss them onto the coals. It will create the most delicate, fabulous taste you can imagine.

Serves 4 in an hour

4 tablespoons olive oil
2 fennel bulbs, tops removed,
   and cut in half, lengthwise
1 whole clove garlic, buds
   separated, smashed with the
   flat of a chef's knife, and
   peeled

salt and pepper to taste
½ cup water

In a 10-inch skillet, heat olive oil over medium heat, then add fennel bulbs and smashed garlic buds. Brown on both sides, about 10 minutes. Season to taste. Add water, cover, lower heat, and simmer until tender when pierced with a fork.

Green Beans with Blackberry Vinegar
[Oregon's Own Gourmet Vinegars]

Serves 4 in 30 minutes

1 pound fresh green beans,
   ends nipped but left whole
   water to cover
4 tablespoons butter

¼ cup Oregon blackberry
   vinegar (see mail order
   section)
¼ cup chicken stock

Parboil beans in boiling, barely salted water to cover until just al dente, about 10 to 15 minutes. Drain. Replace in pan and add butter, vinegar, and chicken stock. Boil, uncovered, until liquid reduces to 1 tablespoon. Serve immediately.

Green Beans and Elephant Garlic

Elephant garlic, as garlic-growing purists will tell you, is not a true garlic. But it is wildly popular on the West Coast. Why? Perhaps because it's so big. Perhaps because it's so new. Or, perhaps, just because it's so tame. You can slice elephant garlic in very thin pure-white slices and intermix it with many vegetables to good advantage—the taste is subtle, gentle. You won't even notice anybody taking a discreet step away from you after lunch.

Serves 4 in 20 minutes

1 tablespoon peanut oil
1 pound fresh green beans,
   ends trimmed, cut in 3-inch
   lengths
1 large elephant garlic clove,
   peeled and sliced paper thin

2 tablespoons red wine
   vinegar
2 tablespoons Shoyu soy sauce
   few drops hot pepper oil
¼ cup water

In a wok or 12-inch skillet, heat oil to smoking and stir-fry beans and garlic for 2 minutes. Add vinegar, soy sauce, hot pepper oil, and water. Cover. Reduce heat and steam until beans are cooked and liquid is reduced to no more than 2 or 3 tablespoons, about 10 minutes. Equally good piping hot or at room temperature.

Broiled, Stuffed Zucchini Grande

I swear, that story, Jack and the Beanstalk should have been Jack and the zucchini vine. And, of course, the bigger they get, the less flavor they have. If you have precious courgettes (baby zucchinis with the blossoms intact), just steam them a moment and serve with butter. But if you've turned your back on the garden long enough for the invasion of the body snatchers to take place in your own backyard, here's one way to use a monster squash—aside from a fast game of Zuke frisbee.

Serves 4 in 20 minutes

1 large zucchini (1 pound)	3 tablespoons homemade or
1 green onion and top, finely	best-quality mayonnaise
sliced	1 teaspoon cornstarch
2 tablespoons minced fresh	salt and freshly ground
parsley	black pepper to taste
3 tablespoons freshly grated	additional Parmesan for
Parmesan cheese	sprinkling

Precook whole zucchini either by parboiling for 10 minutes or, in the microwave, whole and unsullied, for 3 minutes. Slice in half lengthwise. Scoop out flesh, leaving generous shell.

Chop zucchini flesh and combine with remaining ingredients. Stuff into shells. Sprinkle with additional Parmesan. Broil 4 inches from heat for about 5 minutes, or until top browns. Cut each piece in half and serve to 4 people.

Mousseline of Carrot and Turnip

As sure as death and taxes, you will find vegetable mousses served on the West Coast. Some are wonderful, some bear an uncanny resemblance to wallpaper paste. The difference, it seems, lies in technique.

There are subtle variances in texture, depending on what method you choose to achieve the purée. The old-fashioned way is to use a trusty potato masher. The new, easy way is to use a food processor. The traditional French way is to use a food mill. The texture achieved by a food mill is superior to either of the other choices; you get a "riced" effect, which has more granularity and is the least like you had been secretly opening Gerber's jars in the privacy of your own kitchen.

If you do elect to use a food mill, heat milk and butter separately, then whisk into the riced vegetables using the lightest touch. Adjust seasoning to taste.

The combination presented here is hearty winter fare, best suited to roast-meat entrées. Using produce seasonally, you can create your own mousselines. Just try to include one root vegetable in any combination you consider.

Serves 4 in an hour

4 medium carrots (1 pound), pared and cut into coarse pieces

3 medium turnips (1 pound), pared and cut into coarse pieces

pot of boiling barely salted water to cover

½ cup milk or cream or yogurt

2 tablespoons butter

¼ teaspoon ground nutmeg

Boil carrots and turnips in boiling salted water, uncovered, until tender. Drain. Purée and combine with remaining ingredients. Serve immediately with roast or grilled meats.

Oven-roasted Yellow Finnish Potatoes

Diane Worthington, in *The Cuisine of California*, introduced me to the splendid notion of roasted Finnish potatoes. Here is one version. The golden yellow meat of the Finnish potato, when encrusted by a brown roasted hide, is so irresistible that I can never get the darn things to the table. Put them out on the sideboard while I'm getting the rest of the dinner together and they vanish. Eaten. Wham.

Serves 4 in an hour

2 pounds yellow Finnish potatoes, scrubbed, skins left on, and cut into 2-inch wedges

¼ cup olive oil

1 teaspoon salt

⅛ teaspoon cayenne

¼ teaspoon paprika

¼ teaspoon finely ground black pepper

Preheat oven to 425°. Place potato wedges on cookie sheet with sides.

Combine remaining ingredients, mix well, and coat potatoes. Bake 45 minutes, turning every 15 minutes, until tender and well browned. Adjust seasonings to taste. Serve immediately.

Tamari Sunflower Potatoes

Here is a good emergency dinner. Low fat, low sodium, high fiber, not to mention great taste. You really don't need much else, maybe some sliced tomatoes and a glass of milk. If you have cold baked potatoes to begin with, you can turn this out in a hurry.

Serves 4

2 large russet potatoes (2
   pounds), baked and cut in
   half, lengthwise
¼ cup yogurt
   salt and cayenne to taste
2 cups (½ pound) grated
   Longhorn cheese
4 green onions and tops, cut
   fine
1 cup Tamari sunflower seeds

Preheat oven to 350°. Place halved potatoes in baking dish. Coat the top surface of each with a teaspoonful of yogurt, then sprinkle with salt and cayenne to taste. Top with cheese, onions, and sunflower seeds. Place in preheated oven and bake, uncovered, until cheese begins to bubble and brown, about 15 minutes. Run under broiler to make fine, brown crust, no more than 3 minutes. Top with remaining plain yogurt.

Buttered Phyllo Envelopes Stuffed with Mushroom-Carrot-Walnut-Raisin Filling
[Adapted from Plymale Cottage]

Here is a gorgeous, golden butter-tinged vegetarian entrée, which is suitable only for feeding eight at a time (it does not keep well and it's too much trouble to cut the recipe for two or four). If you have not worked with phyllo before, just remember to keep it between damp cloths so that it doesn't dry out, and try to be as parsimonious as you can about the butter you use to paint between the layers. The first time I made this dish it dripped with butter. But, as I became more experienced with using phyllo, I was able to back off on the butter. I have found that using a pastry brush sometimes helps. Serve this fabulous, rich phyllo envelope with the plainest green salad, a dry California Gewürztraminer, and just a piece of fruit for dessert. This main dish is such a stunner that you needn't offer anything else beyond the simplest accompaniments.

Serves 8 in 2 hours

¾ cup raisins
⅓ cup brandy
¼ cup butter
¾ cup (4 ounces) finely chopped yellow onion
¾ cup (4 ounces) finely chopped celery
2 garlic cloves, pressed
8 cups (1½ pounds) sliced fresh mushrooms
1½ cups (¼ pound) grated carrots
¾ cup (3 ounces) finely chopped walnuts

1½ teaspoons white pepper
¾ teaspoon cinnamon
¼ teaspoon nutmeg
salt and pepper to taste
1 large egg, beaten until frothy
1 cup fine, dry bread crumbs
½ pound phyllo pastry sheets
1 cup melted butter
1 cup (¼ pound) grated Swiss cheese (see mail order section)

Preheat oven to 350°. Combine raisins and brandy in cup and soak until raisins are soft. (You can plump them in a microwave set on low in 2 or 3 minutes; otherwise, it's 30 minutes.)

Heat butter until it sizzles in a 12-inch skillet over medium heat. Sauté onion, celery, and garlic until soft, about 8 to 10 minutes. Stir in mushrooms and carrots. Cover and cook until vegetables are soft, about 10 minutes. Add walnuts, raisins and brandy, and all seasonings. Cook and stir until liquid is absorbed. Remove from heat.

Beat egg and whisk into vegetable mixture. Stir in ¼ cup of the bread crumbs and stir; the filling should be fairly stiff.

Now comes the hard part. Generously butter an 11-by-15-inch Pyrex baking dish. Dampen two clean tea towels. Lay one on countertop and carefully unroll ½ pound phyllo leaves on damp towel. Place second damp towel on top. Melt butter, get ready to make a mess, do some breath holding and cussing because this gets tricky. Just keep this in mind: every time you remove one sheet of phyllo, put the damp tea towel back over the ones you're not using, otherwise, they get like the fallen leaves outside. Dry. Dry. Dry. Worthless.

Place melted butter, filling, bread crumbs, cheese, and the prepared Pyrex pan nearby. Get out your finest spatula and get ready to lift these ornery things. They are fragile. Lift damp tea towel. Butter a pastry brush or your fingers and lightly butter one layer of phyllo. Place in bottom of buttered pan. Now. Here we go.

Place a sheet of phyllo on countertop. Using pastry brush or fingers, lightly butter, then sprinkle bread crumbs on top. Fold in half. Again, butter and crumb top. Using a ½-cup measure, place filling in center. Add a generous pinch of cheese. Now fold, envelope style—sides first, then ends. Carefully lift with spatula and transfer to baking dish, placing seam side down. Don't panic if you tear this stuff here and there. It will get easier. And it tastes good, even if it looks bad the first time you try it.

Arrange envelopes in baking dish, sides touching. (You will get eight of them, all nestled together.) Using remaining melted butter, drizzle over tops, using your fingers to smear it all over.

Bake in preheated oven 45 minutes, until flaky and golden. Serve immediately.

Filbert Phyllo Diamonds
[adapted from the Oregon Filbert Commission]

If making the stuffed phyllo envelopes didn't turn you away from phyllo forever, because it's so blasted hard to work with, and since you may have half a pound in the freezer, here's an easier vegetarian phyllo entrée. Serve that clear, astringent Sopa de Tomatillo first, then this hazelnut entrée, and a cool sorbet, say raspberry, and you will have balanced textures and tastes so well that people will be on their knees, begging for another invitation to dinner.

Please refer to preceding recipe for Buttered Phylo Envelopes Stuffed with Mushroom-Carrot-Walnut-Raisin Filling for instructions regarding the handling of phyllo.

Serves 8 in 1½ hours

8 cups (1 pound) chopped fresh spinach leaves

2 cups (4 ounces) vertically sliced fresh mushrooms

½ cup green onions and tops, cut in 1½-inch pieces, then sliced vertically into thin slivers

¼ cup coarsely chopped Italian parsley leaves

2 garlic cloves, minced

2 cups (4 ounces) grated Swiss cheese

3 large eggs, lightly beaten

1 teaspoon dillweed

salt and a freshly milled black pepper to taste

1 cup finely chopped roasted hazelnuts

½ pound phyllo leaves

1 cup melted butter

Combine spinach, mushrooms, onions, parsley, and garlic in a 10-inch skillet. Cover and cook until spinach is wilted (about 3 minutes). Remove from heat. Stir in cheese, beaten eggs, and dillweed. Season to taste.

Preheat over to 325°. Generously butter a 13-by-9-by-2-inch Pyrex baking dish. Place a layer of phyllo in dish. Coat lightly with melted butter. Repeat with half the phyllo sheets, lightly buttering every other sheet. Top with spinach mixture. Sprinkle hazelnuts over, then top with remaining phyllo, brushing every other sheet with butter as you lay it on. Using a very sharp knife and a sawing motion, score top into 8 phyllo diamonds.

Bake in preheated oven for 45 minutes or until golden brown. Serve immediately.

Fresh Berries in Orange Sour Cream

The berry season is swift and evanescent. Whether you are a gatherer or simply a forager in the produce section of your neighborhood supermarket, when you find perfect, ripe, luscious berries, you will want to serve them that same day. Berries are fragile and begin converting sugar to starch from the moment they are picked. Here is a simple, smashing way to serve any berries you may find: blackberries, olallieberries, dew berries, strawberries, raspberries, blueberries, or the myriad wild varieties. Taste the berries first. Most berries require no sugar whatsoever. If, however, you find the berries too tart, simply shake sugar, by the tablespoon, over them, and set aside to draw juices while you proceed with the cream.

Serves 4 in 40 minutes

1 pint fully ripe berries
  sugar to enhance sweetness
  if necessary
¼ cup sugar for sauce
  zest from half a navel orange
  rind

½ cup fresh orange juice,
  strained
½ cup sour cream, or sour half
  and half, or plain Russian-
  style yogurt

Wash and hull berries, cutting larger berries in half. Sweeten only if necessary. Cover and refrigerate.

Combine sugar, orange zest, and orange juice in small saucepan. Over high heat, raise to a boil. Reduce heat and simmer 10 minutes. Remove from heat. Combine with sour cream or yogurt. Cover and chill until time to serve (at least 30 minutes).

When ready to serve, puddle orange cream in individual footed dessert dishes then arrange berries on top. Good with black butter shortbreads and fresh-ground French roast coffee.

Lemon-Ginger Sorbet
[Judyth's Mountain]

This pungent sorbet is as well suited a palate cleanser for pork dishes as it is a light dessert following a solid winter meal. You will find the flavor matures if made a day ahead.

Serves 4 in 3 hours

1 cup ginger jelly (see Judyth's
  Mountain in mail order
  section)
1 cup water

1 cup lemon juice
1 teaspoon grated lemon zest
  paper-thin slices of lemon or
  candied ginger for garnish

Combine ginger jelly and water in a small, heavy-bottomed saucepan. Raise to a boil, then simmer for 5 minutes. Remove from heat and stir in lemon juice and zest. Refrigerate until cold. Transfer to 9-inch square metal cake pan, cover with plastic wrap, and freeze until solid (at least 4 hours). Whirl in food processor, using off and on bursts until a velvet slush. Replace in pan, re-cover, and refreeze. Remove from freezer a few minutes before serving time. Scoop into footed glasses using an ice cream scooper. Garnish with paper-thin slices of lemon or candied ginger.

Raspberry Sorbet

You can use this method for any berry or sweet fruit to good advantage. The main thing here is to use berries or fruits that are completely ripe. In fact, you can even use bargain berries that look too weary for the table. The riper the fruit, the better the flavor.

Serves 4 to 6

2 cups sugar	1 large egg white
2 cups water	pinch cream of tartar
3½ cups fresh raspberries	
2 tablespoons fresh lemon juice	

Combine sugar and water in medium saucepan and bring to good, rolling boil. Stir to completely dissolve all sugar granules. Remove from heat.

In processor, purée berries with syrup. Strain into a metal bowl. Set the bowl in an ice-water bath, taking care not to slosh water into fruit mixture. Add lemon juice. Paddle until chilled.

Beat egg white with cream of tartar until it forms stiff peaks. Fold fruit mixture into egg white. Place in ice tray, cover, and freeze. Ten minutes before serving, remove from freezer. Give it a spin in the processor just before serving for a perfectly smooth, crystal-free texture. Yum.

Zinfandel Sorbet

Crimson ice, both sweet and tart, this can be used as a palate cleanser in a red-meat meal, or garnished with flame grapes and fresh mint leaves, as a cool, refreshing dessert. Make one day ahead.

Serves 4 for dessert; 8 for between courses

¾ cup sugar	1 bunch red flame grapes, for dessert
1 cup water	fresh mint leaves to garnish
1½ cups Zinfandel	
1½ cups white grape juice	
¾ cup freshly squeezed lemon juice	

Combine, sugar, water, and wine in a small heavy-bottomed saucepan. Raise to a boil, then simmer for 5 minutes. Remove from heat. Stir in grape and lemon juices. Refrigerate until cold, at least an hour.

Pour mixture into a 9-inch square cake pan, cover with plastic wrap, and freeze until solid, at least 4 hours. Remove from freezer and let stand 15 minutes. Whirl in food processor or blender, using off and on bursts to make a velvet slush. Replace in pan, cover, and refreeze. Will keep a month. Remove from freezer 30 minutes before serving. Scoop into footed glasses using an ice cream scooper. Garnish with grapes and mint leaves.

Baked Bosc Pears with Coffee-Almond Sauce

When Mona Palmer Onstead of Judyth's Mountain invented coffee jellies, she didn't quite realize what a Pandora's box she had opened. She says that she got the idea from a law professor at Brandeis University. Last week he called her to say that he'd used the coffee-almond jelly folded inside an omelet. He says almond like a Yankee, Mona says, but it's one more use for this splendid jelly. Since I have gone crazy for Rogue Valley pears, I tried it last night over a baked Bosc pear. What a flavor combination. The "ugly" pear, as the Bosc is called, baked to golden perfection with this pungent coffee sweet sauce. Who needs dinner?

Serves 4 in 30 minutes

4   **perfectly ripe well-shaped Bosc pears**
4   **tablespoons softened butter**
     water

¼   **cup dry white vermouth**
½   **cup coffee-almond jelly (see Judyth's Mountain in mail order section), warmed**

Preheat oven to 350°. Coat a 9-inch glass baking dish with butter. Peel and core pears, leaving bottom end of the pear in place so that butter will not leak out. Rub soft butter atop each pear, then stuff each opening with remaining butter. Arrange pears in baking dish, and pour vermouth over them. Now pour ½ inch water in bottom of dish. Place in preheated oven and bake for 20 to 25 minutes, until tops have browned slightly and pears are tender when pierced with a fork. Place pears in footed glasses. Warm jelly and spoon atop warm pears. Serve immediately.

The Pasta Shop

THERE'S A GUY HERE IN ASHLAND who has opened a business known as Past-abilities. He makes and supplies the most divine fresh-made pastas in three or four varieties to our three little grocery stores. From time to time I see him at the refrigerator case, working like a beaver, stuffing in fresh pasta, pulling out yesterday's. Every time I see him, I have to fight the urge to go over and kiss him. Because I'll tell you the truth, that man can make pasta as well as I can, and it certainly is a lot less trouble for me to pick up the fresh pasta he made this morning than to make it myself. These pasta shops are springing up all over. I am grateful. I fully expect to see pasta machines overrunning Goodwill shelves before long. Who would make from scratch something he could buy for $.89? Let's face it. We've won. All sorts of cottage kitchens are making food products with no preservatives or chemicals, and making them fresh every day and stocking stores with them.

The great advantage of pasta entrées are their speed of preparation. But need I tell you that that advantage is lost if you begin with inert flour. For the diehards, I have included one recipe for semolina pasta. Go ahead. Be a glutton for punishment. Make it at home. See if I care. As for me, I am a loyal Pastabilities customer and a good sauce maker—and time ahead because of it.

But, if you really want to try it, here's the basic procedure.

Semolina Pasta

Serves 8 in 1 hour

3½ cups semolina flour
3 large eggs
1 tablespoon oil

1 teaspoon salt
water by the drop to moisten

Place flour in bowl of processor. Break eggs into flour. Add oil and salt. Process until dough forms a ball that leaves the side of the bowl. If too dry, add water by the drop until it forms a ball; if too sticky, sprinkle additional flour in until it leaves the sides of the bowl. Knead by running machine for 60 seconds. Remove dough from work bowl, cover with plastic wrap, and allow to rest for about 20 minutes.

You may also make the dough by hand, mounding the flour on a work surface, making a dent in the center, and breaking the eggs in. Fold flour over and over to coalesce with eggs. Sprinkle oil, drops of water, and salt in, and knead by hand for 10 minutes, then proceed, letting the dough rest, covered, for 20 minutes.

Divide dough into 4 parts, flattening each into thin oval. Dust with flour. Pass through pasta machine with rollers set at widest setting. Fold dough in thirds and turn a quarter. Dust again with flour and repeat rolling. Fold and turn 4 times. You may also roll and turn by hand, using a rolling pin and a well-floured surface.

Lightly flour rectangles, decrease width of the rollers, and once more pass through the rollers, several more times, using an ever thinner setting until you have a long, thin strip of dough. Hang the dough out over the back of a chair, or over a drying rack, for 10 to 15 minutes to dry. When dough feels dry but still pliable, cut into lasagna shape using pasta machine or by hand. To cook fresh, drop into a large stew pot of boiling water for no more than 60 seconds. Drain and toss with olive oil. So, after reading all these directions, aren't you thankful for the local pasta shop? Personally, I wouldn't make pasta at home unless I was snowed in, 50 miles from the nearest town, and *desperate.*

Tortellini with Tomato-Orange-Walnut Sauce

If a pasta shop in your neighborhood is making spinach tortellini, by all means try this recipe with fresh pasta. Otherwise, you can use those good, imported dried tortellini found in bulk in Italian delis. The sauce is splendid atop plain spaghetti or cheese raviolini, as well as tortellini. The last time I made this, I bought equal parts green-spinach tortellini and creamy cheese raviolini, boiled them separately, made strips of each on the plate, and covered them in the red sauce. Good grief. It was the Italian flag.

If you're making this sauce for fresh pasta, remember to cook the pasta last so that the sauce will have time to develop. Serve on a warmed plate with a generous dusting of freshly grated Parmesan cheese.

Serves 4 in 30 minutes

Sauce:

3	tablespoons best quality olive oil		pinch of oregano, fresh or dried
2	large yellow onions (¾ pound), coarsely chopped	⅛	teaspoon dried thyme leaves salt and freshly milled black
3	garlic cloves, pressed		pepper to taste
½	cup coarsely chopped walnuts		water (to thin sauce as needed)
1	cup sliced mushrooms		
1	cup tomato sauce	¾	pound spinach tortellini
1	cup fresh orange juice		barely salted water to cover
12	fresh basil leaves or ¾ teaspoon dried	½	cup freshly grated Parmesan cheese

First, make the sauce. In a 10-inch skillet, heat olive oil over medium heat. Sauté onions, garlic, and walnuts until onions are clear. Add mushrooms. Cook and stir, covering with lid in between stirrings, until mushrooms are cooked and limp, about 10 minutes. Add tomato sauce, orange juice, herbs, and salt and pepper to taste. Place a pitcher of water nearby and dribble a little in as needed to maintain a buttermilk-like consistency. Stir from time to time to keep from sticking. When pasta is cooked, sauce should have been in process about 30 minutes, mature enough to serve.

Boil tortellini in large pot of barely salted water until just al dente (5 minutes for fresh; 25 minutes for dried). Drain. Because tortellinis are pretty, I always serve this dish by pooling sauce in a wide-rimmed soup bowl and spooning tortellinis atop. Dust tops with Parmesan. Serve with crusty French bread.

Tortellini and Raviolini Vinaigrette

Buying two kinds of filled pastas, one green and one white, boiling them separately, then marinating them together in a delicious vinaigrette, will produce a summer lunch to remember. The pasta needs at least four hours to marinate, and if you can remember to make it a day ahead, the flavor will be best. My favorite kind of accompaniment to this summer lunch is a thick slice of beefsteak tomato topped with several leaves of fresh basil and sage, over which I drizzle a few drops of extra virgin olive oil. A hot loaf of sourdough bread. Sweet butter. Sliced kiwi for dessert. Zinfandel to drink. Now that's lunch.

Serves 4

Dressing:

1   teaspoon Dijon-style mustard
1   tablespoon plus 1 teaspoon red wine vinegar
⅓   teaspoon brown sugar
1   teaspoon water
⅓   cup good quality olive oil salt and freshly ground black pepper to taste
½   teaspoon snipped fresh chives

⅓   pound cheese raviolini, cooked in boiling water

⅓   pound spinach tortellini, cooked in boiling water
1   bunch green onions and tops, white part sliced paper thin, and tender green tops cut into ½-inch lengths
1   cup sliced mushrooms
¼   cup sunflower seeds
½   cup freshly grated Parmesan cheese freshly milled black pepper (be generous)

Combine all dressing ingredients in jar and shake to mix. Pour over warm, drained pasta, stirring to coat each piece thoroughly. Add remaining ingredients—onions, mushrooms, and sunflower seeds. Dust with Parmesan. Cover, refrigerate, and marinate at least 4 hours (better overnight). Flavors are aromatic best at room temperature.

Taglierini with Sonoma Sun-dried Tomatoes
[Timbercrest Farms]

First- and second-generation Italian immigrants in Sonoma County, California, always have sun dried the excess bounty of their tomato crop. All of a sudden, Italian sun-dried tomatoes have become stylish, and the Sonoma Italians figured they might as well sell some of theirs. So Rancher Waltenspiel of Healdsburg and Frieda Caplan now offer California sun-dried tomatoes. The primary difference between theirs and the Italians' is price. Needless to say, you have saved yourself the shipping charges from the Mediterranean (see mail order section). Both dried and marinated-dried tomatoes are available. I have a hard time cooking with the marinated ones; I can't seem to keep them around long enough. You can marinate your own, by the way, and save quite a bit of money (see Special Ingredients section).

This particular dish is one of those splendid Italian pasta entrées that combines hot pasta with raw eggs and seasonings for a rich, aromatic mélange. If you've ever made Spaghetti Carbonara, it's the same idea. You combine eggs and flavorings in the bottom of the serving bowl, pour the hot drained pasta on top, and toss with two forks until egg is cooked and sauce is well distributed. This particular recipe is so redolent of garlic and those wondrous smoky tomatoes that you may want it once a week. I do.

Serves 4 in 20 minutes

2	eggs	½	cup chopped Italian parsley leaves
½	cup marinated dried tomatoes, cut into ⅛-inch strips	2	garlic cloves, pressed
¼	cup olive oil	1	tablespoon lemon juice
½	cup freshly grated Parmesan cheese	¾	pound taglierini
		3	quarts water
			salt and pepper to taste

In large serving bowl, whisk to blend eggs, tomatoes, oil, Parmesan, parsley, garlic, and lemon juice. Set aside.

In a 6-quart saucepan, cook taglierini in boiling water, uncovered, until tender (about 6 minutes for dried; 1 minute for fresh). Drain. Add to egg mixture. Lift with 2 forks to mix. Adjust seasonings to taste. Serve immediately.

Seashells and Oregon Scallops

The scallop, like its other seagoing sisters and brothers, is primarily water. If you overcook it and leach out the water that inflates its cells, you'll wind up with a tough, leathery dinner. In any recipe calling for scallops in a sauce, make the sauce first, cook and season it thoroughly, and then toss in the scallops just at the last minute.

West Coast fresh fish shippers have, from time to time, scallops in the shell for sale. I wish you could see those silly things swimming in their shells in briny bathtubs. If you want the freshest scallops possible, order them live. They'll come sloshing to your doorstep in a Styrofoam container. (See mail order section for fish.)

Serves 4 in 30 minutes

4 tablespoons butter	1 tablespoon all purpose flour
2 garlic cloves, pressed	¼ cup beer
2 small onions (½ pound), thinly sliced	1 cup whipping cream
½ teaspoon red pepper flakes	1 pound scallops
1 large green bell pepper (½ pound) thinly sliced	6 ounces (1½ cups) fresh Parmesan, freshly grated
1 large fresh jalapeño (1 ounce), diced	2 tablespoons butter
12 ounces small-shell macaroni, cooked in 4 quarts of barely salted water	1 cup fresh parsley leaves, loosely packed

Heat butter in a 10-inch skillet over medium-low heat; then sauté garlic, onion, red pepper flakes, bell pepper, and jalapeño.

While vegetables are cooking, prepare pasta according to package directions.

Once onion is clear and limp, about 12 minutes, sprinkle flour into skillet. Cook and stir to make a golden roux. Add beer and stir to make a thick sauce; thin with cream. Cook and stir until you have a good, rolling boil. Adjust seasonings to taste (salt lightly if at all). Add scallops and cook until just tender, no more than a minute or so.

Once pasta is cooked, just al dente, drain and place in serving bowl. Toss with fresh grated Parmesan, butter, and parsley. Pour sauce over and serve. And just pray that there'll be some left over to eat tomorrow—cold. Yum.

Vegetable Lasagna Pinwheels with the Basic Tomato Sauce

This dish presents in a most attractive way, with the lasagna noodles rolled up, end on end, stuffed with a spinach-mushroom-ricotta filling and dressed with a basic tomato sauce.

It is better the second day. If you can arrange to make it one day ahead, you'll be happy you did so. At our house, we usually eat it two days in a row, wishing every time that we had waited for that second day before beginning.

Serve with sliced navel oranges, over which are sprinkled some minced fresh basil leaves and a few drops of extra virgin olive oil and half a teaspoon of fruit-scented vinegar. I never serve bread with these pasta entrées; just some gelato for dessert, a square-shouldered bottle of red wine, and good, strong espresso to wrap it up. A good company dish.

The work is divided into stages for this recipe. First, make the sauce, which needs to simmer for two hours. Of course, this can be any two hours of your life; it freezes well. The second stage in the preparation of this recipe is cooking the noodles. The third stage is mixing the filling. We do this in a big stainless steel bread bowl. When you get the filling mixed up, it looks like it'll be enough to feed Coxey's army. Keep rolling. You'll use it all. Finally, the dish is assembled, baked, allowed to stand for ten minutes, and then served. It can be reheated successfully in the oven or in the microwave, and it freezes admirably.

Serves 8 in 1½ hours
beginning with cooked sauce

Makes 1 quart in 2½ hours

Basic Tomato Sauce:

4 tablespoons olive oil
1 large yellow onion (½ pound), finely chopped
8 garlic cloves, pressed
1 celery stalk, finely chopped
½ large bell pepper (¼ pound), finely chopped
2 medium zucchini (½ pound), grated
1 medium carrot (¼ pound), grated
½ cup loosely packed parsley leaves
2 1-pound cans tomatoes and juice, finely chopped

1 6-ounce can tomato paste plus 1 can water
20 leaves fresh basil, crushed, or 5 tablespoons dried
6 tablespoons fresh oregano, crushed, or 3 tablespoons dried
½ teaspoon dried red pepper flakes
½ teaspoon sugar
salt and freshly milled black pepper to taste
1 pound lasagna noodles

Filling:

1 pound lasagna noodles	8 ounces ricotta
1 pound fresh spinach, well washed, drained, and coarsely chopped	1 egg
	1¼ cup freshly grated Parmesan cheese
½ pound fresh mushrooms, thinly sliced	¼ cup freshly grated Romano cheese
1 cup raw sunflower seeds	

For sauce, sauté onion and garlic in oil in a large soup pot until onion turns clear. Begin adding vegetables, one at a time, cooking 3 or 4 minutes after each addition: celery, bell pepper, zucchini, and carrot. Once these vegetables have cooked down, add parsley, tomatoes and juice, and tomato paste and water. Stir to mix. Season with herbs, sugar, and salt and pepper. Simmer, uncovered, for 2 hours, adding water as necessary to maintain a thin soupy consistency, until last 15 minutes, when you raise heat, stir, and allow the sauce to reduce to a thick spaghetti sauce consistency.

About 1 hour before serving, cook lasagna according to package directions, just al dente, then drain and let stand in cold water while making the filling.

Mix filling ingredients together, setting aside 1 cup grated Parmesan to top the dish.

Assembling the dish

Preheat oven to 350°. Using a ½-cup measure, scoop filling onto strips of cooked lasagna, roll up, and place in an 11-by-15-inch baking dish, with cut edges up to get a pinwheel design. Repeat until all noodles and filling have been used (not that it ever comes out even). Pour cooked tomato sauce over lasagna noodles, sprinkle with remaining 1 cup Parmesan, and bake for 45 minutes. Let stand 10 minutes before serving.

Oregon Scallop Seviche Quenelles
with Saffron Sauce
[Heather Bryse-Harvey]

In Portland, where Oregon scallops are most often available, Heather Bryse-Harvey uses them whenever she can. (Other scallops can be substituted with good results.) When Heather makes quenelles for her catering business, Yours Truly, she makes them early in the day, drains them on a cloth, and covers them with Saran wrap so they don't dry out. There are three steps involved: the pâte à choux (cream puff pastries); the quenelles; and the saffron sauce.

Serves 6 in 1½ hours

Pâte à Choux:

½ cup water	6 tablespoons unbleached white flour
3 tablespoons butter	
½ teaspoon salt	2 eggs

Bring water to boil in heavy-bottomed saucepan. Add butter and salt. When butter melts, remove pan from heat and immediately add all flour, beating vigorously with wooden spoon until mixture forms a ball and cleans sides of pan. Add eggs, one at a time, beating vigorously the entire time and making certain that each egg is incorporated before adding the next. Cool. Now, the quenelles.

The Quenelles:

1   recipe's worth cooled pâte a choux
½   pound fresh Oregon (or other) scallops
½   teaspoon grated lime zest
2   teaspoons fresh lime juice
1   green onion and top, finely chopped

1   garlic clove, pressed
½   teaspoon dillweed
1   cup finely chopped cilantro
½   cup whipping cream
    salt and white pepper to taste

Place scallops, lime zest and juice, chopped green onion, garlic, dillweed, and chopped cilantro in bowl of processor. Purée. Remove and place in bowl set in ice; beat over ice with metal whisk until chilled and massed together into a kind of gummy texture. Gradually add pâte à choux, beating over ice. Add whipping cream and beat to a smooth mixture. Season to taste.

Bring 2 quarts of water in a 10- to 12-inch skillet to a simmer; add 1 teaspoon salt. Using 2 teaspoons, scoop mixture from one to the other until forming an egg shape, then drop into water. Work fast until all quenelles are in the simmering water. Poach in this barely simmering water (180°) for about 15 minutes, or until quenelles have nearly doubled in size and roll over easily in the water. Lift from water with slotted spoon.

Drain on cloth towel. Serve hot. You may make these early in the day, cover with Saran, and reheat by steaming for 1 minute just before serving.

Saffron Sauce:

1   cup fish stock
¼   teaspoon saffron threads
2   tablespoons butter
2   tablespoons flour

1½   cups whipping cream
¼   cup sour cream
1   tablespoon lemon juice
     salt and pepper to taste

Combine fish stock and saffron in pan; boil to reduce to 2 tablespoons. Strain and reserve.

Make a golden roux in heavy-bottom saucepan by combining butter and flour. Stir and bubble about 3 minutes. Add reduced fish stock and whipping cream. Continue stirring until sauce thickens and comes to a boil. Remove from heat. Add sour cream and lemon juice. Stir to mix. Season to taste. Pour over hot quenelles and serve at once in wide-rimmed soup bowls.

Gnocchi and Goat Cheese
in a Chanterelle Broth

Once you have mastered the choux paste, you can make wonderful main-dish meals using California chèvre (goat cheese), to spike the gnocchi, and floating the lovely potato dumplings in a chanterelle broth. If you can't get the apricot-hued chanterelles, you can try shiitake, or even plain supermarket button mushrooms. Each mushroom variety will produce a subtly different result. I have used Sadie Kendall's goat cheese, which has the texture of a fine cream cheese and blends superbly with the subtle apricot aroma of chanterelles.

You can make the gnocchi days ahead and freeze, saving the final cooking for 30 minutes before serving time.

Please see preceding recipe for the Oregon Scallop Seviche Quenelles with Saffron Sauce for instructions for making pâte à choux.

Serves 4 in an hour

Gnocchi:

2 cups peeled and boiled potatoes, run through a Foley food mill or otherwise mashed	4 ounces California chèvre salt and white pepper to taste flour to coat cutting board
1 cup warm pâte à choux	3 tablespoons melted butter

Stir mashed potatoes over medium heat in heavy-bottomed saucepan until potatoes begin to film bottom of pan, about 5 minutes. Remove from heat and beat in choux paste and 3 ounces of chèvre, reserving last ounce to sprinkle on top when baking. Adjust seasonings to taste. Roll on lightly floured board to form 2½-by-1-inch cylinders.

Cooking gnocchi is not difficult, but you must keep the water at a temperature no higher than 180°, otherwise the dumplings may disintegrate. Heat a teakettle full of water to boiling. Generously butter a 12-inch skillet, and lay gnocchi in it. Pour boiling water over to cover by 1½ inches and place over low heat. Use candy thermometer; do not let water get above 180°. If temperature seems to be rising too fast, lift skillet off heat. Otherwise, you may wind up with a pot of well-flavored glue. Cook, uncovered, at this below-the-simmer temperature until gnocchi are done. Like quenelles, they will rise to the top, swell, and roll over easily when done. Takes about 20 minutes. Remove with slotted spoon and drain on cloth. You may now refrigerate or freeze until mealtime.

Preheat oven to 375° 30 minutes before serving. Arrange poached gnocchi in heavily buttered glass baking dish. Sprinkle with reserved, crumbled chèvre and melted butter. Bake until bubbly and brown, about 25 minutes.

Chanterelle Broth:

2   cups chopped chanterelles
½   cup finely chopped onion
4   tablespoons butter
2   tablespoons unbleached
    white flour

1   quart rich chicken broth
    salt and pepper to taste
    about 3 tablespoons lemon
    juice

In a soup pot, sauté chopped mushroom and onion in butter until mushrooms collapse and onions turn clear. Stir from time to time. Takes about 10 minutes. Sprinkle flour over vegetables and stir to cook flour and make a roux. Stir in broth and bring to a boil. Simmer 10 minutes. Season to taste with salt, pepper, and lemon juice.

Serve mushroom broth in wide soup bowls with gnocchi floating in broth. Garnish with fresh trimmed chives. Begs for a piece of sourdough bread and sweet butter. Little green salad. Fruit for dessert. Riesling to drink.

Spiked Polenta

All along the West Coast, from Baja to British Columbia, are Italian settlements. In Vancouver, the Italian community is known as Little Italy and is centered on Commercial Avenue. The red, green, and white Italian flag flutters outside many shops, and even though the weather may be briskly Canadian, the mood is definitely Mediterranean. Italian food ranks right up there with French and Chinese in world-class cuisines, and in Vancouver and other Italian communities up and down the coast, you'll find Italian grocery stores that stock pastas, dried chestnuts, and the fabulous gelatos that make their reputation.

Polenta comes from the rural areas of the South and is a hearty, robust starch dish designed to satisfy the gnawing hunger of a pastoral people. If you don't have access to an authentic Italian grocery store, you can substitute coarse yellow cornmeal for the polenta. But remember, polenta is like the French roux. You must cook and stir the cornmeal or the flour until the grain molecules have exploded. Otherwise, you wind up with a raw-grain taste. Patience is the watchword. Cook and stir this mush, tasting from time to time, until the cornmeal loses that raw, alkaline taste and takes on a smooth, bland, cooked-corn flavor. You can make polenta ahead, even days ahead, and bake it just before serving. Here, I have spiked it with red pepper flakes; though you can flavor it in other ways. Pine nuts. Italian parsley. Slivers of elephant garlic. See what you can come up with.

Serves 4 in 45 minutes

1   cup polenta or coarse yellow
    cornmeal
3   cups water
1   teaspoon salt
1   teaspoon red pepper flakes
    generous grinding of fresh
    pepper

2   tablespoons butter
1   cup freshly grated Parmesan
    cheese
    dusting of Hungarian paprika

Combine polenta or cornmeal, water, salt, and peppers in a large saucepan. Over medium heat, cook and stir until it is a thick mush that is no longer raw tasting, at least 20 minutes. (This will thicken a good while before it is actually cooked, so stir frequently to prevent sticking.)

When cooked, remove from heat and stir in butter. Generously grease a 9-by-13-inch baking pan and pour mush into pan, smoothing it into a flat cake. Top with grated Parmesan and dust with paprika. Cover and refrigerate.

About 10 minutes before serving, preheat oven to 400°. Cut polenta into 2-inch squares and bake, uncovered, in the oven until cheese melts and begins to brown, about 5 minutes.

Quick and Easy Risotto

Cal-Rose rice, which grows in California's Central Valley, is short grained and pearly and will do in any recipe calling for Italian short-grained rice. Here is a streamlined method for producing that Italian favorite, risotto. And you don't have to stand and stir for an hour, the way the old-fashioned recipe says.

Serves 4 in 20 minutes

2½ cups chicken broth
salt to taste
1 tablespoon olive oil
1 small onion (4 ounces), finely chopped

1 garlic clove, pressed
1 cup short-grained white rice
⅓ cup freshly grated Parmesan cheese

Bring chicken broth to a boil in a saucepan. Season to taste. Meanwhile, in a 10-inch skillet, heat olive oil over medium heat. Cook onion and garlic until clear, 3 to 4 minutes. Add rice and stir to mix thoroughly. Add boiling chicken broth. Cover, reduce heat, and simmer for *exactly* 15 minutes. At this point, the broth should be almost absorbed. Remove lid and cook and stir until rice looks creamy but not dry. Remove from heat. Add Parmesan. Stir thoroughly and serve.

You can make this a main dish by adding bits of leftover meat or fish. You also can toss in some blanched sugar pea pods.

Curried Brown Rice with Sesame Seeds and Flame Grapes

On the West Coast, brown rice has become the standard. Many Chinese and Thai restaurants now offer a choice of white or brown rice; some even offer a choice between long and short grain. For curry, eaten with a fork, long grain is preferred. This fruity, crunchy rice dish is outstanding with the Mixed Grill Kebab.

Serves 4 in an hour

1	large yellow onion (⅓ pound), coarsely chopped	2½	cups chicken broth
2	tablespoons butter	½	cup sesame seeds
1	cup long-grain brown rice	½	cup seedless flame grapes
1	tablespoon Madras curry powder		salt and fresh ground black pepper to taste

Sauté onion in butter in a 10-inch skillet over medium-high heat until onion is clear, about 5 minutes. Stir in rice and curry powder, coating all grains with butter and curry. Add broth. Cover, reduce heat to low, and simmer until rice is done (about 50 minutes).

Meanwhile, toast sesame seeds in a 350° oven (about 5 minutes), one layer deep, taking care not to burn. When rice is cooked, stir in sesame seeds and grapes. Season to taste.

Chanterelles in a Parsley-Rice Ring

If you walk through the Pike Place Market in Seattle during the autumn, one produce item fairly leaps out at you. At almost every produce stand, you see big boxes of wild chanterelle mushrooms, and for only about $3 a pound. If you have never tasted the precious chanterelle, with its apricot color and faint apricot taste, I urge you to do so. This presentation is one of the most luxurious vegetarian entrées I know of. Lovely rice and parsley ring with a mound of apricot-colored mushrooms. Bountiful. Bountiful.

Chanterelles keep well, about a week in the refrigerator in a brown paper sack, and are good shippers. You can call Peter Hasson (see mail order section) for availability and price. Hasson Brothers Fruit & Produce, in the Pike Place Market, employs its own mushroom pickers and sells about 150 pounds of chanterelles a week during September and October.

Serves 4 in under 1 hour

Rice:

1½	cups Cal-Rose short-grain white or brown rice	1	tablespoon butter salt and pepper to taste
3	cups rich chicken broth		
1	cup loosely packed Italian parsley leaves		

Mushrooms:

⅛	pound (¼ cup) butter	2	tablespoons fresh lemon juice
2	garlic cloves, pressed		
1	medium onion (4 ounces), finely chopped		
2	quarts (1 pound) chanterelles, wiped clean and chopped		

Cook rice in simmering chicken broth, seasoned to taste, covered, until done (20 minutes for white, 50 minutes for brown). While rice is cooking, prepare mushrooms.

In 10-inch skillet, heat butter over medium heat until foamy, then sauté garlic and onion for 2 minutes. Add mushrooms. Cook and stir until liquid released from mushrooms is reduced to about ⅛ cup. Add lemon juice, stir to mix, adjust seasonings to taste, and cover and reserve.

Prepare a 9-inch, 1-quart ring mold by buttering generously. Once rice is cooked, combine with parsley leaves and butter, season generously with salt and freshly ground black pepper to taste. Pack into mold, making firm, dense ring. Place mold in 10-inch skillet. Pour cup of hot water into skillet, taking care that none splashes into rice. Place skillet over medium-low heat, uncovered, and allow water to simmer for 10 minutes.

To serve, unmold rice onto a flat 12-inch platter, spoon hot mushroom mixture into the center, and top with a sprig or two of fresh parsley leaves.

The Main Course

ARBITRARILY, I'VE DECIDED to call animal-protein recipes the main course. In this chapter you'll find poultry, fish, and meat dishes. But the truth of it is that here on the West Coast almost anything can be a main course. If it's at the peak of the season, perfect in every respect, and available in bountiful measure, we may make it the main course. One day in spring, when they were just coming into full flower, we made a full meal from sugar peas steamed whole, with a simple cream sauce on the side. A mountain of sugar peas with only hot buttered bread to accompany. We do that a lot around here. Forget balanced meals. Just enjoy the best of the harvest. All you can eat.

But to get back to this chapter, I've called the main course meats. And there's another arbitrary decision here based on the simple, healthful food preparation that characterizes the New West Coast Cuisine. These meats are either roasted, grilled, or sautéed. No frying or deep-fat frying.

Grilling is nothing new, but I have a couple of pieces of advice about the grill. One is to invest in one of those electric starters for charcoal. This eliminates the hint of petroleum you get in the smoke from using lighter fluid. The second piece of advice is to resist the urge to buy high-priced mesquite, except perhaps to use as you would hickory chips—for flavor. The difference in grill temperature is hardly worth the difference in cost.

On a visit to one of the toniest grill restaurants in Los Angeles, I asked the chef if he used mesquite exclusively. He looked positively horrified. No, no, no, he said. Too expensive. I did see a 50-pound sack of Western Family charcoal standing in the back of his kitchen. Designer fuels will not a good cook make. Be patient. Before you begin cooking, let the charcoal get so hot that the coals are fully covered with a white ash. Watch the food like a hawk. Turn frequently. Move the food around from hot spot to cooler spot. Practice, practice, and soon you'll get to be as good as a chef who stands before a 750° grill night after night. And, since you only do it once in a while, you may not even burn the hair off your arms like that poor fellow does.

Mixed Grill Kebab

The "mixed" in the title of this recipe does not refer to the mix-up in the use of the term "grill," but we may as well get clear on what a grill is, what "to grill" means, and what you can do if you don't have one—a grill, that is.

Grilling means cooking food over a very hot open fire on a slatted surface so that the juices from the food drip down onto the heat surface, smoke, and come back up to flavor the food. The extreme heat sears the surface of the food, holding in the moisture. The combination of high heat and smoke create the special effect that only grilling can produce.

Backyard barbecuing is the most common form of grilling (and it is not barbecuing, by the way, unless the barbecue is covered, as the Weber Kettle is, for example). So, to clear up the first misperception, keep in mind that when people say they "barbecued" the chicken in the backyard, nine times out of ten they did no such thing; usually they grilled it. The Japanese call their grill a hibachi. Americans sometimes call theirs a Jenn-Aire. The plain truth is that it makes little difference what the heat source is: charcoal, wood, gas, or electric coil. But to grill, the food must be *over* the heat source on a slatted surface so that the juices can drip down, smoke up, and flavor the food.

I thought about buying a Jenn-Aire, but I didn't think I could live with the nuisance of only two burners, and I didn't like the price. So I went to the Goodwill and found a small electric grill for $3. It works pretty well. It will blow the fuse if you turn on too much stuff at the same time. But properly preheated it works as well as any other indoor grill.

Now, what if you don't want to fire up the backyard barbecue, you don't have an inside grill, and you still want to try some of these grill recipes? There are a couple of things you can do. The tried and true solution is to broil in the oven. If the broiler is properly preheated, you will get a result close to grilling, although you can see that the food drippings just go into the pan and don't smoke back up onto the food. Another solution is to "pan-broil," which means to cook food on a dry skillet that has been preheated until it's as hot as a pistol. You will get some drip-smoke action with this method, but whatever method you choose, the idea of grilling is appealing, if for no other reason than it is fast. You can have a succulent, flavorful dinner in short order, cooked by the hot, direct heat of the grill. Why else do you think restaurants favor the grill? They can cook to order in a hurry.

Serves 4, marinates in 2 to 8 hours;
grills in 10 to 20 minutes

Meat:

3	center-cut pork chops (about 1 pound), boned, visible fat removed, and cut into 3-by-½-inch strips	3	half chicken breasts (about 1½ pounds), skinned and cut into 3-by-½-inch strips

Marinade:

½	cup fresh lemon juice (approximately 2 lemons) zest of 1 lemon	4	garlic cloves, pressed
		⅓	cup soy sauce

Vegetables:

1	large green pepper (⅓ pound), cut into strips	8	cherry tomatoes
2	small onions (½ pound), cut into quarters	8	bamboo skewers

Peanut Butter Sauce:

	reserved marinade	½	teaspoon hot red pepper flakes
4	tablespoons smooth peanut butter	¼	cup plain yogurt
½	cup honey		

Place pork and chicken strips in shallow glass dish. Make marinade by combining lemon juice and zest, garlic, and soy sauce. Pour over meat strips. Cover and refrigerate at least 2 hours, and up to 8 hours.

Cut bell pepper into strips about same size as meat strips. Cut onion into quarters.

Weave meats and vegetables onto 8 skewers, alternating colors and texture in appealing way. Reserve marinade.

Preheat grill. Cook skewers of meat and vegetables, turning frequently, just until meats are done (no more than 10 to 15 minutes).

While meats are grilling, make sauce. Pour reserved marinade through strainer and into small saucepan. Bring to a boil. Add peanut butter, honey, and hot pepper flakes. Boil hard 2 to 3 minutes. Remove from heat and stir in yogurt.

Once meats are cooked, serve 2 skewers on a bed of brown rice to each diner. Serve sauce on side.

San Diego Chicken

The combination of Oriental and Mexican ingredients, grilled to perfection, California style, gives you a West Coast classic. Do note that California chile pepper is not the same thing as chili powder. This pure-ground capsicum, of the variety grown best in the hot Southern California sunshine, can be found in grocery stores in those cellophane packets hanging on a rack, usually near the produce section. The brand available to me is called Mojave.

You can make this dish using whole wings, or even thighs, but it's best with only the largest section of the wing. Butchers sometimes call these "drumettes." Isn't that an annoying term? Makes the poor chicken sound like a cheerleader.

Serve with polenta spiked with red pepper flakes, and alfalfa sprout and artichoke salad. Simple. Calls for a wine that can stand on its own two feet. A stout zinfandel, perhaps.

Serves 4; marinates in 2 hours; grills
in 20 minutes

3 pounds chicken wings	½ cup Shoyu soy sauce
2 tablespoons grated gingerroot	2 tablespoons ground California chile pepper
2 garlic cloves, pressed	2 tablespoons brown sugar
½ cup dry red wine	
1 small onion (¼ pound), thinly sliced	

Place wings in glass utility dish. Combine remaining ingredients and pour over chicken, coating all surfaces. Cover and marinate in refrigerator at least 2 hours.

Grill over charcoal, turning wings frequently, and dipping in marinade with each turn. You have to watch this like a hawk, because the marinade has sugar in it, and it will burn. This isn't one of those preparations where you can sit down and knock back a glass of white wine while it's cooking.

Pay attention and soon you'll have succulent, golden wings that will make you practically take flight. Good cold the next day, too.

Lime-grilled Chicken with Honey Butter

Here is an entrée with no salt, low cholesterol, and if you are dieting, you can do without the sauce. Yet it is pungent, citrus sharp, and works so fast you can be in and out of the kitchen in an hour. If you don't wish to grill it, try broiling instead.

Serves 4 in 1 hour

2   chicken breasts, boned, skinned, and halved
¼   cup fresh lime juice (approximately 2 limes)
3   garlic cloves, pressed

a generous grating of fresh pepper
1   teaspoon honey
3   tablespoons soft sweet butter

Place boned, skinned chicken breasts in glass dish. Combine lime juice and garlic and pour over. Pepper meat generously. Cover and let marinate about 45 minutes, turning 2 or 3 times.

Preheat grill. Cook chicken over very hot grill, turning frequently until just done (no more than 5 to 10 minutes).

Mix honey and soft butter to make sauce. Serve meat with a dollop of sauce on top.

Pollo Margarita

The Mexican technique for quick, even grilling of a whole chicken requires splitting the bird down the backbone and laying it out flat, butterfly style, on the hot grill. In Los Angeles, restaurants known as Pollo Loco have sold a million of these glistening, golden birds.

I wouldn't go so far as to suggest *drinking* the marinade that whitens the flesh and brightens the bird, but you wouldn't mind making a little extra for yourself. Because this marinade is, at the heart, your basic margarita.

Serve with Cranberry Salsa, Spanish Rice, and Green Beans with Elephant Garlic (see index for recipes). Margaritas to drink, of course.

Serves 4; marinates in 1 hour;
grills in 20 minutes

1 whole fryer (about 3 pounds) split down backbone and laid flat	⅔ cup lime juice
	1 tablespoon Triple Sec
	1 teaspoon salt
⅓ cup tequila	¼ cup soft butter

Lay bird out flat in Pyrex baking dish. Combine tequila, lime juice, Triple Sec, and salt. Pour over bird. Cover and marinate at room temperature for up to 1 hour, turning bird several times.

Preheat grill thoroughly. Just before grilling, slather bird in soft butter. Place skin side down first. Use tongs to turn meat so that you don't pierce the flesh and lose juices. Watch chicken. Turn until you feel it is done (usually about 20 minutes for a whole bird). Pierce bird at thickest point and see if juices run a clear yellow. If juice is pink, keep cooking and turning. Carve bird into quarters and serve on a bed of Spanish rice.

Oregon's Own Blueberry Chicken
[Marsha Johnson]

Using fruit vinegars instead of wines for reductions makes for piquant, subtle sauces. Marsha Johnson serves this chicken with blueberry-laced sauce in two ways: with whole chicken breasts sitting in a pool of sauce, or with chicken breast strips folded into freshly made crêpes. Following this recipe, I have included a recipe for cornmeal crêpes, which adds a nice crunch to the texture of the chicken dish. Serve with green beans, a rice pilaf, and some spectacular chocolate dessert. This is a meal for company. And, if you had the dessert made up ahead, a company meal ready in less than an hour.

Serves 4 in 30 minutes

4 half chicken breasts, boned and skinned	¼ cup whipping cream
2 tablespoons butter	1 tablespoon finely minced tomato (about 1 cherry tomato)
¼ cup finely minced shallots	
4 tablespoons Oregon's Own Blueberry Vinegar	optional: 20 fresh blueberries
¼ cup chicken stock	optional: 12 cornmeal crêpes (recipe follows)

In a 10-inch skillet, sauté breasts in butter over medium-high heat, turning frequently, until golden brown on all sides (about 3 minutes on each side).

Remove breasts from pan and reduce heat. Add shallots and cook until tender, about 2 minutes. Add blueberry vinegar. Raise heat and cook until liquid is reduced to a tablespoon. Add stock, whipping cream, and tomato. Cook and stir for a minute. Return breasts to pan and simmer in sauce, uncovered, until cooked through, about 5 minutes. Remove and place on serving platter. Add berries to sauce in pan, cook 1 minute, and pour around breasts on platter. Serve at once.

If you wish to fold chicken into crêpes, tear meat into bite-size pieces before cooking and increase whipping cream to ¾ cup to increase sauce quantity. Lift cooked chicken with slotted spoon, placing tablespoon of cooked chicken into each crepe. Roll and place, seam side down, in Pyrex baking dish. Pour sauce over. Bake at 350° for 20 minutes and serve at once.

Cornmeal Crêpes

Makes 16 to 18 6-inch crepes

1 cup flour	1½ cups milk
½ cup yellow cornmeal	2 eggs
pinch of salt	vegetable oil

Combine flour, cornmeal, and salt. Stir in milk and eggs. Whisk until smooth. Batter should be thin and soupy. Using a 6-inch lightly oiled skillet or crepe pan, heat over medium heat. Measure out scant ¼ cup batter and pour into hot skillet, tilting pan to coat bottom evenly. Cook over medium heat until top is dull and underside is delicately browned. Turn and cook second side, about 15 seconds. Remove to a square of waxed paper. Stir batter. If necessary, oil skillet again. Repeat cooking procedure until all crêpes are cooked. This can be done hours before the meal is served, but crêpes should not be combined with sauce until you are ready to heat and serve.

Chicken Avocado Velvet
[Hilary Miller]

This chicken dish is fast, it is dramatic, it is fit for company, and it makes for very few dirty dishes. Served with the California Christmas Fruit Salad (see index for recipe), a spinach soufflé, and a bottle of Oregon Perry, you've got a great dinner in under an hour.

Serves 4 in 20 minutes

4 boneless chicken breast fillets (about 1½ pounds)	a little melted butter to brush on meat
salt and pepper to taste	

Avocado Velvet:

1 large dead-ripe Hass avocado	¼ cup dry sherry
	¼ cup finely chopped walnuts

Preheat broiler and broiler pan at least 5 minutes. Salt and pepper fillets and brush lightly with melted butter. When pan is hot enough to sizzle if you flick water onto it, place the fillets, serve side up, on pan. Broil about 5 inches from heat for about 5 minutes. Turn when serve side is light golden brown. Broil on other side about 3 minutes.

While chicken is cooking, prepare Avocado Velvet. Whip avocado until perfectly puréed; then fold in sherry and walnuts. Place a dollop of this atop each fillet and continue to broil until a lovely golden brown (about 5 minutes).

Poached Breast of Chicken
with a Ginger-Scallion Sauce

Besides the fact that this tastes so good, it is a wonderful recipe because it can be made ahead at your convenience. It is served at room temperature and is good with brown rice, stir-fried vegetables, and a good dry white wine.

Serves 4; marinates in 1 hour

2   whole chicken breasts
½   cup peanut oil
6   green onions and tops, thinly sliced
½   cup fresh gingerroot, grated
4   tablespoons soy sauce
2   tablespoons dry sherry
4   tablespoons brown sugar

Place chicken in sauce pot. Cover with unsalted water, bring to a boil, then reduce to a simmer. Poach chicken until just done, about 20 minutes. Remove from heat and let stand in liquid until lukewarm. Remove chicken from broth, skin, debone, and cut julienne.

Arrange chicken in a shallow glass baking dish. In a 6-inch skillet, sauté green onions and grated gingerroot in peanut oil for about 30 seconds, then remove from heat and sprinkle over chicken. Add soy sauce, sherry, and sugar to skillet. Boil briefly, then pour over chicken. Cover and let marinate at room temperature about an hour. Serve at room temperature.

Squash Blossom Chicken

The first requirement for this recipe is access to a summer garden loaded with squash or pumpkin plants. With the growing interest in baby vegetables, you don't even have to have your own garden to get blossoms. Webb Ranch, for example, just outside Palo Alto, sells squashes, courgettes—baby zucchinis with blossoms intact—and just plain blossoms. If the farmer's market you patronize doesn't offer blossoms, lean on your produce person.

If you can get your hands on about a quart of squash flowers, you can create a summer dish as subtle and complex as a dish seasoned with the more expensive saffron. Your squash blossom chicken will be colored a pale yellow and laced with the golden threads from the stigmas of squash flowers, instead of the stigmas of *crocus sativus.*

It is best to gather blossoms early in the morning, while they are still fully opened. If you don't wish to impede the crop, gather only male blossoms. You can easily tell male blossoms from female: the male blossoms appear at the end of a slender green stalk; the female blossoms have a bulge beneath the bloom that ultimately will become the fruit. Choose blossoms that are virtually dirt-free, and don't use blossoms that have been sprayed. Without washing, place about a quart of these in a large bowl and cover with plastic wrap. Refrigerate for the day. By supper time, they will still look delicate and fresh picked. Hold out the most opulent one to garnish the dish, then proceed with the recipe.

Serves 4 in 1 hour

1   cup brown long-grain rice, cooked in 2½ cups barely salted water
2   tablespoons olive oil
3   tablespoons Madras curry powder
1   medium onion (¼ pound), coarsely chopped
2   garlic cloves, minced
1   quart squash blossoms (about a dozen)

2   whole chicken breasts (about 2 pounds), boned, skinned, and torn into strips, using 2 forks
2   cups chicken broth
    salt and pepper to taste
2   tablespoons cornstarch, dissolved in ½ cup cold water

Simmer rice in salted water in covered saucepan for 50 minutes. Reserve.

In a 10-inch skillet, heat olive oil over medium-high heat until hot. Stir in curry powder and sauté for 2 minutes, stirring. Add onion, garlic, and blossoms. Sauté until blossoms collapse. Break up blooms with spoon, then add chicken strips. Sauté, stirring, until onion is clear. Now pour in chicken broth, cover, lower heat, and simmer about 25 minutes, or until chicken is cooked thoroughly. Season to taste. Stir in cornstarch dissolved in water. Cook and stir until sauce is clear and thick, about a minute. Remove from heat.

Arrange rice on large flat serving dish, making a well in the middle. Pour chicken and sauce into well. Garnish with reserved squash flower. Serve immediately.

On the side, you may serve any or all of the standard curry condiments: riced, hard-cooked egg; finely cut green onions and tops; minced parsley; almonds; peanuts; sunflower seeds; sesame seeds; chutney; raisins; and Royal Anne cherries. Fresh, thin strips of cucumber and a fine-chopped onion in yogurt, laced with chili powder, also is a successful accompaniment.

Lemon Roasted Chicken

The combination of high heat and a thoroughly lemon-marinated bird produces a well-seasoned dinner in less than an hour. You will find the meat tender and succulent, while the outside is a luscious, crisp golden brown. Do note that there is no oil in this marinade. And if you strip out all the yellow fat, you will have made a dieter's dream. Just remember to begin marinating the bird in the morning; then you can go off to work, come home, and have a fantastic dinner in less time than it takes to stand in line at a good deli. It's wonderful with a side dish of risotto and sautéed mixed julienned vegetables, yellow and green squash and red bell pepper.

Serves 4 in about 1 hour

1   chicken (about 3 pounds), quartered
1½ cups fresh lemon juice (about 4 lemons)
4   cloves garlic
1   cup loosely packed Italian parsley leaves
½   teaspoon red pepper flakes
salt and pepper to taste

Place chicken pieces in an 11-by-15-inch Pyrex baking dish. Squeeze lemons, press garlic, finely chop parsley, and combine all ingredients to make a pungent marinade. Pour over chicken, cover, and refrigerate 4 to 8 hours. (This is loose; I even have left this in the refrigerator overnight when I got a late invitation to eat out.) Turn chicken pieces when you think of it.

About an hour before serving, preheat oven to 400°. Place chicken and marinade in hot oven, uncovered, and roast for 45 minutes. Delicious. Serve piping hot.

Roast Pheasant with Sunchoke Stuffing
[Michael Earney]

Sold as Jerusalem artichokes until Frieda Caplan christened them "Sunchokes," these rough brown tubers look like rounded pieces of gingerroot but have a flavor as distinctive as the big round sunflower, of which they are the root. Frieda gets most of her crop from San Diego County, where the plants practically jump out of the rich hot ground. Stuffing a pheasant with Sunchokes is one more example of stuffing a bird with something he used to stuff himself with, for pheasants are wild about sunflower seeds.

You can use this stuffing with chicken, Cornish game hen, or turkey with equally good results. Last week, I found *boniatos,* the South American sweet potato with white flesh, in the store, and it was outstanding with the stuffed bird. A California Christmas Fruit Salad, some good brown bread, and you're set.

One of the nice side benefits of this preparation is the remaining pot liquor. When I cooked this last week, I ran some water in the Dutch oven while we ate so that the pan would be easier to clean. After dinner, my husband, who was carrying in the dishes, asked, making stock, eh? Well, I answered, I hadn't thought about it, but why not. Lord. I turned the burner on and let the water-and-pheasant drippings and sunchoke flavor simmer along for about an hour. I threw in an onion and a piece of celery. I tasted for salt and added just a whiff. The color was a clear caramel, and the flavor was sweet and rich, intense and complex. My God. The broth was as good as the dinner—and that is saying something.

Serves 4 in less than 2 hours

1 pheasant, 3 to 3½ pounds freshly ground black pepper to taste	2 garlic cloves, pressed
	1 celery rib, finely chopped
	¼ cup raw sunflower seeds
2 tablespoons soft butter	1 bread heel, crumbled
1 pound Sunchokes, scrubbed and coarsely chopped pheasant giblets, chopped	¼ cup milk salt and freshly ground black pepper to taste
1 medium onion (¼ pound), finely chopped	

Preheat oven to 450°. Place rack inside a roasting pan with lid. Oil rack lightly.

Wash and dry bird. Generously pepper and coat with soft butter. Set aside.

In a large mixing bowl, combine chopped Sunchokes with remaining ingredients, adjusting seasonings to taste.

Stuff loosely into bird cavity. Also stuff some into neck cavity. Most instructions tell you to truss the bird closed. What the hell. I never trussed a bird in my life. Just poke the stuffing in fairly firmly, and if a little falls out, who cares? Place bird on rack and in preheated oven for 20 minutes. Now cover bird, reduce heat to 325°, and continue to cook for 30 minutes. Remove cover and finish cooking until done, about 10 more minutes. You can tell poultry is done by piercing the flesh in the thickest part, all the way to the bone, and see what color the juice runs. It should be clear yellow; if pink, keep cooking.

If cooking a domestic bird, you needn't cover for the middle part of the cooking period. But when cooking game birds, it is always a good idea to steam them a while to ensure tenderness.

Fruited Cornish Game Hens
[Danielle Lapp]

This is a meal that can't miss. Easy, foolproof, and delicious. A poultry dish for company that is ready in an hour, looking golden, glistening, and luscious. The roast poultry and fruit mélange fills the air with such a pungent aroma that you'll have to beat them back until it emerges from the oven. If you work all day and don't get home before six, you can serve this to company without even hustling. Serve it with rice pilaf, soak the golden raisins in brandy, and have small condiment dishes of coconut and cashews to pass around. The fruit you choose depends on what's available. Here on the West Coast, we usually have a good selection from the tropical varieties: papaya, mango, carambola, kiwi, cherimoya, even banana. Any of these soft, sweet tropical fruits will work admirably. I just made this dish using peach chutney from Berry Creek Farm. That chutney is so good you can eat it with a spoon (see mail order section). As I mentioned, half a bird is plenty for each serving.

Serves 4 in 1 hour

2 Cornish game hens
4 tablespoons softened butter
1 tablespoon Madras curry powder
½ cup peach chutney
¼ cup fresh-squeezed lime juice

2 cups sliced exotic fruit: any or a mixture of the following: papaya, mango, kiwi, banana, carambola

Preheat oven to 375°. Wash and dry birds thoroughly. Mix soft butter and curry powder and coat birds inside and out with this mixture. Place on rack in open roasting pan and in preheated oven for 30 minutes.

Meanwhile, mix chutney and lime juice. When 30 minutes is up, spread chutney mixture over birds and continue roasting for 15 more minutes.

When the birds are almost done, slice fruits. Place in bottom of roaster around the golden birds (after about 45 minutes of cooking). Leave in oven just long enough to thoroughly heat through (no more than 10 minutes).

Cut birds in half and serve on a rice pilaf bed with cashews and shredded coconut to accompany. Mound fruit on top of browned bird. Yum. Simple steamed broccoli with a squeeze of lime. Gelato for dessert. Easy. Easy.

Rock Cornish Game Hens with Sunflower Seed Stuffing

Here is the New West Coast Cuisine at its best. Hulled sunflower seeds, sold in bulk either plain, roasted, or Tamari-marinated, are wonderful kitchen staples. Not only are sunflower seeds good kid snacks, they give a splendid crunch to starch dishes, such as this fairly traditional bread stuffing. People who quit smoking swear sunflower seeds help kick the habit; and the seeds even provide a modest amount of vegetable protein.

Conventional wisdom calls for one Cornish game hen per diner. Each of these birds weighs roughly twenty ounces and, when stuffed and glazed, becomes quite a substantial entrée. Although restaurants don't care about waste, home cooks do. Try splitting a bird just before serving, place it cut side down on a plate, and see if you don't find that half a bird is plenty of food for one serving. I find it's less intimidating and somehow less carnal-looking on the plate. If you wish to serve a whole bird to each diner, simply multiply this recipe by the number of mouths you have to feed. One thing about this dish, it's not much more trouble to cook ten birds than two. You just need a bigger roasting pan.

Serves 2 to 4 in 1½ hours

2   **Rock Cornish game hens (20 ounces each), rinsed and patted dry**
¼   **cup melted butter for basting birds**

Stuffing:

¼   **cup butter**
3   **tablespoons minced shallots**
1   **garlic clove, pressed**
3   **mushrooms, minced**
½   **celery rib, finely chopped**
½   **cup hulled sunflower seeds**
6   **fresh leaves or ½ teaspoon crumbled dried sage**

fresh cilantro leaves for garnish

¼   **teaspoon white pepper**
2   **cups cubed dry good-quality bread (say, old English muffins or heels from 9-grain bread, or any mixture of substantial breads)**

Glaze:

¼ cup sugar
1 tablespoon white wine
   vinegar
¼ teaspoon cream of tartar
¾ cup fresh navel orange juice
   (approximately 1 orange)
   zest of one orange, cut in
   fine julienne

¼ cup mango chutney (Major
   Grey's, peach, pear, or
   homemade)

Preheat oven to 400°.

For stuffing, sauté shallots, garlic, mushrooms, and celery in butter in a 10-inch skillet until soft (about 5 minutes). Remove from heat. Stir in sunflower seeds and seasonings; add bread. Toss bread lightly to coat all surfaces. Taste and salt. Stuff into birds' cavities. Close and place birds on rack in open roaster. Sprinkle with pepper and brush with melted butter. Roast in open pan in 400° oven for 30 minutes, then reduce heat to 350°, and continue roasting for 15 minutes more. Brush hens with glaze and continue roasting for 30 more minutes, basting with glaze every 10 minutes. Once leg joint moves freely, remove from oven. Remove trussing strings. Either split each hen and serve half to a diner, or serve whole birds. Garnish with cilantro. Good with bulgur.

During first 30 minutes of birds' oven roasting make glaze. In small stainless steel or enameled pan, combine sugar, vinegar, and cream of tartar. Cook over moderately high heat, washing down any sugar crystals clinging to sides with a brush dipped in cold water, until the syrup is pale amber. Remove from heat and immediately add orange juice and julienned rind. Reduce temperature to moderately low, return to heat, and simmer for about 5 minutes, until rind is perfectly soft and glazed. Remove from heat and stir in chutney.

When cutting julienne strips of any citrus rind, use potato peeler or one of those little bar tools for making a lemon twist, like they throw into a martini.

Whatever tool you use, be especially careful to cut away only the colored part of the rind. The white spongy pith is bitter and will ruin whatever food you add it to. I learned this through one, dare I say, bitter, lesson, when I tried to just run lemon rind through the food processor. A ruined recipe. Ugh.

Mama Stamberg's
Cranberry-Horseradish Sauce

The night before Thanksgiving, I was driving along listening to *All Things Considered* on National Public Radio when Susan Stamberg gave out her mother-in-law's recipe for cranberry sauce. I nearly wrecked the car writing and driving. But, boy, was I thankful. You will be too. This cranberry sauce will perk up that tired old roast turkey so much that he may arise from the platter and dance across the table.

All I've done to alter Mama Stamberg's original recipe is to replace sour cream with yogurt. Goodbye fat. Let me tell you, though. It's no wonder Susan Stamberg gets all those calls about this cranberry sauce. It is the best I have ever eaten. Not only is it delicious, but it is also a dazzling hot pink color that looks wonderful. And made with our impeccably fresh Tulelake horseradish, it is without peer. Try it. Served icy cold, it's like the most amazing cold-hot sorbet you ever tasted.

Serves 8 in 10 minutes; freezes in 1 hour

2 cups fresh cranberries	2 tablespoons fresh prepared
1 medium onion (3 ounces)	horseradish
½ cup sugar	1 cup plain yogurt

Combine cranberries and onion in processor bowl or food grinder, and grind together. Add sugar, horseradish, and yogurt; spin to mix. Remove to small refrigerator dish, cover, and place in freezer. About 15 minutes before serving, remove from freezer. Whisk lightly just before serving. The frosty ice crystals add a texture to the pungent ingredients that make it irresistible. You'll be eating it with a spoon.

Cranberry Salsa

Fresh cranberries, combined with chiles and cilantro, make a nouvelle salsa splendid with grilled poultry. Serve icy cold with shards of cranberry ice for a magnificent texture contrast to the smooth white flesh of a chicken breast.

Serves 4 in 10 minutes; marinates in 1 hour

1 cup fresh cranberries	green chiles
½ small onion (2 ounces)	20 cilantro leaves
2 fresh green chiles (2	2 tablespoons fresh lime juice
ounces), deseeded and	(½ lime)
minced, or 2 ounces canned	¼ cup sugar

Combine cranberries, onion, and chiles in processor bowl. Reduce to coarse purée. Stir in cilantro leaves, lime juice, and sugar. Cover and freeze at least an hour. Remove from freezer 15 minutes before serving. Whisk before serving; should have the texture of a fruited sorbet. Serve alongside grilled poultry in its own footed dish.

Elderberry Shallot Sauce for Roast Poultry

During the last lush days of Indian summer, from Southern California all the way up to British Columbia, in that string of mountains that girdles our region, you will find wild elderberry trees heavy with masses of bluish purple berries. It rather dignifies the humble elderberry to call it a tree; actually it is more like a weed—a tall, gangly cane-stemmed weed that grows so vigorously it's as big as a tree.

Anywhere on the West Coast, when you drive into the conifers, beginning at about 3,000 feet, you will start to see single and sometimes whole stands of elderberries. Wildlife love these berries. You may well see deer browsing, or band-tailed pigeons hanging upside down on the branches, simply gorging themselves on the bursting berries. On the ground you may see a family of quail with half-grown chicks busily eating the berries that have fallen.

If you are lucky enough to find an elderberry with both ripe berries and those staggering white blossoms, you're in luck. You can batter and deep fry the blooms for a taste of North American Indian gourmet flavor.

I extract berry juice with a steam juicer, so I have pure undiluted juice for use in a sauce such as this or for making jelly. If you don't have a steam juicer, simply place berries in a large heavy kettle, mash slightly with a potato masher, add a little water to the bottom of the pan, cover, and bring it to a boil. Boil gently for ten to fifteen minutes to extract juice. Allow it to stand until cool, and then strain it through a double-cheesecloth-lined colander. Be patient; don't mash it. You will soon have crystal-clear berry juice for making sauce or jewellike jellies. (You can just discard the berries.)

If you do not have access to wild elderberries, you can substitute cranberries, sweet cherries, blueberries, raspberries, or blackberries. Elderberry juice is not sweet at all, so if you substitute other juices, taste for sweetness. More than likely you will need little if any additional sugar. Steam-released juices are not watered down and are quite thick. If you wish, you can substitute pure, unsweetened frozen juice instead, in which case you should delete any additional water.

This sauce keeps well in the refrigerator, and it is good over Cornish game hens, pheasant, quail, grouse, or band-tailed pigeons, not to mention the lowly chicken when roasted to golden perfection.

Makes 1½ cups in 20 minutes

1 tablespoon butter	¼ cup sugar (again, less for
1 shallot, minced	sweeter berries)
⅔ cup elderberry juice	1 teaspoon arrowroot
⅓ cup water (less for sweeter	½ cup cold water
juices)	

Sauté shallot in butter in small saucepan until shallot is clear. Add juice, water, and sugar and bring to a boil.

Combine arrowroot and cold water until it becomes a smooth mixture. Add to boiling berry sauce, stirring constantly. Cook until sauce is clear. Taste and add salt if you wish. The sauce is fairly thin and simply coats birds with a glistening fruit-flavored glaze.

Theme and Variation on a Strawberry Sauce for Grilled Poultry

I intended to devise a berry sauce for poultry that would go well with grilled breast of chicken or turkey. The plan was to create three variations, then see which was best. However, each one of the variations was so good, I decided to give it to you just the way I did it. You make the three and see which one you like best. Berries and poultry are so good together. Try this principle with other berry varieties—raspberries, olallieberries, cranberries, blueberries.

Grill breast of chicken or turkey that you have lightly coated with butter and sprinkled with freshly milled black pepper. For a really outstanding look, make three ribbons of the vari-colored sauces on a white plate and place the grilled breast of chicken on top. Garnish with a twist of lime. Serve with asparagus spears and a rice pilaf. Good brown bread. Fruity Riesling to drink. Gelato for dessert. Can't you see the menu taking shape? And none of it's hard to do.

Makes 1 pint in 20 minutes

1 pint perfectly ripe	1 tablespoon poppy seeds
strawberries	2 tablespoons fresh lime juice
1 tablespoon grated red onion	¾ cup rich chicken broth

Purée strawberries; then divide equally among 3 bowls. In first bowl, stir in grated red onion; in second, stir in poppy seeds; in third, lime juice. Now, into each bowl stir in ¼ cup chicken broth. Taste. Which one do you like best? What do you think? Seems like a draw to me.

Notice the difference in color. Strawberry and lime juice is the purest strawberry red. The poppy seeds give a smoky purple cast. The onion pales out the color to pink and seems to gel the berry purée.

Cover and refrigerate the 3 sauces. You can make these days ahead if necessary. Serve cold.

Oysters on the Half Shell Hot-Cha-Cha

Removing an oyster from its shell is not as difficult as you might imagine. When we were in Portland, visiting Louis and Dan's Oyster Bar, we were given a dozen oysters in the shells, a funny-looking knife, and a sheet of directions. Essentially, what you do is cut the oyster loose from its moorings by nipping off a little piece of shell then slipping the knife in, up against the shell, to detach the oyster on both sides. When you open the shell, the oyster will still be alive, and will retract slightly at the touch. You can eat the oyster plain, with a squeeze of lemon, with horseradish, or the Mexican way—with a little salsa on top. Here's how.

Serves 4 in 20 minutes

24 live oysters in the shell
¼ cup fresh lime juice (about ½ lime)
1 dead-ripe tomato (½ pound), peeled, seeded, and finely chopped
1 cup minced cilantro leaves
4 garlic cloves, pressed

2 green onions and tops, minced
1 fresh jalapeño, deveined, seeded, and minced
1 fresh red chile pepper, deveined, seeded, and minced
   optional salt to taste

Shuck oysters and place 6 to the plate, taking care not to spill oyster liquor from shell. Combine remaining ingredients. Salt to taste if you wish. Place a dollop of salsa on each oyster and serve with hot French bread.

San Francisco Sourdough Crab Sandwich

This version of the San Francisco classic comes from the Mission district, heart of the Latin population. The addition of jícama and red bell pepper gives this favorite a welcome crunch. If you would like the freshest, most flavorful crab meat, buy a live crab and boil him alive (screaming help, help, in his little crab voice). Or, buy one in the shell and pick the meat yourself. The third solution and sliding into hardly worth it is to buy crab meat already picked and in a carton. Last and certainly least is to buy a can of crab meat. Just keep this in mind: all shellfish begin to oxidize the minute they are separated from their shells, so within a day or two they're as tasteless as Styrofoam. You're best off if you begin with a live shellfish. Deliver the coup de grace yourself and enjoy.

As we all know, there is no substitution for San Francisco sourdough. The bread just doesn't sour the same way any place else. If you want to get the real thing, turn to the mail order section.

Serves 6 to 8 in 45 minutes

1 12-inch round loaf San
   Francisco sourdough bread
½ pound Dungeness crab meat,
   fresh picked from shell
1 cup (¼ pound) shredded
   Swiss cheese
½ cup jícama, cut into match-
   stick julienne
3 green onions and tops, finely
   sliced

½ red bell pepper (2 ounces),
   cut into match-stick julienne
¼ cup plain yogurt mixed with:
1 tablespoon mayonnaise and
1 tablespoon lemon juice
   salt and freshly grated black
   pepper to taste

Cut top off bread, making a hat. Scoop out soft bread inside, forming a bowl. Throw inside of the bread out into the backyard to feed the birds.

Preheat oven to 375°. Combine remaining ingredients, stir to mix well, then stuff into bread bowl. Replace hat. Wrap bread in foil. Bake for 25 minutes. Cut into wedges to serve. Serve with kiwi and peach slices and a good, cold California Gewürztraminer.

Blue Sea Scallops Deglazed with Blueberry Vinegar

Here is a Northwest local dish that uses the best of sea and shore, is quick, delicious, and gorgeous to look at. The scallops are harvested offshore, the blueberries hail from the Cross's farm, and the oyster mushrooms are grown by the Mackys. You can mail order it all. Even if you live in Cincinnati.

Serves 4 in 15 minutes

½ cup sweet butter
5 tablespoons blueberry
   vinegar (Canter-Berry)
¼ pound fresh-sliced oyster
   mushrooms (Full Moon)

1½ pounds fresh sea scallops
¼   cup chopped parsley
    optional salt to taste

Melt butter in a 10-inch skillet over medium-high heat. Add vinegar and mushrooms. Sauté 1 to 2 minutes, or until mushrooms are about half cooked. Add rinsed and dried scallops to skillet and cook over high heat, about 1 minute on each side. Serve on warmed platter and sprinkle with parsley; add salt to taste if you must.

Sautéed Oregon Bay Scallops
with Parsley and Garlic

The Oregon scallop is distinct from its Atlantic counterpart. Smaller, with a crisp, sweet flavor and a buttery texture that clearly sets it apart from the grainy Eastern scallop, it is hard to find in fish markets but well worth the hunt. As I understand it, Eastern scallop beds are stable and reliable, but here in the Pacific, Oregon scallops tend to migrate—in herds, they call them—based on some logic known only to scallops. Fishermen, who have mortgage payments to make, hate to go chasing some skittish bivalve with muscles for brains, so the availability of Oregon scallops in the market is spotty, at best. But if you do see them—grab them. Anyway, you can make this dish using any superfresh scallop.

Serves 4 in 15 minutes

1 pound Oregon bay scallops	2 medium garlic cloves, pressed
2 tablespoons flour	½ cup fresh Italian parsley leaves
salt and white pepper to taste (just a whiff)	1 lime, quartered
2 tablespoons olive oil	
2 tablespoons butter	

Coat scallops with seasoned flour. Combine oil and butter in 10-inch skillet and heat. Press garlic into hot oil and cook for a minute. Add scallops and cook, turning only once, until golden on both sides (about 5 minutes). Remove to warmed plate. Stir parsley into pan juices and cook just to wilt the leaves. Pour over scallops. Serve with a wedge of lime. Rice with mushrooms is a natural bed for sautéed scallops, and an Oregon Perry wine complements the presentation.

Quick Stir-Fried Cashew Shrimp
[Bob Lampley]

Prepared along with cellophane noodles, and served with just picked mandarin oranges, this one's fresh fast-food, West Coast style.

Serves 4 in 20 minutes

¼ cup peanut oil	1 pound snow peas, blossom ends removed, and strung
1 garlic clove, minced	½ cup whole cashews
3 tablespoons grated fresh ginger	¼ cup brown sugar
1 pound small mushrooms, cut into halves	½ pound mung bean sprouts
¼ cup soy sauce	1 pound medium shrimp, peeled
1 tablespoon Worcestershire sauce	

Lay everything out in a line, close at hand, and begin heating dry wok. When good and hot, add oil and heat thoroughly.

Add ingredients in this order—garlic and ginger; mushrooms, soy sauce, and Worcestershire sauce; snow peas, cashews, and brown sugar; and bean sprouts and shrimp—stirring and tossing no more than 20 seconds after each addition.

Sprinkle with 2 to 3 tablespoons water. Cover and let steam for 2 minutes. Serve immediately.

Grilled Salmon Steaks
with Juniper Berries and Gin

The Pacific Northwest has lots of salmon and lots of juniper berries. American Indians combined the two five hundred years ago in a flavor marriage that seems to be a natural. Since gin is flavored with juniper berries, you can toss in a little of the clear flavorful liquor to further intensify the result. When the Indians cooked salmon with juniper berries, they just jerked the berries right off the bush; they didn't use any gin at all. At least not until the Hudson's Bay Company came out West selling firewater. Gin on the steaks sounds like a paleface addition. This preparation begs for wild rice. A tossed green salad. A perfectly made martini is a must before you begin.

Serves 4; marinates in 1 hour

1 tablespoon juniper berries	4 salmon steaks (about 1½
⅛ cup gin	pounds)
¼ cup oil	
freshly milled black pepper	
to coat	

Crush about half the juniper berries and combine with gin and oil. Grate pepper onto steaks, press remaining whole juniper berries into meat, then place steaks in glass dish. Pour gin and oil over, cover, and let stand at room temperature for about an hour. Grill over hot coals, no more than 5 minutes on each side. If you have a juniper bush in your yard, you can break twigs of juniper onto the coals to further enhance the flavor.

Sesame-Marinated Grilled Salmon Steaks

One way to prevent fish from sticking to the grill is to oil the grill well. Another way, as we have learned from the Japanese, is to marinate the fish for a while so that the oil impregnates the fish's surface. Here we have presented nice, thick salmon steaks that won't cook in thirty seconds. By marinating the meat, you can guarantee that the steaks can cook over a very hot fire, and with just one turning get cooked through but still be tender and moist. Sesame oil gives a Japanese accent to the flavor of salmon. If you don't have sesame oil, just substitute regular cooking oil. Serve this salmon steak with boiled new potatoes and parsley and a salad composed of enoki mushrooms, grated carrots, and blanched marinated Blue Lake green beans. Marinate the beans in a rice wine vinaigrette; then spoon the marinade over mushrooms and carrots. This slightly sweet vinaigrette goes perfectly with salmon.

Serves 4; marinates in 2 hours

- 4 salmon steaks (about 1½ pounds)
- ½ cup dry white wine (try a French colombard)
- ½ cup sesame oil
- 2 tablespoons fresh lemon juice
- ½ teaspoon salt
- a fine coating of freshly milled black pepper
- ½ teaspoon rubbed sage
- 2 teaspoons fresh thyme leaves, or ½ teaspoon dried
- 2 tablespoons fresh minced parsley

Combine all ingredients and pour over steaks that have been placed in a glass dish. Cover and marinate at least 2 hours at room temperature, or up to 8 hours in refrigerator. Turn from time to time.

When you are ready to eat, thoroughly preheat grill. Cook steaks over very hot fire, watching all the time, basting with additional marinade. Turn only once. Even with cool fire, this should never take longer than 5 minutes on each side.

Whole Grilled Salmon with Garlic and Rosemary

Since grilled food takes on part of its taste from the smoke that arises to envelope it, you can see that by tossing special twigs and leaves on the fire you can alter the ultimate taste of the food. Here, we toss on rosemary twigs. Rosemary grows like a weed and is one herb that everybody should cultivate at home. It is sturdy, requires little water, and can withstand violent temperature changes; our neighbor in Los Altos had an entire hedge of rosemary. If you don't have a stand of rosemary, toss on dried leaves from a jar. Or substitute fennel, which is different but delicious. You won't get quite the pungent result that can be achieved by using aroma-laden twigs, but you will get a close approximation.

Serves 6 in 30 minutes

1 whole 3 to 4 pound salmon,   ½ cup fresh orange juice
  cleaned and scaled   ½ cup peanut oil
3 garlic cloves, pressed   ¼ cup butter
1 tablespoon fresh rosemary,   small handful of rosemary
  or ½ teaspoon dried   twigs, or 2 to 3 tablespoons
1 tablespoon salt   dried

Dry salmon thoroughly, inside and out. Make paste of garlic, rosemary, and salt. Rub all fish surfaces thoroughly. Combine orange juice and peanut oil. Place salmon in a glass utility baking dish big enough to hold it, and pour liquid over. Cover and marinate in refrigerator for at least 2 hours, basting from time to time.

Prepare charcoal fire. When coals are white, toss rosemary twigs (or dried leaves) onto them. Oil grill carefully so that fish won't stick. Grill first side of the fish from 5 to 10 minutes, dabbing top with butter. Turn only once. Grill second side, basting with butter, until meat barely flakes, usually no more than 5 minutes. Watch this so it doesn't overcook. Dress fish with remaining butter and serve.

Grant Avenue Sand Dabs
[National Fishery Education]

Sand dabs are the smallest of the sole family and are unique to Western waters. They are the flatfish most frequently caught by Central California sportsmen and are also available through commercial sources. These small, delicate fish lend themselves to the subtle flavor of Chinese cookery. If you have a bamboo steamer, haul it out. If you don't, you can jury-rig a steamer using a Dutch oven and a stand—say two empty one-pound cans with holes punched in the tops. Serve these exclusive California fish alongside Mendocino Miso Soup (see index for recipe) and white rice and finish off the meal with one of the stupendous chocolate desserts. Saké is the wine of choice. Warm saké.

Serves 4 in 25 minutes

2 to 3 pounds dressed whole   1 quart boiling water
  sand dabs   ¼ cup salad oil, heated
1 tablespoon peeled, grated   2 tablespoons sesame oil,
  gingerroot   heated
  salt to taste   ⅓ cup soy sauce
4 whole green onions   green onions for garnish

Arrange fish on heatproof platter. Sprinkle with gingerroot and salt. Place whole green onions on top of fish and put platter on a trivet or rack inside a bamboo steamer or large roaster containing boiling water. Cover and cook for 5 to 10 minutes, or until fish flakes easily when tested with fork. Remove fish from steamer. Discard cooked onions and drain off any water from platter. Combine oils, soy sauce, and sauce over fish. Garnish with green onions that have been cut vertically to make delicate shards. Serve immediately.

Sautéed Red Snapper Fillets
in a Mexican Nouvelle Sauce

Serve these savory fillets with a spiked polenta and a salad composed from romaine, tomatillos, tomatoes, and a Haas avocado served in a bowl lined with purple salad savoy cabbage. Make a lime vinaigrette. Get a loaf of crusty French bread. A square-shouldered bottle of white wine. A berry sorbet.

Serves 4 in 20 minutes, marinates in
2 hours

4 red snapper fillets (1½ pounds)	2 fresh jalapeños, seeded and finely chopped
salt	⅛ teaspoon dried oregano
2 garlic cloves, pressed	⅛ teaspoon thyme
¼ cup fresh lime juice (about 2 limes)	2 bay leaves
2 tablespoons olive oil	¼ teaspoon brown sugar
1 medium onion, thinly sliced	2 tablespoons butter
2 cups fresh tomatoes, seeded, finely chopped, and drained	1 tablespoon olive oil
½ cup green olives, finely chopped	cilantro for garnish
	lime wedges for garnish

Place fish fillets 1 layer deep in shallow glass baking dish. Lightly sprinkle with salt, press garlic over, and gently rub salt and garlic into fillets. Add lime juice and marinate at room temperature, covered, at least an hour (preferably 2), turning fish several times.

About 30 minutes before serving time, heat 2 tablespoons olive oil in 10-inch skillet over medium heat and gently sauté onion until translucent. Add tomatoes, olives, jalapeños, oregano, thyme, bay leaves, and sugar. Simmer uncovered for 10 minutes, stirring occasionally. Pour this sauce into warmed bowl and reserve on the back of stove.

Add butter and remaining tablespoon of oil to same skillet over medium-high heat. Sauté fillets until golden on both sides, turning only once (no more than 10 minutes). Remove to warmed serving plate. Discard marinade. Pour reserved sauce over fillets and sprinkle with cilantro. Garnish with fresh lime wedges and serve at once.

Japanese Eggplant, Bell Pepper, Lamb Stir-Fry

This stir-fried dish is good looking, with shiny purple eggplant, bright green bell peppers, and a lamb-spiked sauce. You also can substitute chicken or pork with good results. But lamb is very big now on the West Coast, and it seems that Japanese eggplant is turning up in everything. Delicious over brown rice.

Note the tablespoon of miso used in the sauce. Miso is a fermented soybean paste that provides a sweet acidic undercarriage of flavor; you can find it in natural-foods stores. Store at home airtight in the refrigerator.

Serves 4 in 30 minutes

6 small Japanese eggplants, about 1 pound

2 large green bell peppers, about ½ pound

½ pound lamb shoulder chops, boned and cut into matchstick julienne

3 tablespoons cooking oil

1 1-inch piece of fresh gingerroot, cut into matchstick julienne

3 garlic cloves, pressed

2 teaspoons cornstarch dissolved in 1½ tablespoons cold water

Sauce:

½ cup water

1 teaspoon sugar

1 tablespoon soy sauce

1 tablespoon saké, or dry white wine

1 tablespoon red miso

Cut eggplants and bell peppers into uniform pieces about 1 inch by 2 inches by ½ inch. Discard seeds and membrane from peppers. Cut meat.

Mix all sauce ingredients and set aside.

Heat wok or 12-inch skillet until water sizzles (about 2 minutes). Add 1 tablespoon oil and heat. Now sauté gingerroot and garlic for 30 seconds. Add lamb strips. Cook and stir until meat is gray (about 2 minutes). Remove meat and reserve. Add eggplant and sauté until brown, then add about 2 tablespoons of water, cover, and steam until tender (about 3 minutes). Add bell pepper and continue to cook, stirring, for 2 more minutes.

Pour dissolved cornstarch into sauce. Add meat to vegetables, pour sauce over all ingredients, and mix well. Cook until sauce is clear and glistening. Serve immediately over brown rice.

Roast Leg of Lamb with a Whole Head of Garlic and a Rosehip Glaze

The first thing you have to do to make this dish is to come up with some rosehip jam. You can buy it in a natural-foods store, or you can make it yourself if you have access to wild rose bushes in the fall. Rosehips have the most evanescent, singular rosearomaed taste. When made into a glaze for a leg of lamb, not only do you get a beautiful rose-colored caramel look but the most exotic taste you ever dreamed of. And the roast literally is studded with slivers of garlic. The combination is to die for. Just this very minute, my husband, Joe, came in with a bite of the leftover cold lamb, slathered in Napa Valley's California sweet hot mustard. Yum. Can I possibly tell you how good it was? And he thinks we ought to roast a lamb coated in the mustard next time. Can you imagine what a difficult, demanding job this is? Cooking and eating good food all the time? Oh well. Someone has to do it. I also have made this leg of lamb using crab apple jelly and red currant jelly with good results. If you are absolutely stumped on the rosehips, feel free to substitute. The result will be fine.

In choosing the leg of lamb, remember that the bigger it is, the more likely it is to be mutton. Take the smallest one you see at the market. That's your best shot at getting a mild, tender lamb.

Serves 8 to 10 in 3 hours

1 whole head of garlic
1 leg of lamb, from 4 to 8 pounds
   freshly milled black pepper to coat
⅛ teaspoon ground cloves
⅛ teaspoon Madras curry powder
⅓ cup Rosehip Jam, recipe follows (may substitute crab apple or red currant jelly)

1 teaspoon grated lemon zest
1 tablespoon fresh lemon juice
¼ teaspoon ground ginger
½ teaspoon dry mustard
   salt and freshly milled black pepper to taste

Preheat oven to 450°. Cut bottom off head of garlic and peel all cloves. Cut cloves into slivers. Puncture leg of lamb, all over, at about 1-inch intervals, and bury slivers of garlic in flesh on all sides. Now rub meat with pepper, cloves, and curry powder.

Place lamb on a rack in a shallow roasting pan. Cook for 20 minutes in preheated oven to sear meat. Reduce heat to 325° and cook until done to suit. Place a meat thermometer into the meat at thickest portion; it will read 140° for rare and up to 180° for well-done. (You can estimate the time it will take by figuring 30 minutes per pound for well-done, and 20 minutes per pound for rare.) While lamb is roasting, combine rosehip jam with remaining ingredients for glaze. Coat with glaze 20 minutes before you are ready to remove leg from oven. When lamb is cooked, remove from oven and let it stand for 20 minutes before carving.

Serve thin slices, taking care that each diner gets a thin sliver of the gorgeous glaze as well as meat. A stuffed, baked apple makes a nice accompaniment.

Rosehip Jam

After the first frost, when the wild rosehips have turned a brilliant red, dress yourself in your most thornproof duds and go out and pick about two pounds of the dazzling red seed pods left behind after the bloom is off the roses. Come home, wash the dust off (you didn't pick in a place that might have been sprayed, did you?), and make yourself this treat.

2 pounds rosehips	1 pound sugar for every
2 cups water	pound of rosehip purée

Combine rosehips and water in medium stainless steel saucepan. Raise to a boil. Simmer just until rosehips are tender, about 10 minutes. Rub the softened rosehips through a fine sieve, using the back of a spoon. This is quite a job and may make you scream, but keep rubbing. Combine cooking water and purée. Now weigh pulp. For every pound of pulp, add an equal amount of sugar. Cook and stir until thick, about 10 to 15 minutes. Store in sterilized jars.

Braised Lamb Shanks Patrick
[Patrick Calhoun]

Patrick Calhoun, who owns the Arbor House restaurant tucked away in Talent, Oregon, specializes in West Coast–style cooking. He marries classic techniques to fresh West Coast products, many of which come from his own place. Patrick prepares shanks only when he can get the finest quality Northwest lamb. No strong muttony taste will do. The success of this dish depends on first-quality meat. It is a curiosity for which I have no answer, but the best local lamb comes to market in the fall and winter. You may find that the best "spring" lamb you can buy is available only in November. Don't ponder it. Just buy it.

The shank, served in a wide-rimmed soup bowl mounded with braised mushrooms and onions and celery in an aromatic sauce over brown rice, is a meal intended for cold winters' nights. It may occur to you to start declaiming in King James's English, or to hunt for a dog to whom you could throw the knuckle, once you are done, because this is one hearty winter meal. Try it with a mousseline of turnip and carrot, a winter salad of pomegranate and grapefruit, and a sturdy red wine, say Henry Estates Pinot Noir.

Serves 4 in 1½ hours

3 tablespoons olive oil
4 lamb shanks, about 2 pounds
2 onions (½ pound), finely diced
1 stalk celery (2 ounces), finely diced
4 cups (¼ pound) sliced mushrooms
1 tablespoon oil
¼ teaspoon each: ground cumin, allspice, ginger, salt, and pepper

1 teaspoon turmeric
1 tablespoon flour
1 tablespoon sugar
1 cup tomato sauce
2 cups beef consommé
2 bell peppers (½ pound), cut into match-stick julienne
3 cups cooked brown rice
bunch of fresh parsley for garnish

Preheat oven to 350°. In large dutch oven, heat oil over medium heat, then add lamb shanks and brown on all sides. Remove from pan and reserve. Add onions, celery, and mushrooms to pan. Cook and stir until vegetables have cooked down, about 20 minutes. Remove from pan and reserve.

Add another tablespoon of oil. Add cumin, allspice, ginger, salt and pepper, and turmeric. Cook and stir for 1 minute. Add flour. Make a golden roux, cooking and stirring for 2 to 3 minutes. Sprinkle sugar over and cook for 30 seconds. Add tomato sauce and consommé. Reduce heat to low.

Stir to mix. Replace shanks and vegetables, adding bell pepper. Cover and simmer until meat is tender, about 45 minutes. Serve with brown rice and fresh parsley garnish.

Ashland Avenue Pears and Ribs
[Barbara Schack]

Just imagine going to a buffet where every dish is a winner, yet one stands out overwhelmingly above all. When I judged a Southern Oregon food show that had over six hundred entrants and 68 finalists' best recipes, there was a clear winner. I, along with eight other judges, voted decisively for this dish. The grand-prize winner and creator is Barbara Schack from Los Angeles, who is one of those innovative cooks that simply can't follow a recipe. Barbara begins by seeing what is available fresh and then applying classic cooking techniques to what's on hand. A winning attitude.

For the cookoff, Barbara presented the ribs on a platter with pears on top and a lovely row of nasturtiums on parsley at the bottom. She said she likes to use kumquats, but it was too early in the year for them. You can imagine how beautiful and colorful this platter is. Mahogany ribs, glazed pears, dazzling golden nasturtiums, and good old green parsley. Don't you just want to try it this very minute?

Serves 4 in 2 hours;
marinates in 4 hours

2 pounds meaty pork
    spareribs
3 tablespoons soy sauce
3 tablespoons dry sherry
¼ cup fruit juice (apple, pear,
    orange, whatever's on hand)
3 tablespoons water

2 tablespoons oil
1½ tablespoons honey
1 garlic clove, pressed
½ teaspoon freshly grated
    ginger
3 large fresh bartlett pears

Simmer spareribs in water to cover for 30 minutes. Drain, cool slightly, and cut meat between bones almost through into easy-to-serve pieces.

Combine remaining ingredients except pears and blend thoroughly. Place ribs in 11-by-15-inch Pyrex baking dish, pour marinade over, cover, and refrigerate at least 4 hours, but may be as long as overnight.

An hour and a half before serving time, place ribs and marinade, covered, in 350° oven for about 45 mintues or until ribs are tender. Uncover pan, lower oven temperature to 325°, and bake 20 to 30 minutes longer, turning and basting ribs frequently, until they become a dark mahogany color. During the last 20 minutes ribs are cooking, peel, halve, and core pears. Arrange these in pan with ribs the last 15 minutes of baking, brushing lightly with marinade. Add a little water to pan if rich juices begin to stick.

Serve immediately.

Chutney Pork Chops

This recipe falls into the category of minimum effort for maximum gain. If you use a fine smoked chop, say one you ordered from Roi Ballard of Meadow Farms Country Smokehouse out in Bishop (the matinee cowboys' favorite), with no more than 10 minutes attention, but up to an hour more for baking, you can have a good, delicious dinner. Good with bulgur and a simple salad.

Serves 4 in under an hour

4 large center-cut pork chops
    (about 1½ pounds)
1 medium onion (½ pound,
    thinly sliced)

½ cup chutney

Preheat oven to 325°.

Brown chops in dry skillet over high heat. Remove from heat. Top each chop with onion and generous dollop of chutney. Pour ½ inch of water into skillet, cover, and place in oven until chops are tender—from 30 minutes to 1 hour, depending on thickness of chops. Lift onto warm platter and serve.

Braised Pork Chops in a Nest
of California Wild Rice

The Deer Creek people were the first to grow wild rice west of the Mississippi. Located in Yuba City, they produce a nonshattering variety that is particularly well suited to California's climate. Although wild rice is expensive, its assertive taste makes it the classic accompaniment to game dishes. It expands up to four times its dry volume, so you can even blend it with equal parts brown rice to cut the cost. I am one person who actually prefers it mixed with brown rice, because it is so potent that eating it plain makes me feel a little like a Percheron mare . . . chomp, chomp, chomp. You can buy the wild rice from the Deer Creek people either plain or mixed with brown rice (see mail order section).

Serves 4 in under 2 hours

4 thick center-cut pork chops (about 1½ pounds) salt and freshly ground pepper to taste
2 large onions (¾ pound), thickly sliced
2 large tomatoes (¾ pound), thickly sliced

1 cup raw wild rice, or wild rice mix, presoaked in warm water 15 minutes
2 cups rich chicken broth
1 teaspoon freshly grated gingerroot

Preheat oven to 350°. Brown pork chops in Dutch oven over high heat. Remove from heat and season with salt and pepper. Arrange onion and tomato on top of chops. Add wild rice and pour on chicken broth. Cover and bake until tender, about 1½ hours.

Pork Loin Medallions
with Ginger Cream and Lime

A wonderful winter dish. Pool ginger cream on a dinner plate, place chops on cream, and garnish with lime wedges. Fabulous with a winter mousseline and made complete by the addition of sashimi salad. Finish with a cranberry-walnut torte and you have, indeed, the New West Coast Cuisine.

Serves 6 in 1 hour

1 ¼-pound piece fresh
gingerroot, peeled and cut
into julienne the size of a
wooden match stick
1 pint half and half
2 cups beef broth
1 tablespoon cooking oil
1 tablespoon butter
6 pork loin medallions (4
ounces each), sprinkled with
cracked pepper

1 green onion and top, finely
sliced
1 cup dry sherry
2 tablespoons butter
1 large lime, peeled, seeded,
and segmented

Combine gingerroot with half and half in small saucepan. Heat to just under the simmer (do not let boil or it will curdle) and let simmer for about 50 minutes while you prepare the rest of the dish.

At the same time, in a separate pan, reduce broth to 1 cup by boiling.

Heat oil and butter over medium heat in a 10- to 12-inch skillet. Brown well-peppered pork until golden on both sides (about 5 minutes). Add reduced broth, cover, and cook over low heat until tender, about 25 minutes. Remove meat to heated platter and reserve.

Add green onion and sherry to pan juices, raise heat, and boil to reduce to about ½ cup. Strain in warmed ginger cream; do not boil. Remove from heat, swirl in butter to thicken.

To serve, pool ginger cream sauce on bottom of plate. Place chops on cream and garnish with lime wedges.

Carne Asada con Salsa de Naranja y Tomate

The Mexicans have long combined oranges and tomatoes to make wonderful sauces. This Mexican Nouvelle presentation is pungent, satisfying, and lower in calories than the more classic sauces. Serve with steamed asparagus, *bolillos,* and sweet butter, with a good sturdy zinfandel to accompany.

You can grill the steaks over charcoal, or you can pan grill them. Whichever method you choose, make the sauce first, because the meat cooks in a hurry and you'll want to have the salsa ready for it.

Serves 4 in 45 minutes

2 cups peeled, seeded, and
coarsely chopped tomatoes
(1 pound)
2 large navel oranges
1½ tablespoons olive oil
4 garlic cloves, pressed
½ teaspoon cumin seeds
¼ teaspoon ground coriander
¼ teaspoon dried red pepper
flakes

1 teaspoon tomato paste
salt and freshly ground
pepper to taste
½ teaspoon sugar
4 green onions and tops, finely
chopped
4 6-ounce steaks, either New
York or rib eye

To make salsa, set tomatoes aside in colander to drain. Peel and section 1 orange, discarding all membrane and pith. Set aside.

Juice other orange and reserve juice. Cut zest from ½ of 1 orange and finely chop.

Heat oil over high heat in 8-inch skillet and add garlic, cumin, coriander, pepper flakes, and ½ teaspoon of orange zest. Cook and stir for 30 seconds. Add orange juice and reduce to 3 to 4 tablespoons. Add orange sections, drained tomatoes, tomato paste, salt and pepper, and sugar. Cook, stirring, for 3 minutes.

Stir in onion and reserved orange peel. Pool salsa on bottom of dinner plates and place grilled beef on top. To pan grill steaks, trim any visible fat from meat and place fat in large skillet. Over high heat, render fat; remove solid pieces. Dry steak surfaces thoroughly with paper towel. Generously pepper steak with cracked black pepper, pressing pepper into flesh. (Never salt meat before grilling; you will leach out the juices.) Place steak in very hot skillet and sear for 2 to 3 minutes on each side to seal. Continue cooking until done to suit you—no more than 2 to 3 additional minutes per side. Turn meat with kitchen tongs instead of any fork, so the good juices will not run out and into the pan.

Grilled Flank Steak with Lemon-Parsley Butter

You can serve these succulent strips in several satisfying ways. Fold them inside a warm flour tortilla, dab with sauce, and you've got a great sandwich. Or serve on a bed of brown rice with a side dish of mixed sautéed vegetables. To tell you the truth, you'll be hoping there's some left over, because the next day, cold with Napa Valley sweet mustard and some red-tip lettuce and a bottle of good beer, these make a dynamite lunch.

Serves 4 in 1 hour

1 flank steak (1½ pounds)	4 garlic cloves, pressed
½ cup lemon juice (approximately 2 lemons)	½ cup fresh Italian parsley leaves
⅓ cup soy sauce	4 tablespoons butter
2 tablespoons honey	
½ teaspoon freshly grated ginger	

Pound flank steak on both sides using the side of a saucer or a meat mallet. Using filet knife, slice diagonally into strips about ¼ inch thick. Place in glass dish for marinating.

Combine lemon juice, soy sauce, honey, ginger, and garlic in small bowl, then pour over meat. Cover and let marinate at room temperature for at least 30 minutes.

Preheat grill. Lift meat from marinade (reserve marinade) and grill over hot fire, turning only once. Meat should cook to rare perfection within 3 minutes to the side.

While meat is grilling, make lemon-parsley butter. Transfer marinade to small saucepan, bring to boil over high heat, and reduce to 3 or 4 tablespoons. Stir in parsley. Remove from heat and swirl in butter. Once meat is cooked, swab in flavored butter. Good.

Braised Rabbit with Almonds, Oranges, and Glazed Kumquats

Here is a West Coast special—all our local produce and rabbits to boot. If you can't find rabbit in your local market, see mail order section under meats. Most rabbit comes frozen these days, unless you happen to raise your own. Marinate the rabbit all day in this aromatic blend, then set him to stewing at the end of the day, and within an hour you will have a splendid dinner.

I like to serve this with fresh noodles, cooked at the last minute and tossed with parsley and butter. A good Riesling to drink, date bread to accompany, and plain limestone lettuce and English cucumbers with a simple vinaigrette.

Serves 4 with 15 minute's work;
marinates in 2 to 8 hours;
stews in 1 hour

1	rabbit fryer, about 2 to 2½ pounds	3	green onions and tops, minced
4	tablespoons butter	½	teaspoon salt
¼	cup fresh lemon juice	3	garlic cloves, pressed
1	cup dry white wine	½	cup whole almonds
1	tablespoon soy sauce	1	navel orange, thinly sliced
1	tablespoon Worcestershire sauce	8	glazed kumquats
			fresh parsley for garnish

Place rabbit in large stainless steel or glass container. Combine remaining ingredients except almonds, orange slices, glazed kumquats, and parsley. Pour over rabbit. Cover and let stand at room temperature to marinate for at least 2 hours, but as long as 8 if using frozen rabbit. Turn occasionally if you think of it.

About an hour before serving time, transfer rabbit and marinade to Dutch oven. Cover and place over medium heat, bring to a boil, then reduce heat and simmer until rabbit is tender, about an hour. Ten mintues before serving, remove lid, add almonds and orange slices, turn up heat, and boil down juices. Adjust seasonings to taste.

At serving time, quarter rabbit. Serve quarter to each person on bed of fresh noodles or brown rice, garnished with glazed kumquats and fresh parsley.

The
Dairy Pail

I LOVE THE PROLIFERATION of dairy and cheese stores here on the West Coast. The abundance of good dairy products speaks to the vigorous and healthy dairy industry. Drive into the country, particularly in the verdant Northwest, and you will see pastures full of spotted cows, all calmly chewing their cud. You also may see, more and more, herds of goats, because we've discovered goat cheese—with a passion that borders on obsession.

In this chapter are various recipes that make use of our good West Coast dairy products. Everything from entrées to desserts. And I encourage you to check out the cheese listings in the mail order section. You can order cheeses handmade by time-honored methods. If you have certain preferences or fond memories of an exotic cheese from your childhood, you even can have cheeses custom made to your order.

I've put tofu in this section because it frequently is used in the same manner as a dairy product. Diana Muhs, who owns our local tofu factory, wishes that tofu was kept in the dairy case instead of the produce section, because of its ready interchangeability with cheese. But some kind of concrete thinker must have said to himself, it's made of soybeans, and that's a vegetable, so I'll put it with the vegetables. Oh, well. You and I know where it belongs.

Jalapeño Pie
[Katherine DeFoyd]

Imagine a Pyrex pie plate with six corn tortillas fanned out inside to form a kind of Mexican Nouvelle posy in the bottom of the pan. The tortillas, overlapping and coating the bottom of the dish, make the easiest pie crust imaginable—and one that's nutritious in the bargain. Fill the instant crust with eggs and cheese, lace it with jalapeños, and you have a kind of Mexican Nouvelle quiche. Easy. Delicious. Nutritious.

Serves 4 to 6 in 1 hour

6 corn tortillas
2 cups (6 ounces) grated sharp
   cheddar cheese
   jalapeños, stemmed, seeded,
   and cut into match-stick
   julienne

6 eggs, beaten until frothy

Preheat oven to 275°. In dry 6-inch skillet over highest heat, soften tortillas, one at a time, 15 seconds on each side. Press into 9-inch Pyrex pie plate, overlapping and completely covering pan, fanning the edge of each tortilla out over the lip of the pan.

Place grated cheese over tortillas. Arrange jalapeños on cheese, then pour over beaten eggs. Bake 45 minutes. Serve warm, cut in pie wedges.

Guatemalan Quiche

The title of this recipe is a bunch of nonsense. I only put it there because when I looked up the word, quiche, to see if there was a less loaded synonym I might use, I discovered that the Mayan language of the Guatemalan people also was known as quiche, pronounced *kee-chā*. Now isn't that interesting? And this dish does have cilantro and corn tortillas, so there is some sort of loose connection there. But I'll confess, it's just a bit of literary-culinary license. Don't go to Guatemala and tear down the streets hunting for this one in a restaurant. You won't find it.

This dish is pure California. Beginning with a French quiche technique, this recipe plugs in tofu, seasons the filling with an Oriental flair, and then pours it all into a corn tortilla crust. Is that the West Coast or what?

Serves 4 in 1 hour

2 tablespoons oil
1 medium onion (4 ounces), finely chopped
4 garlic cloves, pressed
1 cup finely sliced fresh mushrooms
15 leaves fresh cilantro, minced, or 1 teaspoon dried
4 cups (½ pound) spinach, washed and chopped
⅓ cup plain yogurt
½ pound tofu, pressed and drained
1 pinch cayenne

1 pinch nutmeg
2 tablespoons soy sauce
¼ teaspoon freshly grated gingerroot
1 teaspoon fresh lemon juice
2 tablespoons tahini (sesame seed paste), or peanut butter in a pinch
1 tablespoon dry sherry
1 large egg, slightly beaten
4 tablespoons freshly grated Parmesan cheese
6 corn tortillas

Preheat oven to 350°. In 10-inch skillet, over medium heat, sauté onion and garlic in oil until onions turn clear (about 5 minutes). Add mushrooms and cilantro. Cover and continue cooking for 5 more minutes. Place spinach over mushrooms. Cover and steam for 2 minutes. Remove from heat and set aside.

In bowl of mixer or food processor, combine all remaining ingredients except tortillas. Mix thoroughly; then stir into onion-garlic mixture. Adjust seasonings to taste.

Soften corn tortillas in dry 6-inch skillet over high heat, 15 seconds on each side. Place in 9-inch Pyrex pie plate, overlapping tortillas to completely cover pan, and fanning edge of each tortilla out over the lip of the pan.

Pour tofu-spinach-onion mixture into shell. Bake until it is firm, about 30 minutes. Let stand 10 mintues before slicing. For an alternative, add 4 slices of thick-sliced cooked bacon to top of the filling before baking.

Baked Lentils with Raw Milk Cheddar
[Danielle Lapp]

You can buy excellent raw milk, rennetless cheeses on the West Coast. In this dish, basically bland with lentils, cheddar is the cheese of choice. You could alter the cheese type for different results. Jack cheese with jalapeños. Swiss. Chèvre would be quite interesting here. See mail order section for all the possibilities.

Try this bean entrée with Four-Pepper Salad, whole wheat bread and butter, and a piece of fruit for dessert. Tastes good. Good for you.

Serves 6 in 2½ hours

1¾ cups dried lentils, rinsed
3½ cups hot water
1 bay leaf
1 teaspoon salt
1 green bell pepper (¼ pound), finely chopped
⅛ teaspoon freshly ground black pepper
⅛ teaspoon leaf marjoram
⅛ teaspoon leaf sage
⅛ teaspoon leaf thyme
2 large onions (½ pound), finely chopped

1 1-pound can Italian plum tomatoes with juice, finely chopped
2 garlic cloves, pressed
2 large carrots (½ pound), sliced into thin rounds
½ cup celery (3 ounces), sliced diagonally
1 cup (¼ pound) grated raw-milk cheddar cheese
parsley for garnish

Preheat oven to 375°. Combine dry lentils, hot water, bay leaf, salt, bell pepper, herbs, onion, tomato, and garlic in a large 2-quart casserole dish. Cover and bake until lentils are tender (about 1¼ hours). Remove from oven and stir in carrots and celery. Adjust seasonings to taste. Re-cover and bake an additional 40 minutes or until carrots are soft and cooked through. Stir in half of grated cheese until it melts. Sprinkle remaining half of cheese on top, then run casserole under broiler until brown and bubbly (about 5 minutes). Garnish with parsley. Let stand 10 minutes or so before serving.

Far East of Denver Omelet

Using tofu hikes protein and drops cholesterol, not to mention that in this recipe it improves taste by introducing the subtle nutty taste of tofu for half of the sulfurous eggs that generally make up an omelet. To tell you the truth, this is not an omelet. It's a frittata.

The technique differs from that used in a classic French omelet in three important ways. A frittata is cooked over low heat, is firm and set, and generally is not folded over. The addition of tofu to a frittata is strictly a West Coast convention.

Here's a quick and easy technique I learned from a tofu manufacturer to remove the whey that wets tofu and makes it difficult to sauté. Spread a double layer of paper toweling on a cookie sheet. Cut a one-pound package of tofu into six slices and lay them out on the cookie sheet. Cover with another double layer of paper toweling. Place a second cookie sheet on top. Weight the layers with about five pounds of something—flour, sugar, the electric mixer. Allow the tofu to stand while you are preparing the ingredients for the recipe. Flip the cookie sheet over once and replace the paper towels. When you are ready to proceed with the tofu, you will find that it is firm, close to the texture of a thick slice of mozzarella. In some stores, you may even find pressed tofu, ready for sautéing with no further ado.

Another hint the tofu maker gave was to buy only tofu that is dated. It is as fragile as a dairy product and deteriorates at about the same rate, so that its natural, nutty taste begins to slide into a rather nasty bitter one. We all know when a bottle of milk has gone, as they say in the country, blinky, but those of us new to tofu may think we don't like it when, in fact, all we have done is innocently picked up an outdated package.

Serves 4 in 20 minutes

2 tablespoons butter	4 eggs
1 medium onion (½ pound), finely chopped	2 tablespoons Shoyu soy sauce
1 jalapeño, finely chopped	1 cup (¼ pound) grated cheddar cheese
1 small tomato (¼ pound), finely cut	dusting of paprika
1 pound tofu, sliced and pressed	

In 10-inch skillet over low heat, sauté in butter the onion and jalapeño until onion begins to brown. Add tomato and tofu. Break up tofu with a spoon, raise heat to medium, and continue cooking until tofu begins to brown.

Mix together eggs and soy sauce and add to tofu mixture. Cover, turn heat to low, and cook for just a couple of minutes until eggs are set. Top with grated cheddar and run under broiler to brown. Dust with paprika and serve in pie slices.

Frittata with Baby Artichokes

The farmers' stands around Watsonville, California, offer artichokes for sale in every stage of development. From small ones not much bigger than your thumb, all the way to the glorious fully opened thistle flowers that are the end result of the artichoke's growth, you can buy it all.

The nice thing about cooking with baby artichokes is that they have no "choke." The choke is the unchewable, indigestible, guaranteed-to-choke-you-if-you-eat-it inside that is around the heart of the mature artichoke. But the babies have no such ugly surprise. They can be deep fried whole, a favorite roadside-stand method, or they can be incorporated into various recipes. If you do not have access to baby artichokes for use in this recipe, remember to dig the choke out of the center of the mature artichoke after you have cut it in half.

This frittata is fabulous looking. Cut the baby artichokes in half and arrange in a spoke design in the bottom of a skillet. Then pour the egg over and cook slowly—frittata style—and you've got a lunch entrée that looks as good as it tastes. Serve with crusty sourdough French bread and sweet butter, fresh fruit of the season, and Zinfandel to drink. Who can go back to work?

Serves 4 in 30 minutes

6 baby artichokes, or 2 medium mature ones, spiny ends trimmed
2 garlic cloves, pressed
2 tablespoons olive oil
¼ cup minced Italian parsley salt and freshly ground black pepper to taste

¼ cup water
3 tablespoons butter
6 large eggs
¼ cup freshly grated Parmesan cheese

Cut baby artichokes in half, lengthwise. Sauté garlic in oil in a 10-inch skillet over medium heat, just until it begins to color. Place artichokes, cut side down, in skillet, and sprinkle with parsley and salt and pepper; sauté just until artichokes begin to brown, no more than a minute or so. Reduce heat to low, add water, cover, and steam until artichokes are tender, about 5 to 7 minutes (as long as 20 minutes for mature artichokes). Once tender (you can tell by tugging at a leaf; it should come free with ease), lift artichokes from skillet and reserve.

Raise to highest heat and evaporate remaining water. Remove skillet from heat. Swirl butter into skillet to coat.

Beat eggs in a bowl until completely blended. Season to taste with salt and pepper. Stir in grated Parmesan and pour into reserved skillet. Arrange artichoke halves in eggs in an interesting spoke pattern.

Over lowest possible heat setting, return skillet to stove and cook, uncovered, until eggs have set and thickened, and only the top surface is runny (about 15 minutes). To finish, run under the broiler to cook top, about 30 seconds. Neither the bottom or top should be brown, just well set. Serve either hot or at room temperature.

Sunny Eggless Salad or Sandwich Filling
[Diana Muhs for Ashland Soy Works]

Diana Muhs, who started a tofu factory in Ashland, Oregon, because she missed the good fresh tofu she'd had in Berkeley, developed this mock egg-salad recipe. She makes and sells gallons of the stuff, pint by pint, to all the best grocery stores around. But you can make it at home. It's good spread on a sandwich of whole wheat or black bread. It's good on a leaf of limestone lettuce. To tell you the truth, it's good on a spoon, snuck out of the refrigerator, any old time.

Makes 1½ pints in 10 minutes

1 pound fresh tofu
1 tablespoon soy sauce
1 garlic clove, pressed
¼ teaspoon turmeric
2 teaspoons Dijon mustard
1 green onion and top, finely sliced

½ cup finely chopped celery
2 tablespoons fresh lemon juice (about ¼ lemon)
mayonnaise and/or plain yogurt to taste

Fine cube tofu into medium-size bowl. Add remaining ingredients and stir to mix. Cover and refrigerate. Will keep up to a week in the refrigerator.

Open-faced Hot Shrimp Sandwich on Bed of Tofu

Here's a power lunch—almost pure protein and complex carbohydrates. Quick to fix and pleasant to look at. A square of sautéed tofu is topped with a sautéed bay shrimp and grated vegetable cake, then served with a pungent vinegar-soy dressing.

Serves 4 in 30 minutes

1 pound tofu
¼ pound cooked bay shrimp
½ medium potato (¼ pound), grated
½ small carrot (⅛ pound), grated
1 teaspoon fresh lemon juice
1 green onion and top, finely sliced

½ red or green bell pepper (¼ pound), cut into match-stick julienne
2 fresh mushrooms, thinly sliced
2 tablespoons cornstarch
1 egg white
3 tablespoons cooking oil

Shrimp Marinade:
1 teaspoon soy sauce

2 tablespoons saké or dry white wine

Dressing:

2 tablespoons soy sauce   1 teaspoon rice wine vinegar

Cut tofu horizontally, into 4 equal slices. Place on cookie sheet between layers of paper toweling, cover with second cookie sheet, and weight with 5 pounds (a sack of sugar perhaps) for 15 minutes. Change toweling once.

Place shrimp in small bowl and add marinade. Stir to coat all pieces. Set aside. Mix soy-vinegar dressing and reserve.

Meanwhile, grate potato and carrot. Place in water to cover which has lemon juice squeezed in, to prevent discoloration. Prepare onion, bell pepper, and mushrooms.

After 15 minutes have elapsed, dust tofu slices thoroughly with 1 tablespoon cornstarch.

Drain potato and carrot and combine with other vegetables and shrimp. Add egg white and remaining cornstarch. Stir to mix. Mound this mixture on top of each tofu slice.

Heat 12-inch skillet for a minute. Add 1 tablespoon oil and heat. Now, here comes the trick. Using 2 spatulas, lift a slice of tofu and flip it into skillet, vegetable-and-shrimp side down. Cook until brown, about 3 to 4 minutes. Add another tablespoon or so of oil to skillet to moisten. Again using 2 spatulas, flip over tofu slices and cook bottom sides. Place on warm serving dish and pour soy-vinegar dressing on top and serve at once.

Green Chile and Goat Cheese Enchiladas

Cascadian goat milk cheese, made by Briar Hills Dairies in the state of Washington, is a mild, white, firm cheese with a delicate flavor. It can be used to good advantage in any Mexican recipe calling for "white cheese." The cheese makers began adding pepper to this cheese for caterers, and now they sell this variety as well. I have used both kinds in this enchilada preparation. Using the pepper cheese makes the enchiladas more *picante.* Serve with Four-Pepper Salad, cherimoya, strawberry, and kiwi slices for dessert.

Serves 6 in 1 hour

Sauce:

2 tablespoons oil

4 large yellow onions (1½ pounds), coarsely chopped

1 15-ounce and 1 8-ounce can tomato sauce
equal amount of water (23 ounces)
salt and freshly milled black pepper to taste

1 tablespoon brown sugar

¾ pound Cascadian white goat cheese, grated

4 green chiles (8 ounces), stemmed, deseeded, and minced, or 1 7-ounce can green chiles, minced

12 corn tortillas
Fresh Green Salsa (recipe follows)

Combine oil and onion in large stew pot over medium-low heat. Cover, cook, and stir until onion is completely limp and clear, at least 15 minutes. Add tomato sauce and water. Adjust salt, pepper, and sugar to taste. Simmer uncovered over low heat until thick as catsup, at least 15 minutes.

Preheat oven to 350°. Grate cheese. Mix half cheese with minced green chiles. Generously grease 9-by-13-inch Pyrex baking dish.

Heat 7-inch skillet over high heat and soften tortillas, one at a time by placing each in hot dry skillet for about 15 seconds. Life with tongs into hot tomato sauce for 30 seconds, then stack them in the baking dish.

Stuff each tortilla with a big pinch of chile-and-cheese mixture. Roll and place flap side down, making neat rows in the baking dish. Repeat until you have stuffed and rolled all tortillas. Spoon remaining sauce over enchiladas, then cover with remaining shredded cheese. Place in oven and bake until cheese bubbles and browns (about 15 minutes). Serve with fresh green salsa.

Fresh Green Salsa

Makes ¼ cup in 5 minutes

4 whole fresh jalapeños,
  deseeded and stemmed
4 garlic cloves, peeled

2 tablespoons white wine
  vinegar
  dash salt

Whirl all ingredients in processor or blender. Serve on the side with any red-sauced enchiladas.

Sweet Cream Cheese Soufflé
[Casey Ellis]

It's kind of a toss-up to say whether this should be served as an entrée or a dessert. Or, to tell the whole truth, even for breakfast. Whenever you serve it, have alongside a bowl of mixed fresh fruits, the best you can find—kiwi and carambola and strawberries and bananas. Serve a dark bread, like the Quick Walnut-Date Rye Bread, and a cup of well-made espresso.

Serves 4 in 50 minutes

6 ounces cream cheese
⅔ cup sour cream
2 tablespoons aromatic honey

pinch of salt
dash of cinnamon
4 eggs, separated

Preheat oven to 300°. Thoroughly mix cream cheese, sour cream, honey, salt, cinnamon, and egg yolks. Beat egg whites until stiff, then fold in yolk mixture. Pour into an *ungreased* soufflé pan, then cook in preheated oven until set (about 45 minutes). Remove from oven when center just trembles a bit. Serve immediately.

Baked Brie with Walnuts
and Fruits of the Season

Here is a dessert so simple, so elegant, you may want it as a standard ending to a dinner that's already gone beyond gourmet. The serendipity of this dessert is that it really requires no recipe. You can buy a wedge of Brie large enough to accommodate the diners—figure about one ounce per person—and use half again as much butter and walnuts, about half a piece of fruit per person, and you can multiply this into a banquet. Piping-hot soft Brie, cold fruit pieces, a good dessert wine, some hot black coffee.

Serves 4 in 10 minutes

1 4-ounce Brie wedge, rind on
2 ounces walnuts, chopped fine
1 tablespoon softened butter

2 pieces of the best fruit you can find: comice pears in winter, peaches in summer, pippin apples in between

Preheat oven to 400°. Place wedge of Brie on ovenproof serving plate. Combine chopped walnuts and softened butter then press into cut edges of Brie. Place Brie, uncovered, into the hot oven for about 4 minutes.

While Brie is heating, cut fruit of the season into good-looking serving pieces. Comice pears or pippin apples are nice in winter; papaya when you can get it; fresh peaches. Just choose something at its peak of sweetness and succulence. Once Brie is heated through and almost beginning to run, remove from oven, arrange fruit around it, and serve.

Some people may wish a flat bland cracker to back the cheese. Remember to give each person a spreading knife as well as a fork to manage this. Cold California Gewürztraminer works well with this combination.

The
Bakery

IS THERE ANYTHING BETTER than a well-made piece of bread? The West Coast made its reputation as the seat of good-for-you cooking with bread. Those who dropped out, who decided to stay at home and do their own thing, began by learning to bake bread. Some of these folks got so good at it that they opened bakeries, started getting up at three in the morning to set the dough to rising, continued by delivering bread to local restaurants no later than eleven, and before long, we all took good bread for granted.

Now, in the hard-driving eighties, bread making once again seems a luxury. But through this evolutionary process, we've all become discriminating as can be about what bread should be. And most of us have access to fine bakeries for the rest of the time, when we haven't the luxury of four hours in which to bake.

In the mail order section of this book you will find sources for that unique West Coast bread, San Francisco sourdough. Don't let anybody kid you. You can't make that at home. They've even tried to ship out the sourdough to other locations and the farthest they can get and come up with the same bread is Oakland. You'll also find the mail order address for what may be the last stone-grinding mill on the West Coast, Butte Creek Mill, which grinds a variety of superior flours the old-fashioned way, between stones that are powered by the fast-rushing Butte Creek. At Butte Creek they also sell a superior yeast, Red Star, which you can get at most good natural-foods stores and some grocery stores. It is worth the difference in price. You know, yeasts taste different, and this one, in my opinion, is the best.

The breads in this chapter make use of grains, seeds, fruits, and vegetables. They'll fill your house with the aroma that properly should be called "home," and in terms of the process, the preparation of any bread is worth two hours with any therapist. Forget analysis. Forget primal scream. Forget having your aura read. Make bread. You'll feel better.

And once you've mastered bread, you'll be ready to move on to the advanced baking class, where you can tackle mouth-watering tortes, tarts, pies, and cakes. I apologize for the overabundance of cranberries in this section. I love cranberries. If you don't, just substitute blueberries, or strawberries, or red currants, or whatever is your favorite. Try not to feel too guilty about lusting over profligate desserts. Everybody's doing it.

Chocolate shops are springing up all over. They represent a fascinating crosscurrent that is running through the food business on the West Coast. While everybody is concerned about purity, health, fitness, low fat, low sodium, everlasting life and love, they are also killing themselves learning how to make the most complicated, chocolate-laden desserts known to man. What I usually hear is this: if I am going to eat a dessert, I don't want to waste the calories on some pumped-up junk food. I want just a morsel of the very best— truffles, a perfect torte, a pastry as good as you can get in a pâtisserie.

One friend of mine swears that there's a trace mineral in chocolate that activates the brain's endorphins and makes you feel as good as running four miles a day, or finding a new lover. Sounds good to me. Read on. Cook on. Sweat and strain baking a fabulous dessert. Now that's exercise. Go for it.

Raspberry Bread
[Carmen Kozlowski]

Here's the bread that Carmen Kozlowski made with Julia Child for a *Good Morning America* special on Sonoma County. Besides being a divine breakfast bread, it also is lovely for afternoon tea with some slivers of Sonoma Jack cheese and some warm spreadable goat cheese from Sadie Kendall. You can substitute other berry jams with good results.

Makes 2 loaves in 1 hour

1 cup butter	½ cup buttermilk
1 cup sugar	3 cups unbleached white flour
1 teaspoon vanilla	½ teaspoon salt
4 large eggs	1 teaspoon cream of tartar
1 cup Kozlowski Farms red raspberry jam	1 teaspoon baking soda

Streusel Topping:

¼ cup brown sugar	¼ teaspoon cinnamon
2 tablespoons flour	¼ cup finely chopped walnuts
2 tablespoons butter	

Preheat oven to 325°. Grease and flour 2 9-by-5-inch loaf pans.

Cream together butter and sugar. Add vanilla, eggs, raspberry jam, and buttermilk. Stir to mix. Combine dry ingredients and sift into raspberry jam mixture. Beat together until thoroughly mixed and light. Pour mixture into prepared pans and top with streusel mixture. (For streusel, cream topping ingredients together and sprinkle atop bread loaves before baking.) Bake until done (bread will spring back when touched lightly in center), about 40 minutes.

Quick Walnut-Date Rye Bread

If you are looking for a bread that is chewy, not too sweet, made with honey instead of sugar, and has wonderful keeping qualities, give this one a shot.

This recipe verifies the old saw about necessity being the mother of invention. I've made date bread forever using whole wheat flour. But with the introduction of bulk buying in grocery stores, I find myself with clear plastic sacks of unidentified raw ingredients. Rye flour looks like whole wheat, no? And when I accidentally substituted it for whole wheat, it gave a more complex result. A darker, more mysterious batter, combined with fabulous Medjhool dates from the desert in Thermal, California, and the first-of-the-fall crop of fresh walnuts, yielded a not-too-sweet bread that made a great addition to a buffet board.

Makes 1 loaf in 1 1/2 hours

1 cup chopped Medjhool dates	1 teaspoon vanilla
¾ cup boiling water	1 cup unbleached white flour
2 large eggs	1 cup rye flour
1 cup mild honey	½ teaspoon salt
1 tablespoon soft butter	1 teaspoon soda
¼ cup brandy	1 cup chopped walnuts

Preheat oven to 350°. Grease and flour 1 9-by-5-by-3-inch loaf pan. Set aside.

Pour ¾ cup boiling water over dates. Set aside; don't drain.

Using high speed on mixer, beat eggs until thick and light. With mixer running, add honey, butter, brandy, and vanilla. Drop speed to lowest setting and add dates and their soaking water.

Combine flours, salt, and soda. Stir into egg mixture along with walnuts, just enough to blend.

Pour into prepared pan and bake until toothpick comes out clean, about 50 minutes.

Cool on a rack. Don't slice until bread is completely cool. Store in a tin. Good plain or with orange Neufchâtel cheese.

Avocado Advocate Bread

Unless you have lived in a California neighborhood with a towering avocado tree, you may not believe that people actually get desperate to get rid of avocados, the way gardeners do about zucchini. For two glorious years, we lived in a house next door to an avocado tree, and from time to time a welcome child would appear on our doorstep with a basket of perfect avocados.

Also noteworthy about the avocado is that dogs are quite fond of them. Our neighbors had one very fat dog of their own, and a gourmet Doberman used to leap their fence from time to time to partake of the perfect avocados with his host, one overweight and slightly frightened cocker spaniel. We did everything with those fabulous Hass avocados. Soup. Salad. Ate them like apples. But one of the best recipes we came up with was this one. With inspiration from Bernard Clayton.

Makes 1 loaf in 1 1/2 hours

1 large egg, beaten until frothy	2 cups unbleached white flour
½ cup perfectly ripe Hass avocado, completely puréed	¾ cup sugar
	½ teaspoon baking powder
½ cup plain yogurt	½ teaspoon baking soda
1 cup finely chopped walnuts	¼ teaspoon salt

Preheat oven to 350°. Prepare 1 9-by-5-by-3-inch loaf pan by greasing generously. Set aside.

Combine egg, puréed avocado, yogurt, and nuts. Combine dry ingredients. Stir to mix thoroughly, then add to avocado mixture, stirring only to moisten.

Pour batter into prepared pan, smoothing the top. Rap the pan on the counter top to remove air bubbles. Place in oven and cook until done (springs back at the touch), about 50 minutes. Remove from pan and cool on a rack.

Allow to cool completely before cutting. Better the next day.

Whole Wheat Tortillas

You simply cannot make a corn tortilla at home as good as you can buy, unless you have access to fresh masa. But with practice you can perfect the flour tortilla and can get results that are better than you can buy. Light handling is the answer. That and resting the dough.

Whole wheat tortillas fall into the category of Cosmic Mexican, and will elicit a response from Mexican purists that gives you an inkling of how the Spanish conquistadores must have felt when they had stumbled over some Aztec taboo by accident. Oh well. Eating the heart of one's adversary has gone out of vogue. Be brave. Try it. You will have increased the nutritional value of the tortillas, you will have completed the protein if you eat them with beans, and (she said, running hard and not looking back) you will have made a tortilla that tastes even better than one made from white flour.

Makes 24 tortillas in 45 minutes plus 45 minutes to rest (the dough rests, you wash dishes).

3 cups whole wheat flour
1 cup unbleached white flour
2 teaspoons salt
2 teaspoons baking powder

¼ cup shortening
1½ cups (approximately) very hot water

Combine flours, salt, and baking powder in large bowl. Cut in shortening using pastry blender or two knives until it resembles coarse meal. Using a regular fork, stir in water, gradually, using only enough to make dough pliable.

Turn out onto a floured board and gently knead 10 or 15 times, turning dough, working in a little more flour—not too much—only if it seems sticky. Cover dough with oiled plastic wrap and let it rest in a warm place for 20 minutes.

Pinch off balls of dough about the size of golf balls, rubbing them between the palms of your hands to get a good globe shape. Re-cover with plastic wrap and let rest at least 20 minutes, but if need be, as long as 3 hours.

When you are ready to cook, preheat a cast-iron skillet or griddle to 425° (hot enough so that water sizzles when sprinkled on). Lightly flour a board or marble surface. With a small, thin rolling pin (a broom handle is the pin of choice by Mexican cooks), roll out a disk using swift, confident strokes, 3 or 4, then turn it a quarter, 3 or 4 more strokes, turn, until you have a thin, relatively round 6-inch tortilla.

Carefully lift tortilla with spatula, and slap it down on the hot griddle. Cook just until bubbles begin to puff on top (about 25 seconds), then turn and cook other side. Don't overcook or you'll wind up with a lifetime supply of shoe leather for your efforts.

Repeat this process, rolling and cooking, until all tortillas are cooked. Stack them as you go, layering tortillas between sheets of wax paper; wrap the entire stack in foil to keep warm. They will (thank god) freeze (3 weeks maximum) and can be reheated successfully.

The preferred way to reheat tortillas (any tortillas) is directly over a low-gas flame. Simply lay the tortilla on a flat burner grid and move it around every few seconds to avoid burning in one spot. Turn once. If you are cursed with an electric range, heat tortillas—dry—in 8-inch skillet over a hot coil, no more than 15 seconds on each side. You also can heat the whole stack, wrapped tight in foil, in 200° oven.

Sesame Seed Tortillas

Once you have gotten the hang of making whole wheat flour tortillas, you may want to experiment—the way we do here on the West Coast. You simply can follow the procedure for making flour tortillas and add different nuts and seeds to see what you like. These sesame seed tortillas are particularly good wrapped around a stick of dill Havarti or Jalapeño Jack cheese. The textures and tastes seem a natural.

Makes 16 tortillas

½ cup sesame seed
3 cups unbleached white flour
2 teaspoons baking powder
1 teaspoon salt

¼ cup shortening
1 cup (approximately) very hot water

Toast sesame seeds, 1 layer deep, on a cookie sheet in a 350° oven, shaking occasionally, until a light golden brown (about 10 minutes). Cool on a plate.

In a large bowl, combine flour, baking powder, salt, and toasted seeds. Cut in shortening using a pastry blender or two knives until it resembles coarse meal. Using a regular fork, stir in water, gradually, adding only enough to make dough pliable but not sticky.

Turn out onto a lightly floured board and gently knead 10 or 15 times, turning dough, working in a little more flour only if it seems sticky. Cover with oiled plastic wrap and let it rest in a warm place for 20 minutes.

Pinch off golf ball–size dough balls, and again, rest them under plastic wrap for 20 minutes or so.

When you are ready to cook, preheat skillet or griddle to 425° (you can tell by flicking water on griddle—it will sizzle and practically jump off, as if it were saying ouch!). Lightly flour board and roll out a disk using swift, short strokes, turning the disk after every 3 or 4 strokes by a quarter until you have a thin, uniform 6-inch disk.

Lift carefully with a spatula and slap it down on hot, dry griddle. Cook about 45 seconds on each side, or until there is just a hint of brown on the surfaces. Repeat this rolling and cooking with all disks.

Stack tortillas as you cook them; wrap in foil to keep warm.

Pistachio Puffs

Cream puffs may say "dessert" to you, but they are equally good as a savory bread. You can use variations on the basic principle and come up with your own splendid airy mouthful. Try different nuts or seeds. Different cheeses. And they can go stuffed or unstuffed. Dungeness crab with a little yogurt and chives stirred in would be heaven here. But really, they are so good plain, that you may not wish to gild the lily, as it were. I like to make these for parties, because I can make them up ahead, cool them thoroughly, and freeze them in double layers of freezer wrap for up to two weeks with no damage. Then, as the party jolts along, I can pop them into a hot oven, just until they are hot through and the surface is crisp. Very good.

Makes 36 puffs in 1 hour

1 cup water	4 large eggs
¼ pound butter	⅓ cup shredded Swiss cheese
1 cup unbleached white flour	¼ cup finely chopped pistachio
¼ teaspoon salt	nuts

Preheat oven to 450°. Prepare 2 cookie sheets by generously coating with butter. Set aside.

Combine water and butter in medium saucepan and bring to a boil. When butter is melted, add flour and salt. Using a wooden spoon, stir vigorously until mixture leaves sides of pan and begins to form a ball. Remove from heat.

Add eggs, 1 at a time, beating vigorously with the wooden spoon after each egg, until mixture is smooth and glossy. Add cheese and nuts and again beat vigorously so that you have a complete blend.

Using 2 tablespoons, 1 to measure and 1 to push batter off the spoon, drop small blobs of batter, about an inch apart, onto prepared pans. Pop into hot oven and bake at 450° for 15 minutes. Then lower temperature to 325° and continue baking for 20 more minutes. Remove from oven. Immediately loosen puffs from pans with spatula and cool on a rack. If you wish to stuff them, allow puffs to cool completely before cutting. Use a serrated-blade knife to cut top ⅓ off for filling.

Klamath Falls Potato Bread
[Paula Cracas]

Paula Cracas is a fine and sensitive poet. When she gets in the kitchen, she proves, once again, that the artist, given the simplest, most common ingredients, can create a work that exceeds the sum of its parts. Here is a bread that meets the description: staff of life. And when Paula braids this into an enormous two-foot-long challah-looking loaf, all glistening gold and sprinkled with poppy seeds, I'd swear that if you had a chunk of this bread, a round-shouldered bottle of Mondavi red, and Paula to read her poetry aloud for you, the whole experience would be so sublime that all you'd need was a box of Kleenex to mop up your tears of pure joy.

Makes 1 24-inch braided bread or 2 regular loaves or 36 rolls

1 large russet potato (½ pound)	2 tablespoons dry active yeast
1 teaspoon salt	¼ cup lukewarm (110°) water
1 cup water	1 teaspoon sugar
¼ pound butter	5 to 5½ cups unbleached white flour
1 tablespoon sugar	1 egg yolk
½ cup powdered milk	1 tablespoon water
3 large eggs	

Peel and coarsely chop potato and combine in a medium saucepan with salt and water. Simmer covered, until tender. Remove from heat and stir in butter and 1 tablespoon sugar. Process or whip until potato is mashed. Add powdered milk and eggs, blending completely.

Dissolve yeast in lukewarm water and 1 teaspoon sugar. Add to potato mixture. Stir this potato-yeast liquid into flour to make a soft dough.

Knead until smooth and elastic, at least 10 minutes. Place in a well-oiled bowl, cover, and let rise in a warm, draft-free spot until doubled in bulk (about 1 hour).

Punch dough down, re-cover with plastic wrap, and refrigerate until you need it. (Dough will keep as long as 10 days. You can pinch off little pieces of it for rolls as you go along, make into 2 loaves, or save the whole thing for 1 glorious braid.) When ready to use, let dough rise at room temperature for a couple of hours. Then shape into rolls, bread loaves, or braid. Place on oiled baking sheet (for rolls or braid) or 2 oiled 4-by-8-inch loaf pans, cover, and let rise again until doubled in bulk, about 45 minutes.

Preheat oven to 425°. Mix 1 egg yolk with 1 tablespoon water and gently paint on top surface of bread. Sprinkle with poppy seeds or sesame seeds.

Bake loaves, rolls, or braid at 425° for 10 minutes, then reduce heat to 350° and continue baking until done, about 30 to 45 minutes, depending on size of loaf, or 20 minutes for rolls.

Saffron Challah
[Barbara Schack]

The addition of saffron to a classic challah intensifies its color to a deep gold and adds a bite to this already rich bread. The loaf, when double-braided and allowed to rise to its full twenty-four-inch potential, is a wonder to behold. You easily could make this the centerpiece on a buffet table.

Makes 1 enormous 24-inch-long golden braid in 3½ hours

2	teaspoons sugar	1½	teaspoons salt
1¼	cups lukewarm (110°) water	2	large eggs
1	tablespoon dry active yeast	3	tablespoons melted butter
⅛	teaspoon saffron threads	1	large egg yolk
5	to 6 cups unbleached white flour		sesame or poppy seeds for sprinkling on top

Combine sugar and ¼ cup lukewarm water in small bowl. Dissolve yeast in mixture. Set aside to proof for 5 minutes.

To release their golden color, heat saffron threads with remaining cup of water to boiling. Cool to lukewarm.

In a large bowl, mix together 4 cups flour, salt, eggs, melted butter, the yeast, and saffron mixtures. Stir vigorously, then add enough additional flour until dough begins to lose its stickiness.

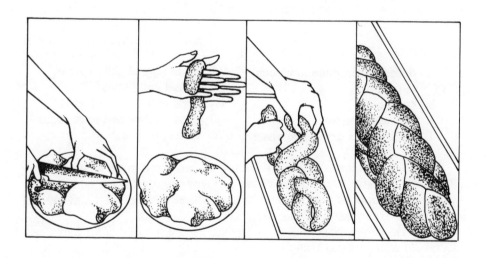

Turn out onto a floured board and knead until smooth and elastic, at least 10 minutes by hand, adding flour as needed.

Oil a large bowl; place dough in bowl and turn over so that oiled side is up. Cover and let rise in a warm, draft-free place until doubled in bulk (about an hour). Punch down, cover, and let rise again, for about 30 minutes.

Turn dough out onto board. Knead a few short strokes, then divide dough into 2 unequal portions, 1 slightly larger than the other. Divide the larger portion into 3 equal pieces and roll each into a long strip about 1 inch in diameter. Form 3 pieces into fat, even braid, pinching top and bottom ends under neatly. Place onto a large, well-oiled baking sheet.

Divide the smaller portion of dough similarly, forming another braid. Tuck ends under, and center the smaller braid atop the first.

Preheat oven to 350°. Cover double-braid loosely with plastic wrap and let rise until doubled in bulk (about 30 minutes). Beat egg yolk in small cup and, using a very light touch, brush entire loaf heavily with beaten yolk.

Sprinkle generously with sesame or poppy seeds and bake for about 50 minutes, or until loaf is a luscious golden color and sounds hollow when rapped on bottom with your knuckles.

Plum Fresh Tomato Bread
[Barbara A. Clancy]

Make this bread in the summer when Italian plum tomatoes are plentiful. Have it for breakfast. It begs for sweet butter and honey. A piece of Gorgonzola cheese. A perfect orange. A cup of café latte. A breakfast to remember.

Makes 2 8-inch round loaves in
under 3 hours

1 dozen Italian plum tomatoes (1 pound)	1 large egg, slightly beaten
½ cup honey	¼ pound soft butter
¼ cup warm water	1¼ cups milk, warmed to 110°
2 tablespoons dry active yeast	5 cups unbleached white flour
	2 tablespoons salt

Bring pot of water to boil in medium saucepan. Drop in tomatoes and boil 2 minutes. Remove from boiling water, slip now-blistered skins, and discard. Cut tomatoes open and squeeze to remove seeds. Place peeled and seeded tomatoes into processor or blender and purée. Set aside.

Combine honey, warm water, and yeast. Set aside to proof for 5 minutes. Combine with egg and butter.

Combine milk and tomatoes. Add yeast mixture and stir to mix. Add flour and salt all at once to liquid, mixing until you have a large ball. Add just enough additional flour so that dough is not sticky; then knead until you have a smooth, elastic texture (at least 10 minutes).

Divide dough in half and form into 2 equal-size balls. Lightly oil 2 8-inch pie pans and place a ball in each one. Cover and let rise until double in bulk (at least an hour).

Preheat oven to 350°. Bake bread in hot oven until golden brown, about 35 minutes. Cool on a rack about 15 minutes (if you can stand it) before cutting.

Tomato Basil Baguette

You can make the most delicate baguettes for sandwiches using this recipe. The possibilities are legion. Ricotta, fresh basil leaves, and thin slices of yellow plum tomatoes. Mozzarella and anchovy strips, run under the broiler until bubbly, brown, and aromatic. Tomato paste and Gorgonzola, broiled until piping hot. Turkey breast, sweet butter, and sprouts. Cold Kir to drink, a sandwich, and an artichoke-and-sprout salad. Truffle for dessert. Here are the makings for a truly decadent picnic.

Or you can make a fabulous party pizza, using this recipe for the dough; you will get one 16-inch pizza pan full. Once dough is flattened into pan, brush dough with extra virgin olive oil then coat with a thin layer of tomato paste or sauce, mozzarella, pepperoni, or whatever else you can think of.

Makes 2 baguettes or 1 16-inch pizza crust in 3 to 4 hours

3 cups unbleached white flour	¼ cup lukewarm (110°) water
¼ cup powdered milk	1 tablespoon honey
12 fresh basil leaves, minced, or 1 tablespoon dried	⅔ cup lukewarm (110°) water
1½ teaspoons salt	⅓ cup tomato paste
3 tablespoons soft butter	1 tablespoon egg plus 1 teaspoon water wash for top
1 tablespoon dry active yeast	

Combine flour, powdered milk, basil, and salt in a large mixing bowl. Cut in butter until mixture resembles coarse meal.

Combine yeast, ¼ cup lukewarm water, and honey in a large measuring cup. Set aside to proof.

Combine ⅔ cup lukewarm water with tomato paste, and add to yeast mixture. Make a well in the flour and pour in. Stir to mix thoroughly. Knead, by hand or machine, until you have a smooth, elastic dough (about 10 minutes). Place in a well-greased large mixing bowl, cover, and set in a warm, draft-free place to rise.

Allow to rise until doubled in bulk (about 1½ hours). Turn dough out onto a well-floured surface. Punch down and toss until no longer sticky. Form into smooth ball. On floured surface, cover with bowl and let dough rest 15 minutes.

Now roll out to form a 14-by-7-inch rectangle. Cut in two, so that you have 2 14-inch pieces. Roll each up tightly, starting with the 14-inch side. Place diagonally on greased cookie sheet. Brush with a mixture of 1 tablespoon egg plus 1 teaspoon water. Slash top 5 or 6 times.

Cover and let rise until doubled (from 30 minutes to 1 hour). Preheat oven to 375° 10 minutes before baking time. Bake until golden brown, about 30 to 35 minutes. Cool on a rack. Don't slice until the loaf is cool enough to handle. Now when did your kitchen ever smell so good? Is there anything better than cooking with herbs?

Fresh Herb and Parmesan Bread
[Mona Rodgers]

The aroma that will fill your house while these pungent pinwheels bake defies description. If you don't have access to fresh herbs, remember to use only a quarter the amount of dried herbs. These pinwheels freeze well and are a real hit at parties.

Makes 40 pinwheels in 3 hours

2 tablespoons dry active yeast
1 cup warm water
3 tablespoons honey
2 teaspoons salt
1 cup warm milk
⅓ cup melted butter
2 large eggs, slightly beaten
3 cups unbleached white flour
3 cups whole wheat flour
2 tablespoons melted butter
1 teaspoon minced fresh parsley, or ¼ teaspoon dried
1 teaspoon minced fresh basil, or ¼ teaspoon dried

1 teaspoon minced fresh oregano, or ¼ teaspoon dried
½ teaspoon minced fresh thyme, or ⅛ teaspoon dried
½ teaspoon minced fresh sage, or ⅛ teaspoon dried
2 garlic cloves, pressed
3 tablespoons freshly grated Parmesan cheese
additional Parmesan and paprika to dust tops

Dissolve yeast in warm water with honey in large bowl. Set aside to proof for 5 minutes. Add salt, milk, melted butter, and eggs.

Gradually add flours, mixing constantly until dough is soft. Add just enough flour so that dough loses its stickiness; then knead until you have a smooth, elastic dough (at least 10 minutes). Divide dough in half, and roll half into a 13-by-18-inch rectangle.

Combine 2 tablespoons melted butter with fresh herbs, garlic, and Parmesan. Brush half of this mixture onto flattened dough. Starting at one end of the long side, roll up jelly-roll fashion; pinch seam to seal. Cut into 20 slices with a wet knife. Repeat with second half of dough.

Place slices, cut sides up and sides touching, on a well-greased cookie sheet with sides. Cover and let rise in a warm place until double in size (about 1 hour).

Preheat oven to 350°. Just before baking, sprinkle with additional Parmesan cheese and dust with paprika. Bake until golden, about 45 minutes. To serve, tear into individual pinwheels. Spread with sweet butter.

Raisin-Rye Yeast-rising Bread
[Barbara Keup Wolff]

Here's a good breakfast bread—less sweet and more complex than most.
Also good as a sandwich loaf or as an accompaniment for main-dish soups.

Makes 4 1½-pound loaves in 4 hours

¼ pound butter	2 tablespoons dry active yeast
⅓ cup molasses	1 teaspoon sugar
⅓ cup honey	¼ cup lukewarm (110°) water
1 tablespoon salt	2 cups raisins
2 cups boiling water	5 to 6 cups rye flour
1 cup cold water	5 to 6 cups whole wheat flour
⅔ cup powdered milk	

Combine butter, molasses, honey, salt, and boiling water. When butter has
melted, add cold water and powdered milk. Mix thoroughly. Cool to lukewarm.

Combine yeast with sugar and warm water. Set aside to proof for 5 minutes.
Once it's good and foamy, add to molasses mixture and stir to mix.

Add raisins and 2 cups flour. Stir to mix thoroughly. Add remaining flour,
a little at a time until dough is firm but not dry.

Knead dough at least 15 minutes, or until it is a smooth elastic texture. Place
in an oiled bowl, cover, and allow to rise to double in bulk in a warm, draft-
free spot (about an hour). Punch down and allow to rise to double in size
again (about 30 minutes). Oil 4 regular 8-by-4-inch bread pans.

Finally, punch down dough and divide into 4 equal pieces. Pat each piece
down into a flat rectangle, the length of which is the same as the bread pan.
Brush top with melted butter. (You may dust with cinnamon if you wish.) Now,
roll into loaf shape and place in well-oiled pan, seam side down.

Preheat oven to 400°. Allow loaves to rise in pans 1 inch over the tops
(about 30 minutes), then place in hot oven. Bake 20 minutes; then reduce
temperature to 375° and bake 25 to 30 minutes longer. Turn out of pans and
cool on rack. For a soft crust, brush tops with butter while still hot.

Gloria's Whole-Meal Bread

Whole-meal breads are sometimes so dense and solid they'd be better
suited to a construction site than to a dinner table. This bread is an exception.
It is light, even textured, and chewy. Makes great toast. Keeps well. I bring
it to you from my last cookbook, by popular demand, as they say.

Technique is the reason this bread has such a fine texture. First you make
a sponge, which you allow to rise for about an hour before you proceed with
the customary bread-making steps. The sponge step acts on the heavy flours,
releasing the gluten so that the whole bread can rise beautifully.

This bread can be an original every time. Note that the last ingredient says
one cup *total* of nuts, seeds, grains, or fruits. Just use what you have. Different
ratios and different choices will produce different breads.

Makes 3 loaves in 4 hours

2 tablespoons dry active yeast	8 ounces plain yogurt
2 cups lukewarm (110°) water	1 tablespoon salt
½ cup honey	1 cup *total* of any or all of the
4 cups unbleached white flour	following: sesame seeds,
4 cups whole wheat flour	poppy seeds, oatmeal,
1 cup powdered milk	chopped nuts, raisins, dates
½ cup oil	

Oil 3 regular 9-by-5-by-3-inch bread pans (or cookie sheets for round loaves) and set aside.

Dissolve yeast in lukewarm water and add honey, stirring to mix. Add half white flour and half whole wheat flour and blend thoroughly (you can do this with a regular mixer). Turn out into a large oiled bowl, cover, and place in warm, draft-free place to rise until double in bulk. This makes the "sponge" and takes about an hour.

Combine dry milk, remaining flours, oil, yogurt, salt, and seeds. Add this mixture to sponge and mix thoroughly. Knead for 10 minutes, either by hand or machine. Maintain a soft dough, adding water or flour to keep it just so. Replace well-kneaded dough in oiled bowl, re-cover, and again allow to rise until doubled in bulk (about an hour).

Once the dough has risen to double in bulk, punch it down and turn out on board. Press it down into a flat rectangle. Cut dough into 3 equal parts. You can form loaves either into the standard loaf shape, or you can make a round free-form shape. For a standard loaf shape, after you've divided the dough, form the piece into a rectangle about the length of bread pan and twice as wide. Roll it up carefully, pinching the edges together, and place it in prepared bread pan with pinched edge down.

If you wish to make a free-form loaf, simply take dough in hand and begin forming a ball, pulling dough down and around until you have a kind of knot on the bottom side. (It should look something like a big mushroom.) When the top is smooth and free of air bubbles, place on a well-oiled cookie sheet.

Brush tops of loaves with oil and allow to rise in warm, draft-free place until doubled in bulk (from 40 minutes to an hour). About 10 minutes before baking, preheat oven to 350°.

Bake loaves in oven for 30 minutes or until done. The way you can tell if a loaf of bread is done is to turn it out on a towel and tap on the bottom with your knuckles, as if you were knocking on a door. It should sound hollow. An undercooked loaf will be wet and doughy and will sound like it would if you knocked on your own thigh with your knuckles. Try it. See how dull that sound is.

Once bread is done thoroughly, remove from pans and cool on rack. If you want a soft crust, rub tops with butter. Allow to cool completely before slicing. (This may require standing guard over the loaves once that aroma pervades the house.) Such great bread. You'll want it once a week.

The Basic Truffle

If you would like to make truffles, but you don't happen to have a master's degree in chemistry or an apprenticeship with a master chocolatier under your belt (so to speak), here is a simple home-cook's method for making truffles that requires no special chocolate thermometer, marble board, or other exotic equipment.

I know that many a cooking purist turns up his or her nose at the very mention of the word microwave, but I must say that in my kitchen the microwave has found one of its best uses in melting chocolate. Chocolate should not be heated above 120° or it will burn, become grainy, and lose some flavor. Although you can melt chocolate safely in a double boiler, I find that the microwave, set on medium-low for about a minute per eight ounces, melts chocolate to perfection. No risk of burning. Quick. The chocolate comes out looking like it did when it went in, but one stir and you will see that it is that perfect liquid consistency required in so many chocolate recipes.

The center of a chocolate truffle is known as the ganache. It depends on flavored cream, combined with melted chocolate, then formed into that familiar round pebble shape.

In the recipe that follows, I have suggested a vanilla bean to flavor the cream. But once you have made these truffles and see how easy this version is, you can begin to fool around with the flavorings. Boil cream with whole coffee beans, or cinnamon bark, or hazelnuts, or any combination thereof. Each flavored cream will result in a subtly different truffle.

See what you can think of. You can get a wide variety of truffle flavors from this one basic recipe simply by varying the flavoring agent and being patient enough to let the truffles develop to their fullest flavor potential before you let anybody see them. My god, these things get eaten in a hurry.

If you can stand it, you should allow the truffles to sit overnight in the refrigerator, so that the subtle flavors can marry and deliver the optimum blended result.

If you have access to a heavy whipping cream that is raw rather than ultrapasteurized (try the Pike Place Market), you will add a dimension of flavor to the truffles otherwise unavailable, though they will be even more perishable. Raw-cream truffles keep no longer than a week, refrigerated in an airtight container. When made with ultrapasteurized cream, they keep at least ten days. You can freeze them for up to two months, suitably wrapped with plastic wrap, then foil, then an airtight container. Then just thaw, unopened, overnight in the refrigerator.

Makes 36 1-inch truffles in 1 hour

½ cup whipping cream
1 vanilla bean, sliced thin in 3
   or 4 pieces
   few grains salt
8 ounces bittersweet
   chocolate, block, squares, or
   chips

1 ounce milk chocolate, block,
   squares, or chips
2 large egg yolks
1½ tablespoons bourbon, rum,
   or liqueur of your choice

Coating:
**Unsweetened Dutch-process
cocoa**

Combine cream, vanilla bean pieces, and salt in small stainless or glass saucepan. Over medium heat raise to gentle boil and allow to cook for 1 minute uncovered. Remove from heat and allow to cool for about 5 minutes. Taste. If flavoring is in the right proportion, you should get a definite punch of the flavor at this time. If it is too subtle, boost it a little, say, with a ½ teaspoon of pure vanilla extract. (Remember, chocolate is a dominant flavor, and if you want this truffle to taste better than the bar of pure unadulterated chocolate that you started out with, you must infuse the cream with a goodly amount of the flavoring of your choice.)

Strain the flavored cream through a fine sieve into a medium-size mixing bowl (preferably stainless steel) that you safely can place in a water bath without danger of splashing water into the chocolate.

Melt chocolates together. You can do this in 1 of 3 ways. The simplest is to combine chocolates in a Pyrex bowl and melt in a microwave set on medium-low for about a minute. Another fairly simple way is to place chocolates in a metal pan and place on a "hot" tray (you know, those plate-warmer things). The third way is to place chocolates in top of a double boiler and melt over hot, but never boiling, water. If water boils, chocolate gets too hot and right before your very eyes will turn to a dull, turgid grayish clay. Inert. Dead. Useless.

Once you have melted chocolates, stir to mix thoroughly. Whisk egg yolks until lemony, then blend into cream. Now whisk in chocolate and liquor flavoring and blend until smooth.

Place the chocolate mixture, known as the ganache, over an ice-water bath, taking care that not a single drop of water sloshes into the chocolate. Using a rubber spatula, paddle gently until it is completely cool, about 5 minutes. Remove the bowl from ice-water bath, and using a wire whisk, whip the ganache, watching it like a hawk, until you see that it lightens in color and begins to form soft peaks (this won't take longer than ½ minute or so). Don't overdo it.

Sprinkle generous coating of cocoa on a sheet of waxed paper in a pan. Using a melon baller or 2 teaspoons, form chocolate balls and drop them onto cocoa-dusted sheet. You should get about 3 dozen 1-inch balls. Once you have formed the balls, tap the pan on the heel of your hand to roll the balls around in the cocoa.

Refrigerate for about 10 minutes. Remove from refrigerator. Dust your palms with cocoa and further form each ball, rolling in the cocoa and in your hands so that you have a mound of earthy-looking truffles, as rare and precious as the natural fungi for which they were named.

Line an airtight tin with foil, then plastic wrap, and place truffles inside, separating layers with foil. Cover tightly and let them stand in the refrigerator at least overnight, so that all the delicious flavors can blend. Well, maybe you could eat 1. I guess 2 wouldn't hurt. Just don't let anybody else know they're made until you are ready to serve. Otherwise it's curtains.

Triple-Chocolate Truffle Terrine
[Heather Bryce-Harvey and Barbara Michel for Yours Truly Catering]

Here is a grand-prize-winning dessert that serves sixteen to twenty people. Complicated to prepare and relying on best-quality chocolate for optimum results, it will, nevertheless, satisfy the chocoholic's deepest desires, for days, for weeks, for as long as it takes to get up the energy to do it again. You can use truffles from a shop or you can make them yourself.

Serves 16 to 20 in 2 hours

vegetable oil (to coat a 6-cup oblong terrine)
1 tablespoon unflavored gelatin (1 envelope)
¼ cup cold water
5 large egg yolks
½ cup sugar
1½ cups scalded half and half
5 ounces finely grated bittersweet chocolate
3 ounces finely grated milk chocolate

Raspberry Sauce:
2 cups fresh or frozen raspberries, mashed and strained to remove seeds

1 teaspoon orange extract
3 ounces grated white chocolate
1½ teaspoons pure vanilla extract
2¼ cups cold heavy whipping cream, whipped and divided into 3 parts
¼ pound uncoated chocolate truffles, rolled into a ¼-inch log shape (see index for The Basic Truffle recipe)

1 10-ounce jar seedless raspberry jelly

Coat inside of 6-cup oblong terrine mold with vegetable oil and set aside. Soften gelatin in cold water and set aside.

Beat egg yolks until thick and pale, gradually adding sugar until mixture is pale and forms a ribbon. Meanwhile, scald half and half in a heavy-bottomed 3-quart saucepan (not aluminum), then thoroughly blend egg and sugar mixture into scalded cream.

Cook over medium heat, stirring constantly with a wooden spoon until mixture coats the back of the spoon, about 10 minutes. *Do not boil.* Remove from heat and stir in gelatin until dissolved. Strain mixture into a 1-quart measuring cup, then divide equally among 3 mixing bowls.

Working quickly, add bittersweet chocolate to first bowl, milk chocolate and orange extract to second bowl, and white chocolate and vanilla to third bowl. Using a separate wire whisk for each bowl, whisk mixtures to dissolve chocolates. Cover each bowl with plastic wrap. Refrigerate the bittersweet chocolate mixture; keep the white and milk chocolates unrefrigerated for the moment.

Whip cream until stiff peaks form, then divide into 3 equal parts. Remove bittersweet chocolate mixture from refrigerator and place milk chocolate inside refrigerator.

Fold ⅓ of whipped cream into bittersweet chocolate and pour into greased terrine. Smooth top and tap the terrine on counter to knock out small air bubbles. Place terrine in freezer for no more than 10 minutes.

Remove milk chocolate from refrigerator and place white chocolate mixture in refrigerator. Fold ⅓ of whipped cream into milk chocolate mixture. Remove terrine from freezer and gently layer over the milk chocolate mixture. Smooth top and gently tap to remove air bubbles. Return to freezer for 8 to 10 minutes.

Remove white chocolate mixture from refrigerator and fold in final ⅓ of stiffly whipped cream. Spread a thin layer on top of the milk chocolate layer, again smoothing and tapping to get an even bubble-free layer. Replace terrine in refrigerator.

If you are using uncoated truffles from a candy specialty shop, roll into 1 long ¼-inch-thick log. If you are making homemade truffles, see accompanying recipe, and form ¼ pound of the homemade truffle into a long thin log.

Cut truffle log into 3 equal-length pieces and lay on top of the white chocolate layer. Cover with remaining white chocolate, filling the space between the rolls and covering them with a thin layer of white chocolate.

Finally, cover with plastic wrap and refrigerate at least 4 hours or as long as overnight.

To make Raspberry Sauce, add raspberries to jelly and warm slightly to facilitate mixing. Chill before pouring around the unmolded chilled dessert.

To unmold, run a knife around the edge of the terrine. Wrap hot towel around mold, invert onto platter, and remove terrine mold. This sometimes is easier said than done. You may find it necessary to add a second hot towel. Just think back to those old cowboy movies where the barber swaddles the cowboy's face in hot towels before the shave. This may help keep you from screaming while the damn thing hangs on.

Once the terrine has turned loose and slid onto the plate, puddle the brilliant red sauce on the plate around it and serve to 20 slavering chocoholics.

Pear-Pistachio Chocolate Torte

Want to make a cake that looks like it came from a pâtisserie? That uses our own native ingredients? Here is one that tastes as good as it looks and takes advantage of the superior pears available from Oregon's Rogue Valley. Ninety percent of America's pears grow there, in five or six varieties, and in such abundance that one routinely can buy them for fifteen cents a pound. Small bartletts, the yellow and the red, or the succulent comice work equally well in this cake. Just choose fruit that is completely ripe but not bruised. Since the pears are presented in halves on top of the cake, choose four that are uniform in size and well shaped.

If you use red-dyed pistachios in this cake, the color will be reminiscent of the old-fashioned devil's food cake, but natural green pistachios are easier to work with and won't dye your fingers red when you shell them. Why did they start dying pistachios anyway? Their natural green is so delectable.

Serves 10 in 1½ hours plus 3 hours
to chill

Poached Pears:

2 cups water	4 small, uniform completely
2 cups sugar	ripe pears, bartlett or
¼ cup fresh lemon juice	comice
(approximately ½ lemon)	water to cover, with juice
zest from ½ lemon	from ½ lemon squeezed in
1 teaspoon ground cinnamon	

Torte:

½ cup finely ground toasted	3 egg yolks
pistachio nuts	⅓ cup poaching syrup
¼ cup all-purpose flour	1 tablespoon bourbon
3 ounces (3 squares)	5 egg whites, whipped to stiff
semisweet chocolate	peaks
¼ cup sweet butter	1 pinch cream of tartar
1 tablespoon sugar	

Buttercream Frosting:

3 ounces (3 squares)	2 tablespoons bourbon
semisweet chocolate	4 tablespoons sweet butter, cut
½ ounce (½ square)	into 6 pieces
unsweetened baker's	
chocolate	

Combine water, sugar, lemon juice, zest, and cinnamon in a medium sauce-pan. Place over medium heat and simmer 10 minutes.

Using a potato peeler, peel, halve, and core pears, leaving stems intact on 4 halves. Drop into a bowl of water scented with a squeeze of lemon juice (to prevent browning). Once you have completed peeling and coring, lift pears from water bath and drop into simmering poaching syrup. Cover and poach until tender throughout (about 10 minutes). Test with a skewer; do not over-cook. Set pan aside and allow pears to cool in poaching syrup while you make the torte.

For torte, shell and toast pistachios in a 350° oven until golden (about 10 minutes). Grind warm nuts very fine. (You can do this in a well-cleaned-out electric coffee mill, or you get a mocha cake in the bargain. Not bad, but not the same.) Leave oven on at 350° to bake cake.

Combine ground pistachios and flour in a small bowl and set aside.

Melt chocolate squares, butter, and sugar in either a double boiler or a microwave set on medium-low. Stir to mix thoroughly and set aside. Beat egg yolks in bowl with ⅓ cup pear-poaching syrup until thick, pale, and smooth (at least 5 minutes); then stir in chocolate mixture and bourbon.

In another bowl, beat egg whites and cream of tartar until stiff but not dry. Sprinkle half flour mixture onto egg whites and then dribble ⅓ of chocolate mixture over. Fold in gently. Repeat until all flour and chocolate are folded into whites.

Generously butter and flour a 9-inch round cake pan. Carefully pour batter into pan, smoothing top. Bake cake in preheated 350° oven for 25 minutes or until a toothpick comes out clean from the center. Cool torte in pan for 10 minutes, then turn out on a rack to cool completely before frosting.

To make frosting, melt chocolates and bourbon together, either in a double boiler or in microwave set on medium-low. Stir to mix thoroughly. Beat in butter, piece by piece, until creamy. If mixture is too soft to spread on cool cake, place bowl in a larger bowl of ice water and continue beating until it stiffens up sufficiently for spreading.

Spread a thin layer of buttercream frosting on cooled torte. Remove pear halves from poaching syrup, and pat them dry using paper towels. Arrange 4 halves on top of cake, stem ends to the center. Press remaining halves into sides of cake. Cover and refrigerate for 3 hours before serving.

Cranberry Walnut Torte
Frosted with Chocolate Truffle Cream, Filled with Brandied Whipped Cream and Fresh Cranberries

The secret to success in assembling the Cranberry Walnut Torte is to have everything cold. Cold plate. Cold cake layers. Cold frosting. Cold filling. Otherwise, everything slides around and you think you're going to scream. No wonder they invented bakeries. You have to be a glutton for punishment or a Grade 9 chocoholic to take on this one. But, my god, there's no bakery that makes it. If you love chocolate, and you love truffles, and you love cranberries, what choice do you have? Go for it.

Serves 12, takes all day and
10 gallons of sweat

The Cake:

¾ cup Dutch-process cocoa	2 cups unbleached white flour
¾ cup butter	1½ teaspoons baking soda
1 cup strong just-brewed French roast coffee	½ teaspoon salt
	2 cups sugar
½ cup chopped fresh cranberries	½ cup plain yogurt
	2 large eggs
¼ cup finely chopped walnuts	1 teaspoon real vanilla

Chocolate Truffle Cream Frosting:
- ½ cup heavy whipping cream
- 1 2-inch piece of vanilla bean, cut in 3 to 4 thin slices
- few grains salt
- 8 ounces bittersweet chocolate, chips, squares, or block
- 2 large egg yolks
- 1½ tablespoons brandy

Frosting:
- 1 cup sugar
- 1 tablespoon light corn syrup
- ¼ cup water
- 2 large eggs
- 1 cup cold sweet butter
- 1 cup cold ganache

Brandied Whipped Cream with Cranberry Filling:
- ½ cup heavy whipping cream
- 2 tablespoons sugar
- 1 tablespoon brandy
- ½ cup chopped fresh cranberries
- additional whole cranberries and perfect walnut halves for the top

Preheat oven to 375°. Generously grease and flour 2 8-inch cake pans.

Combine cocoa, butter, and coffee and heat to melt butter. Mix thoroughly. In processor bowl, chop cranberries and walnuts. Remove and reserve.

Combine flour, baking soda, salt, and sugar in processor bowl. Mix. Pour in cocoa liquid and yogurt. Process until thoroughly mixed, scraping down sides as necessary. Now add eggs and vanilla and mix thoroughly. Stir cranberries and walnuts into mixture by hand.

Divide evenly into prepared cake pans. Bake until the center springs back at the touch, 25 to 35 minutes. Cool layers in pans for 10 minutes. Turn out onto a rack. When the cakes have reached room temperature, cut each layer in half horizontally so that you have 4 equal-size disks.

Wrap layers together in plastic wrap and refrigerate until completely chilled, about 30 minutes, while you make the frosting.

To make Chocolate Truffle Cream Frosting, first make a ganache, the same luscious chocolate you find at the center of truffles.

Combine cream, vanilla bean, and salt in a small saucepan over medium heat. Bring to gentle boil. Simmer 5 minutes. Remove from heat and allow to cool 5 minutes. While the cream is cooling, melt chocolate in a medium-size bowl—either in microwave set on low, or over hot water, or on a hot tray. Stir to get a smooth mix.

Strain cream through a fine sieve into chocolate. Whisk in egg yolks and brandy and beat until smooth. Place bowl of ganache into an ice-water bath, taking care not to slosh any water into the chocolate. Using a rubber spatula, paddle the mixture until it is completely cold (about 5 minutes). Using a wire whisk, whip ganache until it begins to lighten in color and forms soft peaks (about 30 seconds). Using the rubber spatula again, form it into a solid, smooth ball. Cover and refrigerate. Begin the frosting.

Combine sugar, corn syrup, and water in a small saucepan. Over medium heat, using a candy thermometer, bring up to 235°. Use a pastry brush to wet down sides and keep crystals from forming (takes 5 to 10 minutes).

While syrup is heating, beat eggs until light and frothy. Once syrup reaches 235°, pour a thin stream into eggs, beating all the while. Continue to beat at high speed until mixture is completely cool, at least 5 minutes. Reduce speed of mixer to medium and add cold butter, in 1-tablespoon (approximate) chunks. Once you have a smooth mixture, add 1 cup of cold ganache. Beat until smooth. If frosting is too thin to spread, refrigerate until it is cold.

To make filling, whip cream into stiff peaks, dribbling in sugar a few grains at a time. Whip in brandy, then fold in cranberries.

To assemble torte, place one layer of cake on a chilled serving plate, cut side up. Tuck 4 pieces of waxed paper under the edges to catch frosting drip.

Frost first layer with chocolate frosting. Place second layer cut side down, so that you have put back together the first round of cake that you cut in two.

Create a moat of chocolate frosting around the edge, using 2 tablespoons or piping it on. String 3 whole cranberries each onto 3 toothpicks. Place these support sticks in the chocolate moat, at equal distances from each other to hold up second layer. Fill lake you just made with sweetened whipped cream and cranberries.

Carefully lay the third layer on, cut side up. Frost with chocolate truffle cream. Place the final layer on, cut side down, so that you have put back together the second layer of cake that you originally cut in two. Frost completely with remaining chocolate truffle cream.

Garnish top with whole cranberries and walnuts. Refrigerate at least 2 hours before serving.

White Chocolate, Cranberry, and Orange Tart

You remember the old joke about buying a yacht: If you have to ask how much it costs, you can't afford it. About making this dessert, I'd say that if you have to ask how long it takes or how hard it is to make or how many calories it contains, turn the page. But, if you'd like to prepare a tart so good your guests will never forget it, read on.

Serves 12, takes forever

The Crust:

1 **cup unbleached white flour**	6 **ounces orange Neufchâtel**
⅛ **teaspoon salt**	**cheese**
½ **cup butter**	

To make crust, combine flour and salt in bowl of food processor. Cut butter and cream cheese into chunks roughly equivalent to 1 tablespoon each; distribute chunks evenly over flour. Process just until dough forms a ball. Wrap in plastic and refrigerate dough for 30 minutes. (Make glaze during this time.)

To form and bake crust, lightly butter an 11-inch tart pan. Handling dough as little as possible, roll into a 12-inch circle and carefully place in the pan. Press sides into fluted edge of tart pan, doubling the sides with dough that's left over. Refrigerate an hour.

Preheat oven to 375°. Prick crust with fork every inch or so. Bake until light golden brown, about 15 minutes. Remove and glaze.

The Glaze:

1 **cup fresh cranberries**	1 **tablespoon sugar**
½ **cup sugar**	1 **teaspoon cornstarch**
½ **cup water**	

To make glaze, combine cranberries, ½ cup sugar, and water in small saucepan. Boil just until cranberries pop. Remove from heat and purée in food processor. Add additional tablespoon of sugar and cornstarch. Return to pan. Cook and stir over medium-low heat until thick and clear, about 5 minutes. Remove from heat and set aside to cool. When crust is done, you will spread this glaze over it.

White Chocolate Filling:

2 **large eggs**	½ **cup very soft butter**
6 **ounces white chocolate**	⅔ **cup sugar**

To make white chocolate filling, place unshelled eggs into a small bowl filled with hot water. (Warm eggs beat up higher and stiffer than cold ones, and this is one quick way to do it.) Melt chocolate 1 of 3 ways: either in double boiler, in microwave set on medium-low, or on hot tray.

Meanwhile, in mixer, whip soft butter until you have incorporated some air. Add sugar, a teaspoon at a time, with mixer on high, until you have a complete blend and a pale yellow, granule-free mixture. Test by rubbing filling between your finger and thumb; it should be smooth as silk.

Turn mixer to lowest setting and pour in chocolate, scraping sides so that chocolate does not cool and solidify on sides of bowl.

Turn mixer speed to high and add 1 egg. Beat for 3 minutes. Add second egg and beat for 3 more minutes, scraping sides of bowl frequently with mixer running. You should now have a light, smooth-as-satin white chocolate filling to pour over cranberry-glazed crust.

The Topping:

3 **ounces bittersweet chocolate**	1 **teaspoon vegetable oil**
1 **tablespoon butter**	

To make topping, melt together chocolate, butter, and oil in microwave, double boiler, or on hot tray, getting it hot enough so that you can pour it in a thin stream. If you heat this in a 1-cup Pyrex measure with a lip, it makes the final task easier.

Assembling the Tart:

Just to recap. Here is how you order the work: first, make the crust. While crust is in its resting state, make the cranberry glaze. Then bake crust and glaze it with cranberry purée while it's still hot from the oven. Now make filling and pour into glazed crust. Finally, pour on bittersweet chocolate, in a thin stream, making a spiral from outside edge to center. Refrigerate until firm. Pull a dull knife blade lightly over the top from center to edges to get a spiderweb effect. Wipe knife blade after each pull to keep black and white distinct. Let stand at room temperature for 20 minutes before serving.

Swiss Tart with Fruit of the Season
[Nancy Denney Phelps]

You won't believe how gorgeous this is. And it's a fruit-and-cheese course rolled into one. Think of a twelve-inch tart, golden brown and aromatic with Swiss cheese and toasted coconut, topped with the most luscious fruits you can find: blood orange slices and pomegranate seeds, or star fruit and papaya, kiwi and strawberries, red flame grapes and honeydew melon. The idea here is to master the crust, then top it with whatever looks fabulous that day at the farmer's market.

Serves 10 in 40 minutes

½   cup sweet butter
¼   cup sugar
¼   teaspoon salt
1   cup (3 ounces) Swiss cheese, shredded
1¼ cups unbleached white flour
2   tablespoons half and half

1   cup shredded coconut
2   cups fruit of the season
⅓   cup jelly or marmalade
½   teaspoon spirits (optional), such as brandy, bourbon, crème de cassis

Preheat oven to 375°. Place butter, sugar, and salt in processor bowl. Process to combine. Add shredded cheese, flour, and cream and process to make a ball. (You may make this dough traditionally by cutting butter into sugar and salt using pastry blender, then cutting in cheese and adding flour and milk alternately, stirring with a fork until you have a ball.)

Spread dough by hand into 12-inch tart pan, smoothing with hands and creating a slight lip around edge. Bake for 5 minutes. Remove from oven, sprinkle evenly with coconut, then return to oven and continue baking for 15 minutes, or until the crust is lightly browned. Without removing from pan, cool on a rack.

While the crust is baking, slice seasonal fruits into paper-thin, attractive slices. Place sliced fruits on crust in good-looking design while crust is still warm. Now think of a jelly you have that will complement the basic taste of the fruits you have chosen (crabapple, apple, or orange marmalade? Almost anything but purple grape, which tends to look gray and awful). Combine jelly in small saucepan with complementary spirit, heat to boiling, and pour over arranged fruits.

Chocolate Silk Pie
in a Walnut-Butter Crumb Crust

Once you have made this piecrust, you will want to try different fillings in it. In fact, it is so good, you can eat it plain. Or maybe with a vanilla ice cream filling. Just try it once. You'll see. The aroma alone is enough to knock you out. Walnuts, brown sugar, and butter cooked together. Need I say more?

And the filling? Aptly named. If you are patient enough to whip the chocolate, butter, and eggs into the sugar until every granule of the sugar is dissolved, it will produce a texture so silky that you may have trouble deciding whether to eat it or rub it on your body.

Serves 8 in 1 hour

The Crust:

¼ cup brown sugar	½ cup butter
1 cup unbleached white flour	1 cup walnuts

Preheat oven to 375°. Combine all ingredients in processor bowl and process until resembles coarse meal. Now place in 13-by-9-inch baking dish. Bake for 15 minutes. Remove from oven and stir with a fork. Pour into 9-inch pie plate and press with back of fork into pie crust shape. Re-place in oven and cook until light golden brown, about 10 minutes. Remove from oven and cool.

The Chocolate Silk Filling:

¾ cup butter (1½ sticks)	1½ teaspoons vanilla
1 cup sugar	3 large eggs
4 ounces bittersweet chocolate	

To make filling, cream butter and sugar in mixer until fluffy. Melt chocolate (either over hot water, or in microwave set on low) and add to sugar and butter along with vanilla. Add 2 eggs and beat, on high, for 5 minutes. Now add remaining egg and beat until every sugar granule has dissolved, at least 5 minutes but probably 10 or so. (You can tell when ready either by tasting it or by rubbing a bit of filling between finger and thumb; should be silky smooth.) Scrape into cooled crust. Freeze. You may serve either frozen or about half-thawed. Incredible.

Hazelnut Pie

Oregon's hazelnuts, sometimes known as filberts, provide North America with most of its supply of this old-world favorite. They generally come raw, in the shell. To release their flavor to the fullest, here's how to roast them.

Preheat oven to 350°. Place hazelnuts, in the shell, one layer deep on a cookie sheet and place in oven. Roast for about 10 minutes. You will smell the most divine aroma emanating from your kitchen. Now remove and cool.

Crack just the amount you plan to use, and store the rest in a cool place. Don't put them in plastic. One filbert grower I know says, "Thow 'em in an old pillow slip and keep 'em in the basement." Dark and dry. That's the idea.

This old-fashioned nut pie is similar to a pecan pie. The principle used in this pie, which makes it superior, is raising the sugar and corn syrup to a boil to thoroughly dissolve the sugar granules. You can substitute any nut with good results: walnuts, pecans, or almonds. Say, wouldn't a pistachio pie be something? I think I'll try that next.

Makes 2 8-inch pies in 1½ hours

1 cup sugar	4 large eggs
⅛ teaspoon salt	2 cups finely chopped, roasted
1½ cups dark corn syrup	and hulled hazelnuts
4 tablespoons butter	2 unbaked 8-inch pie shells
1½ teaspoons vanilla	

Preheat oven to 350°. Combine sugar, salt, and corn syrup in medium saucepan. Raise to a boil. Stir to completely dissolve sugar granules. Remove from heat. Swirl in butter to melt; then add vanilla. Beat eggs until well blended but not frothy. Blend with sugar syrup. Stir in hazelnuts. Divide between 2 pie shells, and place in oven, immediately reducing temperature to 325°. Bake until a knife comes out clean when inserted in the middle, about 50 to 60 minutes. Cool on a rack.

Serve with unsweetened whipped cream, or even better, with a dollop of crème fraîche.

Louise Hoffman's Black Butter Shortbreads
[Peggy Sammons]

This little cookie is a miracle. It melts in your mouth. People will swear it has essence of almond in it. It is never quite the same way twice, but always tastes positively divine. A splendid accompaniment to any fresh-fruit dessert.

*Makes 3 to 4 dozen shortbreads
in 1 hour*

1 cup unsalted butter	2 teaspoons vanilla
½ teaspoon fresh lemon juice	2 cups unbleached white flour
¾ cup sugar	1 teaspoon baking powder
2 tablespoons milk	½ teaspoon salt

Preheat oven to 300°. Brown butter in medium saucepan until it smells like caramels and is almost ready to burn. Keep heat no higher than medium and stir constantly to avoid burning. But be patient—keep over heat until the very last moment before it burns. Whisk it off the fire and squeeze in a few drops (roughly ½ teaspoon) of lemon juice. Set the saucepan in an ice-water bath to solidify the butter.

Once butter is solid, turn into bowl of mixer or processor. Cream in sugar and beat until fluffy. Add remaining ingredients and mix well. Turn out onto lightly floured surface and knead into a smooth ball. Grease 2 cookie sheets. Pinch off walnut-size pieces, roll into balls, and place on cookie sheets. Flatten with a fork. Bake at 300° for 25 to 30 minutes; cookies should be an even caramel color and should not be allowed to overcook. Cool on a rack. Store in an airtight container.

Dolce Spazio
[Susan Wilson for Judyth's Mountain]

This sweet pungent sauce that relies on Judyth's ginger jelly can be kept on hand and brought from the refrigerator at a moment's notice to top vanilla gelato, orange sorbet, or a little plain cake. I keep it in one of those antique mason jars with a wire bale and a rubber stopper. I can bring it to the table, as is. I like this sauce because it is not cloyingly sweet and because, like Everest, it is there.

Makes 1 pint in 15 minutes

½ cup Dutch-process cocoa
1 cup sugar
1 cup light corn syrup
½ cup half and half
¼ teaspoon salt
3 tablespoons butter

1 teaspoon vanilla
1 cup ginger jelly (Judyth's Mountain)
3 tablespoons minced orange zest

Combine cocoa, sugar, corn syrup, half and half, salt, and butter in saucepan. Cook over medium heat, stirring constantly until comes to full, rolling boil. Boil hard for 3 minutes, stirring from time to time.

Remove from heat and stir in vanilla, ginger jelly, and orange zest. Pour into sterile pint jar, cover, and refrigerate.

Mail Order

ONE NIGHT IN SAN FRANCISCO, we were eating in a fabulous Spanish restaurant on Clement called Alejandro's. In the paella were slivers of ham so delicious that I was picking through the rice like somebody sick with gold fever going through gravel, panning for gold. Boy, I sure would like to have this at home, I said. Me too, said my husband, Joe. And he gallantly called the waiter over and inquired after the ham.

Where did it come from? The waiter, who was about seventeen, enormously eager to please, and on the verge of a panic attack at any request that went beyond the menu, finally stammered that he had just gotten off the plane two weeks ago and his English was "no too good." So I, thinking to save the situation, relayed the request in Spanish. He looked enormously relieved. He bowed. He smiled. He said, in flawless Castilian Spanish, that he didn't know but he would go and ask the cook. He fairly flew into the kitchen. See? I said. That wasn't so hard. It wasn't long before the young man returned. He was smiling from ear to ear. He looked so confident. He approached the table. He folded his hands, as if in prayer. He took a deep breath and spoke. And I quote. "The cook says me, tell them is pig meat from Oakland." So much for finding out about ingredients used in fine restaurants.

But after that night, I got to dreaming. I knew that fine restaurants had their own suppliers, distinct from the supermarkets and retail food shops that most of us home cooks have access to. I knew about the food underground, the sources that were known to people in the business but not available to home cooks. I decided to crack the code. I wanted that damn pig meat from Oakland.

And so I began, kind of stumbling along. One thing led to another, and here is what I found. Tucked away, up and down the coast from San Diego to British Columbia, are a host of new cottage kitchens that grow, produce, and process, in small batches, some of the finest food products available. Home cooking, without preservatives, without chemicals, without bottled color. Home cooking established on a food philosophy that says food should nourish you. A philosophy that says shelf life is not the goal, *life* life is the goal. But it's home cooking that you don't have to do. Home cooking that is as close to you as the telephone. Most of these small entrepreneurial ventures accept telephone orders, take Visa or MasterCard, and will ship out to you food as good as your Aunt Martha used to make.

Some of these people are reviving nearly lost arts. I found cheesemakers who make it all by hand, beginning with feeding and milking the cow or goat. I found jam makers that simmer, in small batches, jams as good as your grandmother could make. I found mushroom pickers who provide bushel baskets full of chanterelles and precious cups of morels. I found people who smoke salmon the way the Indians did, using alder twigs and time. I found specialty produce people who grow all those exotic vegetables you read about in the food magazines. With overnight shipping, you even can get these.

You'll just have to read through this section to believe the variety of fine food products we have here. And thanks to the fast shippers, no longer do you have to live down the road from a cheesemaker to get handmade cheese. Pick up the phone. Order it. And when you get it home, you can use the recipes in this book to make the real New West Coast Cuisine. When I look in my refrigerator and pantry, stocked with foods from these small cottage kitchens, I think, surely, this is the neighborhood that Eve got kicked out of, years and years ago. Do you think I should stay away from apples?

Mushrooms and Vegetables

Seasonal Salads with Wild Herbs and Edible Flowers

Fresh Northwest
13217 Mattson Road
Arlington, Wash. 98223
phone orders: yes/206-435-4648/ Visa/MC: no/minimum order: $10 plus shipping

Say you're having a dinner party for ten and you'd like to really knock 'em out. How about a salad with at least twelve ingredients, some cultivated and some wild, including mâche, or arugula, or cattail shoots. And to complete the salad, an array of edible flowers. Would you believe you can pick up the phone, and the next day, by magical overnight UPS, at your doorstep will appear the ten salads, washed, prepped, and ready to serve? Fresher than if you'd started at the produce section of your supermarket. Now what do you think you'd have to pay for such an extravagance? Would you believe $1.50 a serving? That's it. Just $1.50 a serving. Isn't that incredible?

Mark Musick, the guiding light behind Fresh Northwest, has been supplying the finest restaurants in the Northwest with such salads for seven years. In the trade he is considered to be the master of fast shipping. He has developed shipping techniques that make it possible for him to send his fresh salads as far away as New York. He has provided Chez Panisse with red huckleberries.

Mark also acts as a one-man clearinghouse for a number of small growers in the Northwest. If he doesn't grow or gather some particular exotica that you'd like, nine times out of ten he can tell you where to get it. He and Robin Stern not only grow and compose these fantastic salads, they also sell wild blackberries, red huckleberries, nettles, cattail shoots, and who knows whatall they find in the verdant Northwest woods where they live. Mark Musick is a walking reference book to native foods of the Northwest. You should place your order by phone just for the chance to chat with Mark about what's to eat in the Northwest.

Oyster and Shiitake Mushrooms

Full Moon Mushroom Co.
P.O. Box 6138
Olympia, Wash. 98502
phone orders: yes/206-866-9362/ Visa/MC: no/minimum order: no

You can buy shiitake (Japanese Forest Mushrooms) from Mike and Barbar Maki for $6 a pound plus shipping; or what may be even more fun, you can buy your very own oyster mushroom farm for $7. The Makis have become quite the experts in mushroom cultivation and will even custom grow "garden giants" or other edible species. Call for price and availability. They'll even provide mushroom spawn, quality hardwood sawdust and chips, pasteurized straw, and other proper bedding products in case you'd like to get into cold framing mushrooms on a large scale.

If you live in the Seattle area, you should visit the Makis at the Pike Place Market on Saturdays from April 15 through December 22. You can call them at their home, order the mushrooms you want, and pick them up at Pike Place on Saturdays. How's that for service?

Wild Mushrooms and Exotic Vegetables

Hasson Brothers Fruit & Produce
1527 Pike Place Market
Seattle, Wash. 98101
phone orders: yes/206-622-1370/
Visa/MC: no/minimum order: no

Peter Hasson, the younger, employs mushroom pickers who bring to his stand at the bounteous Pike Place Market, bushels of chanterelles—two or three varieties. He also gets boletus and matsutakes mushrooms, which he sells for about $15 a pound. (In their native Japan, they go for $100 a pound.) These are the fall mushrooms. In the spring, he gets morels (supplies are spotty). Peter also has access to Washington's famous onion, the Walla Walla (June) and to all the stupendous produce grown in the Pacific Northwest. Asparagus so good you'll faint. Call him up and get a price quotation—he ships at his going rate plus container and shipping charges.

Oregon White Truffles

White Truffle Foods Inc.
1328 S.W. Cornell Street
Lake Oswego, Oreg. 97034
phone orders: yes/503-221-0611/
Visa/MC: no/minimum order: no

Matt Kramer, food and wine writer for *The Oregonian,* says that the Oregon white truffle, served side by side with a fresh Italian white truffle, might not be quite the same, but then again, how often do you have the opportunity to conduct such a comparison? The truffle pluckers of Oregon do not use dogs or hogs to sniff out the truffle found at the base of oaks in Oregon. They use a kind of stick. But they do hope to be able to buy a dog this year.

The Oregon white truffle is vastly superior to anything canned. Jane Grigson says that canning truffles reduces them "almost to a rumour of their extraordinary scent and flavour." Write the Oregon trufflers for price and availability. Sadie Kendall told me that the most outstanding truffle dish she'd ever tasted was served at one of those toney Napa Valley chef-competition things, in which a dish of pasta was dressed simply with Sadie's crème fraîche with Oregon white truffles shaved into the cream. What could be simpler? The main thing to remember when you get your Oregon white truffles is: the less you do to them the better. The most cooking this delicate truffle can endure is to warm it through with a little butter. Otherwise, you may find yourself with Jane Grigson's rumour.

Pickled Blue Lake Beans

Wicklund Farms
3959 Maple Island Farm Road
Springfield, Oreg. 97477
phone orders: yes/503-747-5998/
Visa/MC: no/minimum order: 1 case

If you order a Bloody Mary in any bar in Oregon, chances are it will come with a pickled-green-bean swizzle stick. And chances are that it came from Larry Wicklund, who, using his mother's recipe and basement and $15,000 of borrowed money, began a pickled-bean business. Larry grew up picking the Blue Lake pole beans that the Wicklunds raised for sale, but when automatic pickers made pole beans obsolete (a machine can work over a bush but not a pole), Larry figured out a way to make the family bean patch pay off; he says he did it just to raise capital. He plays with the rock band, Southern Comfort, and hopes to be a creative writer and poet. Stick with pickles, Larry. They're steadier than print. His pickled beans are quite delicious—crisp, tart, just the right blend of spices and sweet and sour. His mother's recipe is a winner. It should keep Larry Wicklund in paper, pens, and sound mixers for a long time.

Fruits and Nuts

Fresh European Chestnuts

Happy Dragon Chestnuts
10110 Wilder Ridge Road
Garberville, Calif. 95440
*phone orders: no/707-986-7526/Visa/
MC: no/minimum order: 3 pounds*

For five or six weeks, long about November, Peggy Etcheverry meets herself coming and going. For thirteen years, she has raised European chestnuts, organically, on a place just east of Sacramento. And when the harvest is on, she picks, packs, and ships her chestnuts to loyal, devoted chestnut fans. Her 1984 prices were three pounds for $11, or five pounds for $15.95 (postpaid west of the Rockies, extra shipping charges east of the Rockies). These beautiful chestnuts are shipped fresh, not dried or processed in any way. Just in time for the holidays.

California Pistachios

Rock Creek Nut Co.
1000 Rock Creek Road
Williams, Oreg. 97544
*phone orders: yes/503-846-6160/
Visa/MC: no/minimum order: no*

Conny and Walter Lindley got into this nutty business by hauling bulk foods to natural-foods stores. Somehow, there seemed to be a preponderance of pistachios in the back of the truck, so the Lindleys decided, what the heck. They began packaging the freshest, biggest pistachios they could get their hands on. Then they hooked up with some people in Ashland who Tamari soaked almonds and cashews. And now, you can buy either plain, undyed pistachios at $5.95 a pound, or a good-looking wooden gift box with a half-pound each of pistachios, Tamari almonds, Tamari cashews, and hickory-smoked almonds for $14.95. These nuts are really fresh.

Dried Fruits and Nuts

Timber Crest Farms
4791 Dry Creek Road
Healdsburg, Calif. 95448
*phone orders: yes/707-433-8251/
Visa/MC: yes/minimum order: no*

Rancher Waltenspiel does a good job. Located just 75 miles north of San Francisco, his orchard grows, dries, and packages a variety of fruits and nuts. All the products Waltenspiel grows are grown organically and are free of added sugar, sulfur dioxide, and preservatives. He ships orders the same day he receives them, and includes recipes with every package. Some of my favorites are his dried apricots, pears, and peaches, and one of his new products, sun-dried tomatoes (see index for several recipes using his California-grown and -dried tomatoes). He also sells those mixed plates of figs, almonds, walnuts, and other dried fruits. You've seen them. The kind they have at the roadside stands. Only if you buy from Rancher Waltenspiel, you know what you're getting. Goodness. Write or call for a full catalog and price list. He's got a lot of stuff. He also welcomes guests to the ranch Monday through Friday 8:00 A.M. to 5:00 P.M., and in December on Saturdays too.

Oregon Pears and Apples

Pinnacle Orchards
P.O. Box 1068
Medford, Oreg. 97501
*phone orders: yes/800-547-0227/
Visa/MC: yes/minimum order: no*

Pinnacle is the Avis of orchards, running harder behind Harry and David (see next entry) to be *the* gourmet pear shipper of America. Pinnacle offers the same high-quality pears from our Rogue valley—comice or bosc—sometimes combined with red or golden delicious apples. Pinnacle has a big gorgeous catalog that you can call and order. They have a full range of quality food products: cheeses, nuts, sausages, salad dressings, and preserves. You can even buy baked goods and bulbs for amaryllis, narcissus, and paperwhites. Whether you shop with Pinnacle or Harry and David, it may boil down to a decision of the Hertz-Avis type.

*The Granddaddy of
Mail Order Fruit Shippers*

Harry and David
Bear Creek Orchards
Medford, Oreg. 97501
*phone orders: yes/800-547-3033/
Visa/MC: yes/minimum order: no*

Knowing that people would rather eat than read, Harry and David began the Fruit-of-the-Month Club way back when. Their first ad, right in the teeth of the depression, was a little one in the back of *Fortune Magazine*. If there is one company in America that sets the standard for shipping fresh food, this is it. They have only the highest-quality products and a sophisticated drop-ship system that guarantees freshness. They sell a variety of food products, not only through their venerated Fruit-of-the-Month club but in infinite combinations. Call for a catalog.

I live about 10 miles from Harry and David and make their Reject Fruit Stand a regular stop on my weekly grocery shopping spree. If you're in the area during the season, you can buy fabulous comice pears for fifteen cents a pound. They always have good quality and good prices. They also have a fine restaurant and a good nursery. It really is a must-see at 2836 South Pacific Highway, in Medford, for any visitor to Southern Oregon.

Jams

Pacific Northwest Berry Jams

Deer Mountain Berry Farm
P.O. Box 257
Granite Falls, Wash. 98252
*phone orders: yes/206-691-7586/
Visa/MC: no/minimum order: 4 jars*

John and Barb Graham make berry jams as good as you can make at home. And with the price they charge for a one-pound jar, $1.90, I swear I don't know how they make a living. Such a deal.

They grow and pick gooseberry, strawberry, raspberry, loganberry, blackberry, boysenberry, and blueberry varieties for their old-fashioned preserves. If you are looking for jam for yourself—or for a gift—that is better than homemade and maybe even less money than you could do it for anyway, this is the place. The colors are pure and translucent. The preserves are solid with fruit. The flavor is a fresh and purely berry as if you were standing there picking them yourself. The truth of it is, if you want a preserve as good as grandma's, you'd better use her recipe. And that's just what the Grahams have done. If you're ever in Granite Falls, call and arrange for a tour through the berry patch. The Grahams would love to have you.

*California Berry Jams,
Vinegars, and Wine Jellies*

Kozlowski Farms
5566 Gravenstein Highway
Forestville, Calif. 95436
*phone orders: yes/707-887-2104/
Visa/MC: yes/minimum order: $20
with credit card*

When Julia Child selected places to visit in Sonoma County for her series on *Good Morning America*, the Kozlowski berry farm was high on her list. She and Carmen Kozlowski made Carmen's famous Raspberry Bread (see index for recipe) using jam made on the farm. This old-fashioned jam simply reeks of raspberries, and is outstanding. Another good product from Kozlowski Farms is kiwi jam. That luscious kiwi green, and with a slight hint of the best figs you every tasted, it is just lovely.

In their farm kitchens, these folks also put up no-sugar jams, wine jellies starting with good California wines, berry vinegars, and a gourmet mustard. If you're sight-seeing and tippling through the wine country north of San Francisco, make Kozlowski Farms one of your stops. They're located just north of Sebastopol.

Puget Sound Berry Preserves

The Maury Island Farming Co.
Rt. 3, Box 238
Vashon, Wash. 98070
phone orders: yes/206-463-5617/
Visa/MC: yes/minimum order: no

Located on an island in Puget Sound, The Maury Island Farming Co. makes preserves the old-fashioned way—using more fruit than sugar, no corn syrup, and small batches. In addition to raspberry, blueberry, strawberry, blackberry, and olympic berry, the best red currant jelly I know of comes from Maury Island. I have used it with great success in the Roast Leg of Lamb with a Whole Head of Garlic (see index for recipe). It makes a Cornish game hen look too good to cut into—no, go ahead, it's too good to leave on the serving board. Maury also offers strawberry apple butter and apricot apple butter made without any sugar, honey, or corn syrup, sweetened only with natural fruit and fruit juice.

If you are on Vashon Island between October and Christmas, you can visit their store just south of the tiny town of Vashon in Valley Center. Puget Sound is so otherworldly, you really should go out and see it. The little town of Vashon seems to shim-

mer in the mist about five feet off the ground. These fog-shrouded islands, with long cool growing seasons but no frost, produce some of the most full-flavored, round-tasting berries in America. And Maury puts them up in small batches and cooks them slowly. Yum.

Low-Sugar Berry and
Fruit Jams

Linn's Fruit Bin
R.R. #1 Box 600
Santa Rosa Creek Road
Cambria, Calif. 93428
phone orders: yes/805-927-8134/
Visa/MC: no/minimum order: 2 jars

John and Renee Linn and their three children run this farm just 10 miles south of Hearst Castle at San Simeon. In June and July, you can make this gorgeous country drive and pick berries to your heart's content: olallieberries, blackberries, and boysenberries. You can also buy baskets of them fresh picked. Last but not least: don't eat lunch before you go. Renee's chicken pies are famous. A whole chicken in every pie, lots of vegetables, and a crust that melts in your mouth. Renee, in her own farm kitchen, puts up low-sugar jams that are bright colored, berry rich, and have fresh fruit flavors. She makes different combinations, but some of the choices are: olallie, raspberry-rhubarb, and kiwi. The Linns welcome visitors 9:00 A.M. to 5:00 P.M. daily, from June to December, and on weekends only from February to May. Call Renee to find out what kinds of jam she's put up this week, and to order. Remember to refrigerate after opening. Low sugar means just like fresh fruit. Perishable.

Organic Fruit Compotes

Cascadian Farm
Star Route
Rockport, Wash. 98283
phone orders: yes/206-873-2481/
Visa/MC: no/minimum order: no

This is a real farm. Growing real certified, organic vegetables and fruits. The strawberry compote that I spread on an English muffin today was dark, deep red, thick as molasses in the winter, and lightly scented with acacia honey. For those who like the taste of honey, these fruit conserves are just like grandmother used to make. Slowly simmered and poured by hand into jars. Besides strawberry, they make raspberry, blueberry, blackberry, huckleberry, loganberry, orange marmalade, apricot, and apple butter. Their kosher dill pickles rival those found at Nate and Al's delicatessen in Beverly Hills. I expect, if you phoned Cascadian in the summer, they'd even ship you some organic potatoes. The state of Washington has just the right soil and climate for growing potatoes. And these are really organic. You can visit any time. Call for directions.

Fresh Fruit Mélanges
Sweetened with Honey

Emma's Jambrosia
Box 142
Crescent Valley, B.C.
Canada VOG 1H0
phone orders: yes/604-359-7166/Visa/
MC: no/minimum order: 1 case for
$27

In the first place, they don't call this spread "jam," because by Canadian law that would imply a certain level of sweetener. And the natural sweetness you find in these "mélanges" comes from fruit, not from sugar. Emma and the women of the collective have added just a touch of honey, a "low-methoxyl" pectin in their fruit spreads, and use only whole fruits and berries

from British Columbia, which has an ideal climate for producing full-flavored fruits. It's all those cool nights. The fruits and berries mature fully on branch and vine before ripening. Nature's answer to fully aged food.

I love this stuff. Blueberry, raspberry, peach, strawberry, and plum. Every flavor is rich in color and thick with fruit and not too sickeningly sweet. In fact, Emma's has fewer calories than any available diet product, and is without chemicals. Good grief. I think you could build a whole diet around it. It's that good. If you buy some, do remember to refrigerate after you've opened it. Without that blast of sugar, it will mold, if left out.

Fresh Fruit Jams, Conserves,
and Sundae Sauces

Berry Creek Farm
337 N.E. Agness
P.O. Box 1084
Grants Pass, Oreg. 97526
phone orders: yes/503-476-8659/
Visa/MC: yes/minimum order: no

This Chuck Islander is a man with good taste. He started making jam up in Grants Pass about five years ago, and it wasn't long before a certain well-known gourmet label asked him to make some jam for them. I can't tell you who that is, but I can tell you that if you buy jam directly from Chuck it will cost you exactly half of what it costs under the designer label, and you get it fresher and faster.

Berry Creek makes seven kinds of jam, including an Oregon blackberry and a sour cherry so good you'd like to slap your grandmother. They make four fruit and nut conserves—blueberry, rhubarb, peach, and peach chutney—four fresh-fruit sundae sauces to make you give up on your diet entirely, and some new raspberry-rhubarb and blackberry-rhubarb preserves that are memorable. For a gift, Berry Creek offers a nice-looking three-jar pack. You get to pick which three you want for $12 flat. If you're in Grants Pass, stop by the Berry Creek Farm Restaurant. If you buy more than a dozen, they'll even knock off a quarter per jar.

Kiwi Jams, Chutneys, and Preserves

The Kiwi Ranch
192 Highway 99E
Gridley, Calif. 95948
phone orders: yes/916-695-1448/
Visa/MC: yes/minimum order: no

Those funny little edible tennis balls do make the most fascinating jam, the expected luminous green with seeds, it reminds me of a high-quality fig with just a hint of strawberry. Gary and Pamela Pigg have been growing kiwis for twelve years. They have numerous gift-pack combinations you can order that include hand-picked kiwis, jam, and/or chutney in almost any conceivable combination. One of their best buys is an item they call the home pack: 100 kiwis for $10 plus shipping. If you ever thought about making your own preserves, here is the buy of the week. These people have gone a little crazy over kiwis and even sell kiwi fruit cookbooks and a board game called "The Farming Game" (about which they say, "it will make you laugh, even in the midst of financial disaster"; now there's a timely game with universal appeal). If you missed out on Cabbage Patch Kids, you can even order from Gary and Pamela a Kiwi Kid, handmade by Granny Radley right there in Gridley, the kiwi capital of the world. Fresh kiwis from the ranch are available from November through Easter, kiwi dolls and board games any time.

Sour-Orange Marmalade

Corti Brothers
5770 Freeport Blvd. #66
Sacramento, Calif. 95822
phone orders: yes/916-391-0300/
Visa/MC: yes/minimum orders: no

I've heard of taking lemons and making lemonade, but this is ridiculous. Darrell Corti, one of the brothers who owns a Sacramento market, says he hates to see anything go to waste, and it just got under his skin to see all those Seville oranges hanging on the trees around California's capital. He asked the parks superintendent if he could pick some. The parks man said, go ahead, but nobody will want them, they're too astringent. But Corti made a sample batch of marmalade using equal parts sugar and oranges and the boiled seeds as pectin. He knew he had a winner. He calls the product "A Capital Vintage Marmalade" and ages it a year before putting it on the market. This year he picked 250 pounds of oranges for next year. These folks aren't kidding when they say "supplies are limited." This marmalade, mixed with bouillon and sherry, makes a complex, mysterious orange sauce and can work as a glaze for poultry. In fact, Corti says the original recipe for Florentine duck and orange sauce calls for bitter oranges. So pucker up. This is the best thing since lemonade. It's so good that Dean & Deluca of New York have placed a big order. Better hurry.

Wild and Raw Honeys

Oregon Apiaries
1118 North College
Newberg, Oreg. 97132
phone orders: yes/503-538-8546/
Visa/MC: yes/minimum order: no

Marita Trunk and her husband started out as entomologists, so it should be no surprise that they turned to gathering honey for their own cottage kitchen enterprise. They have at least five distinctive honeys: fireweed, mild but distinctive in taste; blackberry, mild and light; clover, mild; star thistle, dark, flavorful, a favorite of Marita's and mine; and wild flower, which is both dark and strong.

Marita also makes a splendid almond honey butter and a sweet using honey and filberts that is outstanding. Marita's honeys and honey products are never heated above 110°, and their flavor is full and uncompromised by the pasteurization that you find in grocery-store honeys.

Chutneys, Bombay Sauce for Meat, Preserves, and Marmalades

La Casa Rosa
107 Third Street
San Juan Bautista, Calif. 95045
phone orders: yes/408-623-4563/
Visa/MC: yes/minimum order: no

Since 1935, lunch has been served to discriminating diners at the pink Spanish-style house that was built in 1858. Generations have grown up making the pilgrimage to La Casa Rosa, with its verdant herb garden, for Old California casserole, chicken soufflé, and Ash Blonde to drink. If you ever want to get a handle on what it means to be a native Californian, visit the big pink house. More than thirty years ago, the customers of La Casa Rosa demanded mail order of the fresh-herb French dressing, and it remains a mainstay today. In addition, they now have marmalades, chutneys, preserves, spiced rinds, jellies, and a spectacular Bombay Sauce for

meat. Be sure to stop for lunch if you're in the area. This is the real California.

Salad Dressings, Mustards, Vinegars, and Oils

California Fruit and Wine Dressings, Sauces, and Mustards

Cuisine Perel
P.O. Box 1064
Tiburon, Calif. 94920
phone orders: yes/415-435-1282/
Visa/MC: no/minimum order: 1 case can be mixed (buy small quantities from Oakville Grocery, see listing).

Cuisine Perel perhaps best exemplifies the trend in foods on the West Coast. Silvia Perel says it best: "Our company is really representative of many other California companies. We use all-natural ingredients, and we use what we have around us—fresh fruit and wine, in our case. California creativity is old-world knowledge translated into new ideas."

The Perels came to California from Argentina just three years ago, starting the company by merging their considerable experience and expertise with the bounties of the West Coast. What results is a line of salad dressings, mustards, and fruit/wine toppings that are original, fresh tasting, and divine. The Lemon Chardon-

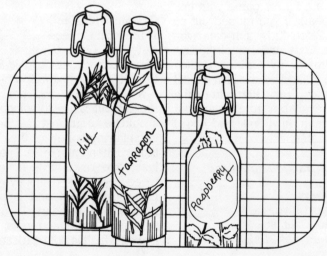

nay dressing won "best of show" prize in the huge National Association Specialty Food Trade show in 1984. I do find people arguing about the Perels. I, for example, got into a vigorous disagreement with a food editor from a metropolitan daily. She swore the Lemon Chardonnay dressing was the best salad dressing in the world. I argued just as vigorously that the Champagne mustard salad dressing was even better, even if it didn't win a prize. The Perels spark this kind of discourse. One major department store removed a well-known East Coast line of fancy food products from its gourmet shelves and replaced it with the seventeen Perel items. I guess I don't have to tell you that their products have no preservatives, colorants, or chemical additives of any kind. Some of the dressings are salt free. Silvia Perel is a respected food journalist and writes Spanish food columns, as well as hosts a cooking show for cable television. But the main thing about the Perels is this: they are originals. They have offered us just a glimpse of what is possible given the right combination. The connoisseurs have called their entire line the "best of its kind." I have to agree.

Pure Salt-Free, Lowered-Calorie Salad Dressings

Victorian Pantry
P.O. Box 222
Saratoga, Calif. 95071
*phone orders: yes/408-734-0907/
Visa/MC: yes/minimum order: 12*

The newest entrant into the salad dressing wars started out making jams. But knowing that wholesome food and exercise meant more to buyers than strawberry jam, the company has shifted gears and now presents salt-free, lowered-calorie dressings that are quite interesting. Red pepper basil in a virgin olive oil base is great for greens; and when mixed with cream, it makes a sauce for omelets, poultry,

or fish. Capers and Cheese combines Parmesan, anchovies, and capers in a light vinaigrette that is good not only on green salads but also as a marinade. Brandy Honey Dressing is made with brandy, honey, brown sugar, mustard, and spices—good for fruits and as a pork marinade. Olive and tarragon combined with white wine, garlic, and lemon juice is good for feta-cheese salads. Besides these interesting salad dressings, the Victorian Pantry also makes chocolate sauces, beautifully packaged, and a full line of jams, chutneys, and conserves.

California Raspberry–White Wine Vinegar and Salad Dressings

Kendall-Brown Foods
P.O. Box 3365
San Rafael, Calif. 94912
*phone orders: yes/415-499-1621/
Visa/MC: no/minimum order: no*

Barbara Kendall was making raspberry vinegar for Christmas presents. Everyone who was so honored said, my god, Barbara, you ought to bottle this and sell it. So she did. She begins with fresh raspberries and uses only the highest-quality California white wine vinegar and has devised a vinegar so good that Jacky Robert, chef of Ernie's in San Francisco, has a standing order. The late Masataka Kobayashi of San Francisco's Masa's said he liked it because a little went a long way. For people concerned about health and fitness, Barbara's vinegar is a must. A little on cooked vegetables makes a great salt substitute. Barbara developed two salad dressings to complement the vinegar: the first, a raspberry walnut, and the second, a dill-horseradish. Both use safflower oil instead of soybean oil, and both can be used for marinades as well as for salad dressings. And best of all, they both taste good.

*Blueberry Jam, Vinegar, Chutney,
and Syrup*

Canter-Berry Farms

19102 S.E. Green Valley Road
Auburn, Wash. 98002
*phone orders: yes/206-939-2706/Visa/
MC: yes/minimum order: $15*

In 1954, Fred and Edith Metzler
bought this blueberry farm. At first it
was a U-Pick place, and blueberries
were fifteen cents a pound. Fred used
to entice people up to the farm by
promising them a piece of Edith's
blueberry pie. One of their four children, Clarissa, stayed on and with her
husband, Doug Cross, now runs the
farm. Last December, the Crosses began putting up, in small batches, blueberry jam, chutney, syrup, and
vinegar. What the Crosses know is that
western Washington is one of the few
areas of the world that cultivates blueberries, and that the soil and weather
conditions provide a world-class
blueberry. The blueberry is quite
sturdy, having a thicker skin than most
berries, and when made up, using old
family recipes, provides a gorgeous
jam with whole berries, a complex
chutney, a syrup with real whole berries that pour out onto the pancakes,
and a vinegar that is superb for de-
glazing and for salads (see index for
Warm Carrot Salad with a Blueberry
Vinaigrette and Blue Sea Scallops
recipes).

Oregon Fruit Vinegars

Oregon's Own Gourmet Vinegars

4307 N.E. Brazee
Portland, Oreg. 97213
*phone orders: yes/503-282-6258/
Visa/MC: yes/minimum order: 3
bottles*

Marsha Johnson made fruit vinegars for her family for years, using
local berries from the fertile Willa-
mette Valley. Raspberry, blackberry,
blueberry. They were all good enough
to drink. Now she sells them. She uses
fresh, whole berries and cold processes the vinegars. After proper ag-
ing, what you get are highly aromatic
vinegars with maximum flavor and a
clarity of color to rival the best aged
wine. Floating in the vinegars are
whole berries—raspberries, blueberries, and blackberries. (See index
for Oregon's Own Blueberry Chicken
and Green Beans with Blackberry
Vinegar recipes.) This truly is a local
production, and still such a new ven-
ture that Marsha got an answering
machine only last week.

Fresh Fruit and Herb Vinegars

Herbs & Spice

P.O. Box 653
Astoria, Oreg. 97103
*phone orders: yes/503-325-1215
(keep trying)/Visa/MC: yes/minimum
order: no*

The only trouble with getting bottles of vinegar from Betty Cier is that
they look so pretty you hate to open
them. Each of the sixteen flavors
comes with some of the flavoring essence floating inside. Right now, on
my desk, is a bottle of garlic vinegar
that's clear with a skewer of three,
plump white garlic buds inside. The
bottle is sealed, then hand-dipped in
violet-colored wax. To finish the picture, there's a violet ribbon and a gold
seal. You talk about a handmade
product. And the second bottle is orange spice with a skewer full of orange zest, a cinnamon stick, and some
unidentified languid seeds. This bottle has orange wax. Okay, I broke
down and opened it. You can drink
this vinegar. Over ice with a little soda.
It's better than that fruit-flavored fancy
water. I wonder if you could reduce
with this stuff? Sure is good. Besides
raspberry and strawberry, Betty has
just begun making cranberry, with
cranberries straight from the bogs.
Now that has got to be good. These
vinegars can be used to deglaze the
pan and to create meat glazes, as well

as the customary salad uses. Betty Cier's daughters raise all the herbs she uses, organically. No sprays. No artificial anything. Just the nicest present you ever got in the mail that you could drink.

California Olives and Extra Virgin Olive Oil

Santa Barbara Olive Co.
P.O. Box 3825
Santa Barbara, Calif. 93105
phone orders: yes/805-683-1932/
Visa/MC: yes/minimum order: no

Do you remember how Dashiell Hammett's Thin Man made constant references to booze? How his true alcoholic nature was revealed through jokes and asides? All I can say about Santa Barbara Olive is, if you are fighting the urge for a martini, stay away from these olives. Because they are so good, so perfect, and so martini, that you will forget all about white wine if you have them on hand. The Makela family grows, manufactures, bottles, and labels these olives in Santa Barbara, and once you taste one, you'll know that the Thin Man may not have been joking when he said he only drank the stuff to get to the olive. And their oil. Such a lovely color. And cold pressed, the first pressing only, a real virgin, and now ordered regularly by the chefs at Hugo's and Spago, as well as by Michael Hutchings and Julia Child. They use no preservatives other than sea-salt brine, white wine vinegar, and purified water. Their martini olives are soaked in vermouth. All the olives are extra large and come in thirteen varieties, from wine-cured to jalapeño-stuffed. Today, I accidently spilled drops of Santa Barbara Olive oil in my coffee while tootling around in the kitchen. I swear, it improved the coffee.

California Mustards

Napa Valley Mustard Co.
P.O. Box 125
Oakville, Calif. 94562
phone orders: yes/707-944-8330/
Visa/MC: no/minimum order: 12 jars

The vineyards in Napa Valley bloom each spring with wild yellow mustard flowers. So inspired, Ruthie Ridman, Sue Simpson, and Ann Grace decided to pool their considerable knowledge and start their own mustard business. The California hot-sweet mustard that they developed first has the texture of a fine creamed honey given the bite of a hot, hot mustard. Of all the mustards I know, this one is my very favorite. You can eat this stuff out of the jar. But its creamed-honey texture makes it a cinch for use in meat glazes, and mixed with a good curry powder, it is a cold knockout for dipping prawns. Their second mustard is German style, with green chile and garlic. A bit of this mustard mixed with butter is great over grilled fish. Neither of these mustards has any additives. The hot-sweet one has no salt, and the German-style only a touch.

Unless you wish to buy mustard by the case, call Oakville Grocery for smaller orders.

Horseradish

Tulelake Horseradish Co.
P.O. Box 636
Tulelake, Calif. 96134
phone orders: yes/916-667-5319/
Visa/MC: yes/minimum order: 3 jars

The University of California, Davis, agriculture department determined that Tulelake had an ideal climate for growing horseradish—cold weather and water making hot roots—and began an experimental patch there. Sure enough, the whitest, hottest root possible in North America developed, and the Tulelake Horseradish Co. was born. I can never understand why anyone would buy horseradish fresh, since you don't know where the root came from and one root is a lifetime supply. Better you should buy it prepared, with no preservatives and no salt. Try Mama Stamberg's Cranberry-Horseradish Sauce (see index for recipe) and make your next Thanksgiving sing. If you're in Tulelake, visit their store at 619 Main. They sell other cottage kitchen products from the area along with some local art.

Oregon-grown Herbs

Pocket Creek Farm
9875 N.W. Lovejoy
Portland, Oreg. 97229
phone orders: yes/503-227-5077 X610 (StashTeas)/Visa/MC: yes minimum order: no

Let's tell the truth. Not all of us have at hand a constant supply of fresh herbs. And most of us do reach for the dried bottled herbs. But here's something I bet you didn't know. Most imported dried herbs have various unidentified weeds mixed in, and they have been sprayed with who knows what—and not only in the field but getting through international ports as well. So what's the solution? Pocket Creek Farm, which organically grows herbs, then dries and bottles them on the farm. What you get are pure, this year's herb crop with no insulting or dangerous additives. These herbs are fresh, green, and aromatic. Once again, Oregon's particular climate, warm long days and cool nights, produces herbs of unparalleled flavor. And they're dried at a low temperature to maintain maximum flavors. Herbes de Provence is my favorite for use in soups and seafood dishes (see index for Chicken & Shellfish Provencal in Broth recipe). Also available are seven herbs combined into Italian Herbs. Sweet Herbs and sweet basil, oregano, and thyme make up the rest of Pocket Creek Farm's pure product line.

Herb and Spice Blends

Canterbury Cuisine
P.O. Box 2271
Redmond, Wash. 98052
phone orders: yes/206-622-0141 (ask for DeLaurenti)/Visa/MC: yes/ minimum order: no

Lynn Kirwan was a city planner for Portland before she moved to the woods. After making a "moth chaser" so effective that her neighbors said she should sell it, Lynn began making potpourri, then kettle blends, and finally spice blends. Lately, she's been making a bean-soup blend she calls Geoffrey's Good and Hearty Bean Soup and another called Grandma Hannah's Sunday Beef Soup. Both of these are so good that her mail since Christmas has grown from one letter a week to six or seven letters a day. They usually begin: "Where can I find this great soup that somebody gave me for Christmas?" Write Lynn for a complete list, or call DeLaurenti to order retail the herb and spice blends that Lynn cooks up way out there in the woods.

Pasta and Meat Sauces

Pasta Sauces to Die for

Judyth's Mountain, Inc.
1737 Lorenzen Drive
San Jose, Calif. 95124
phone orders: yes/(call Oakville Grocery or La Casa Rosa)/Visa/MC: yes/minimum order: no

Mona Olmstead is one of those treasures—an original cook. All the products she offers are so good I didn't know where to classify her. For besides pasta sauces, she makes an outstanding pepper jelly, a ginger jelly known fondly at our house as gj, and a new group of coffee jellies that are not only West Coast exclusives but worldwide exclusives (see index for recipes for Baked Bosc Pears, Dolce Spazio, and Lemon-Ginger Sorbet).

But back to the subject at hand—the pasta sauces she makes could prompt you to give up cooking. A one-pound jar can be left in the refrigerator, spooning out just enough for dinner for one or two. I swear this is the stuff I talk about when I say that if I worked away from home all day, I'd give up cooking. I could live on these sauces. Wait until you hear the choices: herb tomato with bacon, country garden, pepper olive with walnuts, cream garlic, and last but not least, California almond with leeks and capers so good I can't decide whether to eat it or roll in it. Bliss. Sold at I. Magnin, Neiman Marcus, and as they say, "fine food stores everywhere."

San Francisco Barbecue Sauce

Firehouse Bar-b-que
563 Castro Street
San Francisco, Calif. 94114
phone orders: yes/415-864-2693/ Visa/MC: no/minimum order: no

Carl English is a real fireman whose grandfather hooked him on barbecue when he was a kid. He sold barbecue from a pushcart, in Leavenworth, Kansas, using grandmother's barbecue sauce. Which is so good, he has to bottle it and sell it out of his restaurant, just to keep the crowds down. It comes in three temperatures: 1, 2, and 3 Alarm. If you're in San Francisco, visit Carl English's barbecue restaurant on Clement Street, number 501. In fact, you should stay about a week on Clement, just eating your way to the ocean. Block for block, this is the best street in town for restaurants that aren't just for tourists. And Carl English's Firehouse Bar-b-que is right up there with the best of the ethnic choices on Clement.

Smoked Meats, Bacon, and Sausages

Mahogany Smoked Meats

Meadow Farms Country Smokehouse
P.O. Box 1387
Bishop, Calif. 93514
phone orders: yes/619-873-5311/ Visa/MC: yes/write for pricelist

When Bishop, California was the favored location for Hollywood Westerns, Roi Ballard's smokehouse became a popular haunt of the matinee cowboys. Soon they were hauling hams and bacon and jerky back to the mansions of Beverly Hills. Hams and bacon and jerky that so filled their cars and kitchens with the aroma of woodsmoke that people would take a deep breath and say "Where did you get that?" Now Roi Ballard, with only three helpers, makes and ships smoked pork and poultry products to customers from Beverly Hills to Bangkok. Today, we had a BLT made with his bacon. Honey, this is bacon. It does not shrink. It fills the house with an aroma that is worth its $3.50 a pound price tag. This is old-fashioned salt cure bacon made the same way it was when this smokehouse went into business in 1922. The ham is equally famous. *Cuisine* magazine did a taste test and found these hams to be as good as they get, right behind a Vermont smoked ham, and the only ham to buy west of the Mississippi. If you order from Ballard, you will get a batch of papers, his own brand of advertising. Roi brags so much he sounds like a Texan. But his products stand up to the talk. And even the brochures reek of the aroma of mahogany.

Smoked Pork

Macon Bacon

R.D. 4, Box 4831
Gig Harbor, Wash. 98335
phone orders: yes/206-857-4502/
Visa/MC: yes/minimum order: no

We thought it couldn't be found. A ham without water added. But little Macon Bacon, with a retail store in the Tacoma Center, still smokes pork products, the old time-consuming way, and, as they say, "we suffer the shrinkage of 10-20 percent. . . . We do not add water up to 38 percent as commercial packers do. . . ." The cure is an old family secret, the smoking is done with alder sawdust (no horrible liquid smoke chemical junk). If you're in downtown Tacoma, visit them at 1125 Court "C" in the Tacoma Center and pick up just-made barbecue. They also make their own sausages, age hams, and smoke bacon. They're proud of their barbecue sauce, which is made with margarine.

Rabbit and Rabbit Sausages

Triple R. Ranch

Rt 2. Box 393N
Cornelius, Oreg. 97113
phone orders: yes/503-359-9103/Visa/
MC: no/minimum order: no

Hawking rabbit and rabbit sausages at the Saturday Market in Portland, Shari Thomas says that rabbit is more than something just to wrap the baby bunting in. She extols the virtues of rabbit—low cholesterol, high protein, good for you. She makes fine sausage and salami from rabbit with no additives or preservatives. She calls her sausages "lean links" and they're a good choice for those who want sausage for breakfast but don't want their vessels to slam shut. In the Portland area, Shari delivers, and she will, as you may have guessed, even sell you rabbit skins if you want to make your own fur coat.

Fish

Fresh and Live Pacific Seafood

Pure Food Fish Market

1511 Pike Place Market
Seattle, Wash. 98101
phone orders: yes/206-622-5765/
Visa/MC: no/minimum order: no

City Fish Company

1535 Pike Place Market
Seattle, Wash. 98101
phone orders: yes/206-682-9329/
Visa/MC: no/minimum order: no

These two fish companies, both institutions in the Pike Place Market, ship, by air, fish from Puget Sound and the greater Pacific. From either one, you may order a live geoduck clam (you have to see it to believe it), salmon of any variety, mussels, crabs, and various other West Coast fish. As Jeff Amon of Pure Food says, "Let us do the fishing for you."

Troy's Seafood Markets

S.E. 112th & Powell
Portland, Oreg. 97201
phone orders: yes/503-760-2566/Visa/
MC: no/minimum order: no

In Portland, Troy's is the fishmonger with the good reputation. Troy's carries a full range of Pacific seafood and ships daily to customers all over the world. Call for price and availability.

Fresh Whole King Salmon

Johnstons' Seafoods

210 106 Place N.E.
Bellevue, Wash. 98004
phone orders: yes/206-454-6502/
Visa/MC: yes/minimum order: no

This looks like your regular strip center fishmonger. But in addition to a superb array of Northwest Pacific fresh fish, the Johnstons also carry a good assortment of custom-canned fish. They also get daily fresh-flown salmon shipments from Alaska; if you want to ship your brother in Boston a whole fresh salmon, these are the people to call. They are well set up to ship anywhere in the Continental United States using Styrofoam coolers and gel ice. They'll even decorate a whole fancy-baked or kippered salmon for parties. From what the locals tell me, reliability is their middle name. Call them and see what's in today.

Fresh Smoked Oysters

Ekone Oyster Co.
Box 465, Star Route
South Bend, Wash. 98586
phone orders: no/206-875-5494/
Visa/MC: no/minimum order: 1
pound
These beautiful fresh smoked oysters come to you from Nick Jambor's oyster farm. At $22 a pound, they're air freighted, chilled by gel ice, and must be refrigerated upon arrival. Not only is Nick Jambor's smoked-oyster system a West Coast exclusive, but maybe even a U.S. exclusive, since nobody grows, fresh smokes, and ships oysters besides Nick. If you're in South Bend, stop by for a tour, 12 miles south of South Bend in Bay Cities, #192 Bay Center Road, open 8:00 A.M. to 4:30 P.M. Monday through Saturday.

Portlock Smoked Sockeye

Port Chatham Packing Co.
632 N.W. 46th
Seattle, Wash. 98107
phone orders: yes/206-783-8200/
Visa/MC: no/minimum order: no
Arne Lindstrom, owner of Port Chatham, played host to Julia Child when she came to the Northwest in search of an excellent salmon smoker. The visit made its way to *Dinner at Julia's*. Lindstrom holds the most secure place in this business. His black-labeled cans of smoked salmon, sturgeon, sockeye, and coho are seen in the very best places. His Portlock smoked sockeye is frequently in-

cluded in catalogs by other concerns. Write for a catalog. He has a large variety of combinations of canned and fresh smoked salmon products.

Smoked Salmon and Custom-Canned Seafood

Hegg & Hegg
801 Marine Drive
Port Angeles, Wash. 98362
phone orders: yes/206-457-3344/
Visa/MC: no/minimum order: no
Fred Hegg started smoking fish as a hobby. He began selling a little, then just for the fun of it ran a little ad in *Sunset* magazine. That was 26 years ago. Now his smoked-seafood products are shipped all over the world. He still keeps a low profile at home, and sometimes people coming to visit have to tell the natives that Fred Hegg is there. Hegg now does a land office business mail ordering custom smoked salmon, tuna, sturgeon, shad, oysters, crab, clams, and shrimp. He has a salmon and a tuna packed with no salt. His method for smoking salmon is close to the authentic Indian system and produces a dry, flavorful product. It comes vacuum-sealed in plastic.

Gift-packed Smoked Salmon

Specialty Seafoods
1719 13th Street
Anacortes, Wash. 98221
phone orders: yes/206-293-0611/
Visa/MC: yes/minimum order: no
If, for no other reason, you wanted to choose one of the custom packers based on looks, this would be the one to choose. They've won national awards for their packaging, and if you've shopped in Northwest gift shops, you've probably seen their attractive smoked-salmon package. It's a good-looking brown box with great-looking calligraphy and a foil vacuum-packed salmon inside. Their system of vacuum packing fish makes for a moist, tasty product. They specialize

in smoked salmon and oysters. Write for their catalog. You'll see a nice sampling of the best the Northwest has to eat.

Fresh and Smoked Seafood

Karla's Krabs
P.O. Box 537
Rockaway, Oreg. 97136
phone orders: yes/503-355-2362/Visa/ MC: no/minimum order: no

As Karla Steinhauser says, better tasted than told. Her secret method for smoking does produce some of the most succulent Pacific seafood available. She goes to Arizona from November through February, but after that she's back in Oregon, smoking fish, packing the air-freight shipments, and holding forth in the same spot that she's had for twenty years. Go see her when you're on the Oregon coast, one mile north of Rockaway City Center on Highway 101 north. You'll enjoy her restaurant and you can buy fresh and smoked seafood to go or to ship. Karla's Krabs lives up to its reputation: the best smoked fish on the West Coast.

Smoked Rainbow Trout

R&R Aquaculture
2981 Dabob Road
Quilcene, Wash. 98376
phone orders: yes/206-765-3798/Visa/ MC: yes/minimum order: 6 cans

Richard Reinertsen describes himself as the head of operations of the aquaculture enterprise that grows, smokes, and custom cans rainbow trout. Richard is also the tail. This is virtually a one-man operation, and handmade in the true sense of the word. The smoked trout is delicious and great fun for parties. His smoked trout pâté is fabulous in the Pistachio Puffs (see index for recipe) and, when macerated with sweet butter, makes an incredible flavored butter. Richard says to mound this butter in a hol-

lowed green bell pepper cup and serve with vegetable sticks. Can't you see it? I want some this very minute.

Grains, Flours, and Breads

World Famous San Francisco Sour Dough

Boudin Bakery
1995 Evans Street
San Francisco, Calif. 94124
phone orders: yes/415-854-9090/ Visa/MC: yes/minimum order: 6 loaves

Every Tuesday, Boudin ships special orders for bread by UPS Blue Label Airfreight, guaranteed to arrive no later than Thursday. For $20 you get six loaves of the bread that made San Francisco famous. Like the other good breads represented in this section, this is a brand-new recipe; only been making it since 1849. Try it with the San Francisco Sourdough Crab Sandwich (see index for recipe). And if you're in San Francisco, drop by the bakery, 156 Jefferson Street, on Fisherman's Wharf. Boudin also has a gift pack that they ship Tuesdays, which includes an assortment of sourdough bread, cheese, famous San Francisco Italian dry salami, and a bottle of California wine. All you need is $28 and thou on a Thursday to remember why you left your heart in San Francisco.

Armenian Cracker Bread

Valley Bakery
502 M Street
Fresno, Calif. 93721
phone orders: yes/209-485-2700/ Visa/MC: yes/minimum order: no

No new business this, rather an institution in Fresno, which is home to a large Armenian population made famous by William Saroyan. Saroyan turned out a story a week, amazing the editors who bought his work. That same energy is obvious in Janet Saghatelian, second-generation owner of the Valley Bakery. Seeming to be everywhere at once, Janet has enlarged the local bakery into a provider of crackers and breads for a large out-of-town market.

And I'll tell you why. The Saghatelian family's recipe for lahvosh is outstanding. This crisp, pure cracker, sprinkled with sesame seeds, is the perfect backing for good, delicately flavored cheeses. The large fifteen-inch lahvosh, when dampened between towels, can be used for rolled sandwiches and other good things, including one stupendous dessert using whipped cream and almonds. The one thing I can't figure out about the Saghatelian lahvoshs is this: they don't go stale. Period. How come if they're making this bread from only pure ingredients, with no preservatives, it keeps forever? Ask the ancient Armenians. This bread is older than God. And positively sublime in its simplicity. If you're in Fresno, be sure to stop by the bakery, right across the street from the Holy Trinity Armenian Church.

Panforte di Mendocino

Cafe Beaujolais Bakery
P.O. Box 730
Mendocino, Calif. 95460
phone orders: yes/707-964-0292/
Visa/MC: yes/minimum order: no

Margaret Fox has unearthed a medieval recipe for a fruit-and-nut confection first used by the Crusaders to provide high-energy nourishment on their travels through the Middle East that is so potent, you feel as if you could slay the infidels yourself after just one serving. Her traditional Italian nut confection comes with a choice of nuts: almond, walnut, hazelnut, or macadamia nut. To give you an idea of how many nuts are in this pan forte, that's the first ingredient listed. The entire confection is dense, dark, aromatic, and slightly sweet. I love every single one of them. At $19 a twenty-two ounce wheel, they are so good you'll want to keep one on hand. And keep they do. Indefinitely. Out of the refrigerator (remember, they didn't have iceboxes in the Crusades). If you're in Mendocino, do make a stop at Margaret's restaurant, named, you guessed it, Cafe Beaujolais.

Stone-Ground
Flour and Cornmeal

Butte Creek Mill
P.O. Box 561
Eagle Point, Oreg. 97524
phone orders: yes/503-826-3531/
Visa/MC: no/minimum order: no

This grist mill has stood on the banks of Little Butte Creek since 1872 and is a piece of living history worth visiting. Whole grains are ground between big, round, flat white stones that weight 1400 pounds each. The stones were quarried in France, milled in Illinois, shipped around the Horn to Crescent City, and carried over mountains by wagon over a hundred years ago. Visit today and you'll see a real water-powered mill and a real miller at work.

The products offered by the Crandalls of Butte Creek Mill represent a philosophic stance toward sound nutrition. Peter Crandall says, "I am doing a job I believe in. The mill is where it all begins." The Crandalls buy only the best grains, grind the whole product in small batches, and store under refrigeration for optimum taste and nutrition. They grind eleven varieties of flour, including whole wheat, graham, whole wheat pastry, and buckwheat. They also grind yellow and white corn, rye, sunflower and sesame meal, soya, and corn grits.

And the Crandalls are justly proud of their outstanding ten-grain cereal and, believe it or not, their baking mixes. They sell a muffin mix that is served in all the bed-and-breakfast places in and around the area to rave reviews. Write for a free catalog.

California Wild Rice

Deer Creek Wild Rice
680 Jones Street
Yuba City, Calif. 95991
phone orders: yes/916-673-8053/
Visa/MC: yes/minimum order: no

Wild rice is a native American product first harvested by Indians who poled through lakes, bending the heads over the sides of the canoe and knocking the ripe grains into the boat. Deer Creek was the first company west of the Mississippi to grow wild rice commercially. Long known as an expensive gourmet food, commercial production has brought the cost down. And besides that, wild rice swells up to four times its dry size. Deer Creek sells several good-looking gift packs, one in particular packs two six-ounce cans of wild rice and a pound bag of California mixed wild and brown rice in a glorious-looking wicker duck. At $13.95 postpaid in California, this is a nice gift and a good buy. For home use, the mixed California brown and wild rice at $1.25 a pound is an excellent value. If you're ever in Yuba City, call Deer Creek and go take a tour.

Gibbs Wild Rice
8146 Greenback Lane #110
Fair Oaks, Calif. 95628
phone orders: yes/800-824-4932/Visa/
MC: no/minimum order: no

The Gibbs will ship to you, prepaid, either pure wild rice or a white-and-wild blend, a brown-and-wild blend, an instant wild rice, or quick-cooking casseroles. Although not into fancy packaging, Gibbs wild rice is the best quality you can buy, and you can get any quantity that is convenient. Call for price quotation. You also can call Jim Abrahamson and arrange to take a tour through their mill during the summer (now that's something that will keep the Brownie troop busy).

Natural Gourmet Potato Chips

N. S. Khalsa Co.
P.O. Box 664
Salem, Oreg. 97302
phone orders: yes/503-364-0399/
Visa/MC: yes/minimum order: 1
pound box

I first saw these fancy potato chips in Jurgensen's in Beverly Hills. There, in that cozy grocery store doing business the way Main Street America did it forty years ago, free delivery and all, were these old-fashioned potato chips. They were giving out samples that day. Crisp. A little thicker than normal. Heated, they're absolutely fabulous, and they let you know how the whole thing must have begun up in Saratoga Springs, New York, when the potato chip extravaganza accidentally began. You've heard that story I'm sure. Some fussy customer kept sending the "chipped" potatoes back to the kitchen and finally the chef got mad and just sliced them paper thin. Just to get even, I take it. Except they were an instant hit. Only later did they begin dipping them in chemicals and tons of salt to prevent them from going stale. Of course, like other old-fashioned, pure, perfectly simple processes, you will pay for these additive-free, batch-made potato chips, made from only the finest Oregon russet potatoes; they're $8.95 per one-pound box. If you purchase Khalsa's batch-made potato chips, you'll get an idea of what all the excitement was about in the first place. Even if it does cost a scandalous amount of money.

Cheese

Soft-Ripened Goat Cheeses,
Crème Fraîche, and Butter

Kendall Cheese Co.
P.O. Box 686
Atascadero, Calif. 93423
phone orders: yes/805-466-7252/
Visa/MC: yes/minimum order: $20

Sadie Kendall is the one who showed me that goat cheese shouldn't taste "funny." Sadie is a dairy scientist, expertly trained, who is making dairy products in the French farmhouse tradition. She has gone about her business quietly, not seeking publicity, but you can't keep cheeses like Sadie's a secret for long. Julia Child has found her and filmed a segment for *Dinner at Julia's* at the Kendall Cheese Co. The L.A. restaurants have found her: La Toque, L'Ermitage, Les Anges, Ma Maison, Michael's, Newporter Inn, and Trumps. Irvine Ranch stocks her products regularly.

What can I tell you about the cheese? I must agree with all the chefs, Michel Blanchet, Kenneth Frank, Patrick Jamonn, and Patrick a Terrail: Sadie Kendall's Chevrefeuille is as good as any in France. This is a double-creme, soft-ripened, pure goat-milk cheese made exclusively from milk from the Kendalls' own herd of Nubian goats. This cheese is Sadie's own, combining the skills of a French farm housewife with the modern, scientifically controlled techniques for ripening. Because the cheese is hand dipped and double creme, it is delightful young and even more interesting when mature. The Kendalls also produce a pure goat-milk Camem-

bert, reminiscent of a fine Brie; a Chèvre Sec; a new dry-milk cheese; Chèvre Frais, which is a fresh cheese with a variety of herbs on its surface— poivre, fines herbes, romarin, poivre vert, and Herbes de Provence. Chèvredoux is a Camembert made with goat and cow-milk half and half.

If you are a serious chocolatier, you really should order butter from Sadie. This unsalted, ripened-cream butter is produced in the United States only by the Kendalls and isn't even in the same league with grocery store butter. All other unsalted, ripened-cream butter available in the United States is imported from Europe, ghastly expensive, and old besides. But the Kendalls' butter, in very short supply, is the choice for exquisite chocolate making, as well as for simply spreading on breads.

Crème fraîche: The Kendalls' crème fraîche is so thick you can lay a spoon atop and it will not sink. It also is stable and will keep in the refrigerator a month. It will never break down during cooking, and the taste of it is superior to what you can make at home. Let's face it. She's got better dairy products than you can buy to begin with. That's why everything tastes so good.

Soft Sheep Cheeses
in Olive Oil

Sally Jackson Cheese Co.
Star Route 1, Box 106
Oroville, Wash. 98844
phone orders: no/Visa/MC: yes/
minimum order: $10

The Roger Jacksons start by growing all their own hay and grain. They then produce all their own milk, and their handmade cheeses are, perhaps, the most sophisticated available in the state of Washington. Just listen to the choices: soft and semihard goat cheeses with optional herbs, semihard cow cheeses with optional herbs, and soft sheep cheeses in olive oil. And their prices are equally astounding, running from $3 a pound to $3.75. In fact, the Jacksons will even custom make a five-pound wheel of cheese to your own special order, even marbling goat and cow cheese with the herb of your choice. Why these people don't have a phone is beyond me, but if you like really exotic cheeses of the highest caliber, you'll just have to write a letter.

Hard Smoked Goat Cheese

Feather Haven Dairy
5482 Gossett Road
Port Angeles, Wash. 98362
phone orders: yes/206-928-3014/Visa/
MC: no/minimum order: 1 pound

Dave Dickey makes hard goat cheeses, both smoked and unsmoked, using a formula exclusively his own. This is a tiny dairy, and Dickey does everything; you get a truly handmade cheese. The smoked cheese is excellent. His dairy is located 20 miles west of Port Angeles, and if you'll call first, he'll let you come and look around.

Swiss-Style
Raw Goat Milk Cheese

Briar Hills Dairy, Inc.
279 S.W. 9th Street
Chehalis, Wash. 98532
phone orders: yes/206-748-4224/
Visa/MC: no/minimum order: no

I sure was glad to find Briar Hills Dairy. Because up until then, I'd just about decided the only style of goat cheese made locally on the West Coast was that soft cream cheese–type favored by the French. But this mild, white, firm type is well suited to cooking, particularly in Cal-Mex cuisine (see index for the Green Chile and Goat Cheese Enchiladas recipe). Briar Hills makes an elastic-curd type, called Cascadian, and a more crumbly, dry, sharp type they call Briar Hills Natural, which is fine in salad dressings. They even sell this with caraway seeds for snacks or desserts.

Perhaps their most interesting cheese is called Viking Brown Whey cheese; Briar Hills's own version of gjetost. Sweetened with honey and heavy with the aroma of caramelized milk, this cheese is high in potassium, phosphorous, and carbohydrates. It is made from skim milk and is low in fats. It literally melts on your tongue, has the texture of chocolate, and frequently is ordered by joggers, who eat and run. I expect this is what they fed those guys who had to sit in the bottom of the boat and pull the oars while the Vikings crossed the Atlantic. An old Viking carrot and stick.

Gouda and Farmstead Cheese

Pleasant Valley Dairy, Inc.
6804 Kickerville Road
Ferndale, Wash. 98248
phone orders: yes/206-366-5398/
Visa/MC: no/minimum order: 2-
pound wheel (won't ship in hot
weather)

George and Dolores Train milk forty cows every day. They started making cheese because the need for milk fluctuates. After some research, they decided that Gouda was best suited to their climate and situation. Such Gouda! Smooth and creamy and with a subtle nutty quality as if it were a high-toned cousin to Swiss. Every batch takes 850 pounds of milk and is not sold before sixty days. When you order cheese from Pleasant Valley, it comes with a date written by hand on a label over the wax cover. They pack the cheese by hand so no two are quite the same size. They use grade A fresh whole cow's milk that has not been bleached, colored, or chemically tampered with in any way. By now, they have their own starter, they use natural calf rennet (making a few batches of rennetless cheese each season—call for availability). And though the cheese wheels are salted in a brine, Pleasant Valley cheeses test lower in salt than most commercial cheeses. Another type they have just begun to make, they call Farmstead. It is a pale, sharp, smooth cheese with a little more bite to it than the Gouda, but equally good. If you ate two servings of this stuff, you could step outside and yodel.

Canadian Raw Milk Gouda

Grisnich Farmstead Gouda
Bricwell Distributors
1399 Fountain Way #406
Vancouver, B.C. V6H 3T3
phone orders: yes/604-738-5092/ Visa/MC: no/minimum order: 1 10-pound round

I first saw this cheese for sale in the Granville Island Market under a sign that said, "We milk our own cows. We make our own cheese." A creamy white wheel of Gouda, it comes in five flavors: caraway, cumin, herb and garlic, peppercorn, and plain. This is Gouda of the highest quality. The texture is smooth, the moisture content exactly right, and the taste pungent and clear. The Grisnich family makes

this cheese on an emerald green farm just sixty miles east of Vancouver. They use vegetable rennet, no preservatives, coloring, nitrates, or other additives. Their contented cows feed on lush green grass and high-protein alfalfa hay. This cheese is worth the wait at $4 per pound plus shipping COD.

Cougar Cheeses

WSU Creamery
Troy Hall 101
Pullman, Wash. 99164
phone orders: no/509-335-7516/Visa/ MC: no/minimum order: no

Thirty years ago, the Washington State University Creamery developed a smooth dry cheese similar to Swiss or Gouda that they call Cougar Gold, named, as college students are wont to do, for their school mascot. The cheese has become rather famous and is shipped all over the country in thirty-ounce tins. Besides teaching the kids how to make cheese and run a creamery, WSU has developed a cheese that is truly world-class. Their newest addition is Viking, a mild, soft white cheese that is best young, about four months old. Adding diced jalapeños to the Viking, WSU now has Hot Pepper Cheese, which I find to be splendid in Mexican Nouvelle dishes, perhaps superior to Mexico's Queso Fresco, which is the usual addition to Mexican cuisine. As you can see, this is a typical institutional attitude toward the customer (sort of like buying cheese from the post office). All orders must be prepaid, no credit cards and no phone orders. Do you suppose they don't teach marketing up there in Washington? Oh well, at least the cheese is worth the hassle.

Candy and Dessert Sauces

Cranberry Candy

Cranberry Sweets Co.
P.O. Box 501
Bandon, Oreg. 97411
phone orders: yes/503-347-2526/
Visa/MC: yes/minimum order: no

From the cranberry capital of Oregon, right next to the bogs, you'll find this candy shop that's been making cranberry sweets for twenty-two years. If you've read the recipe section of this book you know I am a maniac for cranberries, so you can imagine my response to these candies. That wonderful, sour-sweet cranberry flavor, when mixed with walnuts and pressed into chewy rectangles that are then rolled in plain granulated sugar. That is candy. They also make a similarly outrageous candy using wild blackberries. And the funniest thing they make—now, this really is an Oregon product—is Henry's Beer Candy. Made the same way, only using Henry's Blitz Weinhard beer (we do love Henry here in Oregon). This isn't some dopey idea like Jimmy Carter's brother putting his name on some sorry beer. This is a candy that is—I kid you not—delicious. Perhaps one of the best candies they make is the lemon-pie candy. The same rectangle of filling that tastes for all the world like a fresh lemon pie, and then (can you stand it?) dipped in white chocolate. These candies are all handmade in small batches using no preservatives, no starch, no food coloring or artificial flavorings. Visit them at 1st & Chicago on the waterfront.

Chocolate Truffles

Euphoria Chocolate Co.
6 W. 17th Street
Eugene, Oreg. 97401
phone orders: yes/503-343-9223/Visa/
MC: no/minimum order: Box of 12

Order these once, and you'll know that the company is aptly named. In business for four years, Euphoria only ships during cool months, November 1 through March 15. These nationally recognized truffles are handmade, use the best chocolate for both centers and shells, and take advantage of the perfectly splendid butter and cream that only is available locally in Oregon. Flavors include amaretto, coffee royal, toasted almond, double chocolate, Oregon mint, coffee and cream, and milk chocolate. And if you've ever bought truffles in Beverly Hills, you will be most euphoric over the price. Believe it or not, they only charge a dollar a truffle. If you visit Eugene, you will see a gaggle of guilty-looking ladies who visit Euphoria as faithfully as others in our society visit a methadone clinic. Eating a Euphoria truffle is a terribly dangerous stunt. You, too, could be one of those persons in the raincoats, standing on one foot and then the other, waiting for Euphoria to open up.

Filbert Brittle

Grandpa Buswell's Candy
The Strawberry Patch
26860 Salmon River Highway
Willamina, Oreg. 97396
phone orders: yes/503-879-5377/
Visa/MC: no/minimum order: 1
pound

She still cooks this brittle on the stove, in small batches, so when Judy Buswell says homemade, she means it. Judy uses Oregon hazelnuts (filberts) or peanuts in a brittle that is light and crisp. People write Judy from all over the country saying it's the best brittle they've had, and some of this candy even has made its way to the *Washington Post*. They liked it a lot. But still, Judy keeps it a small business. She said she might sell it in my hometown, Ashland, Oregon, next summer, provided she's willing to drive that far. As Cary Grant used to say: Judy, Judy, Judy. Use UPS. I can't live without your brittle a block away.

Chocolate Sauces

Gretchen's Kitchen
P.O. Box 222991
Carmel, Calif. 93922
phone orders: yes/408-624-3320/
Visa/MC: yes/minimum order: no

Here's that story again. Gretchen Leach's friends said to her, you make the world's greatest chocolate sauce, and she said, maybe so. So now she's bottled it, and it's selling like the proverbial hotcakes. She also has an ice cream sauce destined to win the hearts of Reese's fans—Peanut Butter Fudge. Gretchen says the secret is that she uses the best ingredients she can get; chocolate, cream, and butter, her sauces are all natural. A seventeen-ounce jar is $10 postpaid.

Hand-Dipped Chocolates

Nutty Chocolatier
17200 Ventura Boulevard
Encino, Calif. 91316
phone orders: yes/818-986-NUTS/
Visa/MC: yes/minimum order: no

Untouched by machine hands, these gorgeous chocolates are made entirely by hand. Using pears, pineapple, quince, orange slices, apricots, and peaches, the Nutty Chocolatiers glaze and dip these California fruits into spectacular fruit-chocolate combinations. The nut clusters use every nut you've ever heard of and then some. For gifts, they have hundreds of molded chocolate designs—everything from chocolate golfers to greeting cards inscribed with your own message to chocolate baskets filled with candies of your choice. If you've got an occasion, they've got a mold.

Chocolate Sauces

Paradigm Chocolate Co.
3438 S.E. Radcliff Court
Hillsboro, Oreg. 97123
phone orders: no/503-648-5139/Visa/
MC: no/minimum order: no

Lynne Barra, who with her husband makes all eleven sauces, says that they use the best form of advertising: Taste of Mouth. I can't *tell* you how good these chocolate sauces are; you have to taste them. The Frangelico with hazelnut is so smooth, chocolaty, and nutty that I find myself having to resist eating it out of the jar. I also adore the Jamaican Praline and Gingered Caramel. The other sauces that are, in fact, the Paradigm, include Amaretto, Bailey's Irish Cream, Deep Dark Fudge, Grand Marnier, Kahlua, and Peppermint Schnapps. These sauces aren't too sweet but are terminally rich. The Barras make them in small batches, using no salt, no preservatives, no artificial flavors. They're making something so perfect, that it's worth the calories. I'll tell you the truth. Normally, I don't even like ice cream unless it's gelato, and now I find myself fantasizing about ice cream combos to use with these Paradigm sauces. How do you suppose it would work with Tofutti? Now that would be the ultimate paradox, wouldn't it?

New West Coast Cuisine Grocery Stores

The Oakville Grocery Store
P.O. Box 86
St. Helena Highway
Oakville, Calif. 94562
phone orders: yes/707-944-8802/
Visa/MC: yes/minimum order: no

One of the original "gourmet" grocery stores, Oakville started out in the Napa Valley, up in Oakville on the St. Helena Highway. The old original store is fun to visit. They have intelligent buyers who have good taste and

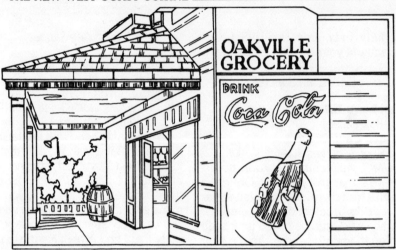

stock the best products to be found from the West Coast. If you're wondering where you can get *anything,* phone Oakville and see if they have it.

DeLaurenti Italian and International Food Markets

1435 First Avenue in Pike Place
  Market
Seattle, Wash. 98101
phone orders: yes/206-622-0141/
Visa/MC: yes/minimum order: no

Aisle for aisle, row for row, De-Laurenti has the most impressive stock I have ever seen, anywhere. Mustards. How about two hundred choices. Cheeses. Hundreds. Jams and Jellies. Who can count? Vinegars. A wall full. If you are in Seattle, make for the Pike Place Market and stop in at DeLaurenti. The only thing I'd skip there is the bakery. Beauty being, as it were, only skin deep.

Latta's of Oregon

P.O. Box 1377
Newport, Oreg. 97365
phone orders: yes/503-265-3238/Visa/
MC: yes/minimum order: no

Judy Latta has combined good taste with a fine design sense to choose and package Oregon food products in a most appealing way. She hired Abigale Anstey to create packages for her food products, and Anstey came up with a stunning "fishwrap" that uses a real fish imprint, made by inking and a brayer. So Latta's fish products, in addition to being carefully chosen for food quality, also are wrapped in such an artistic manner that you almost hate to open them. Besides home-canned seafood, Latta offers fruits, nuts, bread mixes, honey, preserves, fruit chips and syrups, coffee, tea, spices and herbs, and various gift packs. Write for a catalog.

Irvine Ranch Farmer's Market

142 S. San Vicente Boulevard
Beverly Center #101
Los Angeles, Calif. 90048
phone orders: no/213-657-1931/Visa/
MC: no, house charges only

Here is the place that was written up in *Newsweek* for having an absolutely stunning array of fresh produce. But produce is only a part of it. Irvine Ranch has all the good cheeses, a mile-long meat-and-fish counter with everything (even trays full of lamb tongues). If you're hunting something fabulous, call them up and see if they've got it. Chances are, they will.

Trader Joe's

610 S. Arroyo Parkway
Pasadena, Calif. 91005
phone orders: no/818-578-9540/Visa/
MC: yes

This is my favorite kind of store.

Trader Joe began twenty-eight years ago with one little store and now has fifteen scattered all over the greater L.A. area. If you are a bargain hunter in the fine-food category, by all means visit Trader Joe's. Here is where I found the Spanish white wine to rival the best California has to offer at $1.29 a bottle. Here is where I found goat cheese a buck and a half cheaper than at the chichi places. Trader Joe is a shrewd buyer. His prices are great.

*The Best of the
Northwest Gourmet Foods*

Norm Thompson
P.O. Box 3999
Portland, Oreg. 97208
*phone orders: yes/800-547-1160/
Visa/MC: yes/minimum order: no*

Besides being the outfitter for the Northwest, Norm Thompson has sold high-quality Northwest food products through its catalog for a long time. Although the listings change, and the Christmas catalog lists more items than the spring catalog, you can phone and ask for things that don't appear in the catalog, because they carry more food items in the store in Portland than are listed in the catalog. Highly recommended are the custom-canned salmon, beer bread mix, and Hoagland pickled asparagus. It's a free phone call. Just give them a jingle and ask what's to eat today at Norm Thompson's. The stock varies, but the quality is always good. And if you're in Portland, go by the store. It's hard to find but worth the hunt. They have great sales, and free sherry for the customers. So civilized.

*New West Coast
Cuisine Gift Baskets*

To Market To Market
Box 492
West Linn, Oreg. 97068
*phone orders: yes/503-657-9192/
Visa/MC: yes/minimum order: no*

Kathy Parson began as a Portland caterer (Cooking Anonymous), but her designer's eye began to call, and now she combines her good taste with her good eye to put together gorgeous gift baskets filled with West Coast food items. For $25 she has a Gourmet Goose. This funny fellow is a wicker goose basket brimming over with Kathy's own mustard mix that comes in a French canning jar with its own goose-ceramic-handled knife; Thrill of a Dill, which is a superb blend she devised using dill, onion, and Beau Monde Seasoning (I use this stuff in everything. Just now, I sprinkled it on popcorn. Delicious). Back to the basket. Puckered plums, popcorn, jelly bean gems, and three great recipes complete the basket.

Kathy has a series of other baskets, from mini to deluxe. All beautiful. One Portland doctor orders seventy-eight custom baskets from Kathy every Christmas. He says that the people he delivers them to can barely wait from one year to the next. Kathy has put together for us a New West Coast Cuisine Basket that has a copy of the book, as well as a representative sampling of some of the best foods available from West Coast cottage kitchens. The basket comes in 3 sizes, and may include berry vinegar; Thrill of a Dill in the French canning jar with the ceramic-mallard knife; Judyth's Mountain extra hot pepper jelly; Leonardo Perel's fabulous Champagne Mustard salad dressing; Kozlowski Farms kiwi jam; Paradigm Haute Fudge Sauce; Geoffrey's Good & Hearty Beans (see mail order section). A good representative sample of what's to eat on the West Coast. Call for Christmas orders. Kathy also likes to custom make baskets. Call her up and tell her what you want. She has a great eye and good taste.

Index